Beyond Help

A Breakthrough View Of How We Help
Ourselves and Others

Camaron J. Thomas, Ph.D.

authorHOUSE®

AuthorHouse™
1663 Liberty Drive
Bloomington, IN 47403
www.authorhouse.com
Phone: 1-800-839-8640

First published by AuthorHouse 10/26/2011

ISBN: 978-1-4634-3283-6 (sc)
ISBN: 978-1-4634-3282-9 (hc)
ISBN: 978-1-4634-3281-2 (e)

Library of Congress Control Number: 2011913002

Printed in the United States of America

To Sandy,
Thank you for helping me.

To My Husband,
Always.

Acknowledgments

This book has been written many times. It was written once about aging; a second time about a change of heart. When I completed *People Skills for Tough Times*, I thought for sure I'd caught it. But the focus on skills wasn't deep enough so I had to begin again. The opportunity to focus on how we help was a breakthrough for me, and I am owing to many people and others.

I am deeply grateful to all those who supported me during this process: my dear friends, Rosann Mullahey, Laurie Broadwell and Andy Cohen; and the many readers who took their time to review the book: John Morowski, Jim Abdo, Raymond White, Esq., Jo Wise among others. Special thanks go to Christine Packard, Esq., a very skilled and insightful mediator in Burlington, Vermont, who not only read the book multiple times, but willingly offered her wonderful comments and suggestions. Thanks to her selflessness, this is a much better book.

I must thank all my teachers, especially Thomas Lewis, M.D., and the work of Eckhart Tolle, to whom I am forever grateful. And all the "teachers" at the pool – you know who you are – who kept me smiling and inquired regularly as to my progress; and in particular, the special needs adults and their caretakers who have continuously taught me about real help and real joy.

I am not sure what I would have done without Larry Ragan who has come to the rescue too many times and has been a source of strength, ideas, wisdom, and positive energy. And Carol Thomas, for her wonderful skills in photography; the cover is lovely.

Finally, a special thank you goes to my husband...I have no idea why you are always there for me but you are. I especially value your capacity to "try on" some of my zanier ideas...and there have been many. And the girls: thank you Newport, Bennington, Matilda and Samantha for sitting by me as I wrote and re-wrote this book. With so much love, how could one help but find Presence?

Contents

Section Two

Section Three

Introduction

These are difficult times...

World leaders are adrift. Financial powerhouses have lost their strategic edge. The industrial icons we once believed in are in decline or worse, have gone belly-up. Economic growth models, employment and other enduring life cycles have lost their rhythm. Whether we look to banking or the housing industry, health care or transportation infrastructure, the availability of clean water or renewable energy, the government or organized religion, everything -- even the climate -- seems in turmoil. Moreover, conventional solutions aren't working; the tried and true fixes of the past are failing just when we need them most. It sometimes feels as if everything is falling apart.

One could say we live in a constant state of conflict. We are bombarded by media 24/7; in our homes, in restaurants and stores, on computers, even public bathroom mirrors. Slick advertising telling us what to do and buy; loud and abrasive talk shows telling us who's right and who's to blame; shrill commentaries, voyeuristic programming, ceaseless "news", cell phone dramas -- all are clamoring for our attention. Our values have become a source of constant friction instead of a unifying force. And civil discourse is all but forgotten. Even some of our most intimate relationships have lost meaning: church goers who can't find peace, families struggling to hold it together, couples clinging to an image of the way things should be. We live right on the brink of stress and frustration, at a decibel level that is at best, numbing.

But what may be most troubling are the underlying precepts that have been thrown into doubt: the belief that we are here for a purpose; the certainty that the next generation will fare better than the last; the faith we place in education and technology to ultimately save the day; and the confidence we have that at least on some level, things are under our control. Some days it feels like we're beyond help.

And yet, perhaps, conditions are this way for a reason. Perhaps they are pointing to a shift. A shift more significant than any one we can recall from the past; one beyond paradigms and resources, bright ideas and inventions; a shift more akin to the discovery of the wheel, the progression to an upright posture and bipedalism, or the end of the nomadic way of life…a shift that is changing everything.

This book examines the human condition through the prism of how we help. We could have considered any number of human endeavors: the changing nature of child-rearing practices, the rise and radicalization of religious fundamentalism, the history of litigation in business relations, the growing insularity and isolation of many American professions and institutions, even the role pets play in our lives. This is because all of our ventures, our institutions, our problems and our solutions stem from the same source. This source is the reason for the constant state of conflict we live in…it also forms the basis for how we help.

Help became the focus of this book for several reasons. First, how we help takes so many forms; from offering advice, to counseling, to working to repeal a major piece of legislation that we find harmful. There are the more mechanical forms of help, such as training someone to brush his hair or helping a client get dressed in the morning. There are also distinctions between caring for someone and taking care of another human being. Help can involve explaining or clarifying a situation, solving a problem, giving directions or teaching the correct way something is done; from offering suggestions, all the way to proving we're right or know what's best. Despite the many forms help takes, they all involve talking and thinking and meeting needs; conveying what to do or how to do it.

Help was also chosen because it's something we all do, everyday, and in a variety of settings. It is part of the human experience, something we hold dear: we take pride in how we help and that we do so in the first place. We also assume our help is helpful, that it does "good". In fact, *how we help should be the very best part of who we are and yet, at this point of human* *development, it actually <u>adds</u> to the constant state of conflict we live in.* To put it another way, how we help is a reflection of how we live…it reflects where we have evolved to as human beings.

According to the Bureau of Labor Statistics, 1.97 million people in the United States work in the "helping professions". There are more than 594,000 counselors and therapists, 605,100 social workers, 109,200 psychologists, and 440,800 social and human service assistants and community and human service specialists (US Bureau of Labor Statistics, May, 2008). Included among the ranks are marriage and family therapists, mental health counselors, and substance abuse workers; clinical, counseling, and school psychologists; members of the clergy, probation and correctional treatment specialists, and other religious workers.

People who work in these professions provide what we traditionally call "help". Social Workers, for example, have "a strong desire to help improve people's lives…helping them cope with issues in their everyday lives, deal with their relationships, and solve personal and family problems" (ibid., Occupational Outlook Handbook, 2008-9). Counselors "assist people with personal, family, education, mental health, and career problems," while Social and Human Service Assistants fill a variety of roles from assessing needs and determining eligibility for benefits, to helping others "in need of counseling or crisis intervention" and/or to "communicate more effectively, and live well with others" (ibid.). Employment in several of these fields is projected to grow "much faster than average for all occupations" (ibid.).

What these numbers do not reflect are the throngs of people who might fall under a broader definition of helping professions: health practitioners, psychiatrists, law enforcement professionals and first responders, educators, coaches, physicians, family court attorneys and law guardians, educational trainers, ombudsmen, massage and related "healing" therapists, human relations specialists, spiritual leaders, child care workers, etc. Nor do they include the elders we turn to for guidance; the caring friends and family who listen when we're upset; or you and me, who offer our advice daily.

Much of what we deal with when we "help" involves conflict in one form or another. And the conflict people face is deafening. Some of it is inner conflict over guilt, abuse, shame, self esteem, success or failure, unmet expectations, and authenticity. We struggle with ourselves over food issues, addictions, insecurities, personal crises, and feelings of regret. Many of us fall short of cultural norms and rules. We wrestle with a plethora of "should's": who we should be, how we should live and what we should believe. We wonder why we can't live up to an image, why others don't understand or support us, what we can do to be a better person, and how we will endure our losses.

We also conflict with one another. Our relationships ebb and flow. One day at work we're on the top of the world. The next, we've lost a big client or are doing battle with a supervisor. One day we're in line for a promotion. The next we're competing with some up-start who doesn't know the territory. We fight over power, clout, position, reputation, advancement and money; company direction, contracts, ideas, credit, workload and assignments; policies, decisions, next steps and wording; even office space.

But conflict at work often pales to what we confront when we get home. Conflict at home often simmers just beneath the surface. We often call it something else; arguments, spats, disagreements, or quarrels. But discord in our most intimate relationships can ignite at a moment's notice, over any trigger, among those who know our triggers best. We find ourselves complaining at work and with friends about the "situation at home": our failed marriage, misbehaving teenager, stressed out life, former partner, unfulfilled promises, unmet needs…

Add to this the cultural conflict we confront at nearly every turn. High conflict has, in effect, become the norm. As Deborah Tannen wrote in her book, *The Argument Culture*:

> Our fondness for the fight scenario leads us to frame many complex human interactions as a battle between two sides…Approaching situations like warriors in battle leads to the assumption that intellectual inquiry is a game of attack, counterattack, and self-defense. In this spirit, critical thinking is synonymous with criticizing (1998, pp. 18; 19).

High conflict can grow pretty tiring and not surprisingly, in some quarters, the public outcry for civility is louder than ever. We *argue* that we *should* be able to disagree without screaming at one another…which has spawned yet another helping profession: alternative dispute resolution where we seek to resolve our conflicts with the "help" of a mediator, arbiter, ombudsman, or other so-called "neutral".

But what if when we help, we don't? What if the very premise of help is…*broken*?

To be sure, there are many helping professionals who face each day with a renewed sense of spirit and commitment. They are there to serve, to do a service. They genuinely care about their clients, unselfishly give of themselves, and value even the smallest success. There are also those who blindly apply their trade; who follow a prescribed set of procedures day in and day out, and are convinced they can accurately diagnose a given condition at fifty paces. Other helpers become so committed to their mission, they grow militant: every drink is a sign of alcoholism, any infringement is domestic violence, and separation means the kids are in jeopardy. These folks cannot comprehend how anything is more important than what they do and how they do it; fiscal crisis or not, their mission needs funding.

Still others have lost their zeal. Their daily grind is painful and their moments of satisfaction, rare. The frustration, which can be endemic to the field, has drained them. They follow the rules, fill out the forms, and file the reports; while the number of those "in need" continues to climb and the cases grow even more violent and dysfunctional. In private, they wonder whether their clients are beyond help; some of their clients may wonder the same thing.

The broken nature of help however, is more than a matter of how much we care, how hard we work, or the passion we bring to our mission. It comes from something more fundamental, more basic to the human experience. And it's forcing us to ask the harder questions: What if we simply can't solve another person's problems? What if when we help, we foster a cycle of dependency or worse, dis-empower or devalue the seeker? What if, by helping, we actually serve our own needs – we somehow use help to prop up ourselves? These concerns are by no means limited to the helping professions. They extend to *all human relationships*. In fact, "help," as defined in this book, reaches far beyond those who help others for a living. It speaks to each and every one of us; every time we offer our opinion, give advice, or be the voice of experience. Every time _we know_.

Consider the following scenarios. Three siblings sit down to discuss how to care for their ailing mother:

Sibling 1: "It's time. You know it's time. I've been here from the beginning and I can't take the full burden. It's too much for me to continue to care for her. I need a break. I simply don't know how to make you two understand what I've been through. The doctors, the meds, dealing with Medicaid, the home health aides…it's just too-"

Sibling 2: "Good God, can you give it a rest? This is a serious time. This isn't about you. There are major financial issues here to consider. How can we afford the care she needs?"

Sibling 1: "How can you talk about money at a time like this? You've never been there for her and you know it. We're talking about hospice and you're talking about cash. How typical of you."

Sibling 3: "You know, I've said all along, she would be better off in a setting that could watch over her 24/7."

Sibling 1: "So you're saying I've not been there for her. That's what you think, right? You're saying I haven't done more than my fair share. I've been the one…"

Sibling 3: "I'm saying we need to all calm down and think this through logically. We need to do some research, talk with the doctors, project out a timeline, analyze the different options, review the costs. We need to approach this with compassion, yes, but with foresight and planning."

Sibling 2: "She is on death's door for Christ's sake and you're doing a Gant chart. Are you out of your mind? You've got a lot of nerve falling back on your 'I can handle everything routine' when the time for that was months ago, not today. I am so sick of your attitude, I could just-."

Sibling 1: "This is so sad. Not one of you is thinking of her. I know what she wants, she's confided in me. She trusts me; she always has. I know she wants a DNR order, what dress she wants to be buried in. I have a handle on this stuff because I've always been there…"
And then the real battle begins.

Or, take this typical business exchange:

Contractor: "We have a contract. You signed the contract. I did the work to spec. Now you need to pay. That's how it's done in the business world…I assume you know that."

Home Owner: "Look. I contracted with you to get my backyard resurfaced and to bury the debris. You may think the work has been done to spec but it's not what we agreed to in the contract. There's crap all over the yard. What little may have been buried is still showing up through the dirt and if that is level, I need to take up drinking."

Contractor: "Oh, so now you're the authority on level! That yard is level and far better off than it's ever been. We actually did *more* work than what the contract called for and we're waiting – patiently, I might add – for payment."

Home Owner: "Well it might have helped if you'd returned my calls. I've been trying to talk to you for weeks."

Contractor: "Look. I agreed to meet with you to settle this thing. I am trying to help here. We can litigate this but it's going to cost a lot of money and lost time. I suggest you make a list of what you think needs to be done and I'll have my attorney look at it."

Home Owner: "I can make a list until the cows come home but it won't make a bit of difference. You are not going to fulfill the contract and I am not going to pay for shoddy workmanship; I don't care what your attorney thinks. I suggest we both go over there right now and I will show you the deficiencies directly. Then you can tell me how you are going to straighten out this mess."

Contractor: "You're cheap. That's your problem. I know folks like you. They just grind you down. You'll never fulfill your –"

Home Owner: "You don't know me at all. I'm not cheap and never have been. And when I make a contract, I fulfill it…unlike some of the stories I've heard about you."

Contractor: "You little weasel. I do a good business. People know me as a quality businessman who keeps his word. You just want to weasel your way out of paying. You've probably got some short man complex or something. You can't admit when you're wrong and you won't live up to your obligations."

This could go on for hours.

The funny thing about help is that it's often met with resistance. We make a suggestion and the other person gets defensive. We recommend a better approach and someone reacts angrily. We offer our assistance and the other guy snaps back a retort. Clearly in the first scenario, everyone wants to help Mom; they just each have a different version of it. The same is true of the business exchange. Both parties think they're helping. If asked, both would say they offered concessions and met the other more than half way.

But ours is a society of fixers. We each know the perfect solution. We know precisely what to do and how to do it. And we know with certainty, that we're right. The fact that our help may not solve the problem, shuts-down the person seeking it, or is self-serving to any degree, rarely gives us pause. According to recent research on the human brain, our desire to help is innate. Science tells us that in humans:

> The "sympathetic circuit" is hard-wired, at least in most of us…The brain is designed so that acts of charity are pleasurable; being nice to others makes us feel nice (Lehrer, 2009, pp. 188; 183-184).

In other words, we help because it feels good. But how we help gets cluttered with personal needs, one-upsmanship, and unfinished business from the past; with beliefs and judgments; with sarcasm, accusations, and competitive tit-for-tats. While well-intended, it comes off as something else entirely and is received accordingly. Instead of helping, we end up *adding* to the constant state of conflict we live in.

Most conflict begins with a difference in perspectives and dissolves into an argument…along with the anger, temper, hurt feelings, and wounded pride that come with it. We may state our opinion as fact, or sound critical and patronizing; we may believe what we're doing is best, or simply see an issue differently. Regardless of how it happens, instead of welcoming our assistance, it's resisted: people stop listening past the first sentence, they take things personally or try to defend themselves, they declare broad truths or look for someone to blame. We end up trying to convince one another that we're right, locked in a power struggle to prove ourselves. We never get past the words. After that, people rarely take our advice or make the choices we want.

But this is the nature of how we help at this moment in time. In fact, it's the nature of many present-day human relations. That's because they all stem from the same source, the same presupposition: **a person-self… the one that knows and needs**. How we help is a reflection of where we have evolved to as human beings. It validates the very mental constructs that create conflict in the first place: the deeply ingrained sense of self, an ego that needs, and an addiction to thoughts and thinking. This person-self is the source of all difficulties; it's the reason for the constant state of conflict and the broken nature of help.

The problem is not helping per se; nor the helpers, let alone those who seek help. _It's how we help_: we help one person-self to another. We grow attached to a particular outcome, a specific way of getting there, or to helping itself. When we help, we need "to get them to _____": to make the right choice, do the right thing, do things our way; take the best job offer, get some professional help, stop doing this or that. Then helping hurts: it's our way and their situation, our solution and their reality. "They" become separate and other. Whenever we try to force our ideas on others, naturally they resist. This kind of help is prescriptive and directive. It causes defensiveness and competition. Meanwhile the kind of help we need is in critically short supply.

Clearly, the broken nature of help deserves special attention; in part because it's mirrored in so many other human endeavors. But what's really important is **what it's pointing to**. Not surprisingly, how we help doesn't respond to new programs or paradigms, or an influx of funds because the situation is pointing to something much deeper. As Einstein said, we can't resolve the problems of the world from the same level of consciousness that created those problems. So too, we can't resolve conflict from the same consciousness that creates both conflict and the way we help.

This book acknowledges a next stage in human awareness; not some pleasant, Pollyannaish panacea but a natural next step. Just as the universe evolves, so too does human awareness. Moreover, this transition is already happening, as numerous authors and spiritual teachers have pointed out and described. Many other people are coming to this same conclusion at the same moment, acknowledging that what we're doing, clearly, is not working; that we're evolving beyond a wholesale reliance on conceptual thought and all its trappings. This next state of awareness is changing and will change _everything_, including how we help.

Helping holds the seeds of the next state of awareness. Further, those who help will likely be among the first en masse to usher it in. But what makes this book a breakthrough is not that that it too, ascribes to a next state. **What makes this book a breakthrough is that it _applies_ it: it envisions how help will evolve in the next state of human awareness**, without being prescriptive or directing how things should be. As the next state takes root, how we help will grow beyond training; beyond knowledge, advice, and ideas. It will come from a place deeper than the heart. The next state will bring about a simultaneous shift in how we see, how we are, and where we're going which will change everything we think we know about how we help.

This book is divided into three sections. The first section addresses the constant state of conflict we live in. It examines the many causes of conflict: the role of compulsive thinking, our needs-based orientation to the world, and the ultimate source of conflict. It makes the point that conflict isn't natural but at least for now, it serves a fundamental purpose: we need it to survive. This section introduces the notion of the person-self, its link to the mind and its various attachments. It also examines conflict and the person-self from the vantage point of neuroscience to explain why we see the world as we do and how perception contributes to the prevalence of conflict.

The second section of the book considers the role of helping in resolving conflict and why our current concept of "help" doesn't work. It addresses everyday help – the kind of help we offer others everyday, in terms of the advice and assistance; the work of professional helpers; and social help – the help offered on a mass scale by organizations and institutions.

Chapters in Section Two examine the prescriptive and directive way we help. This section considers several fields such as counseling, court systems, family support networks, etc., and explores one field in particular, that of mediation, to describe how help is broken. Mediation was chosen because of all the helping professions, it prides itself on empowering participants to formulate their own solutions: technically speaking, it should be non-directive, neutral, and reduce conflict. The final chapter in this section considers who's to blame for this, the human condition, highlighting personal, cultural, and collective rationales. It reviews the kind of help that is offered by such institutions as education and organized religion, among others. It also draws on recent advancements in neuroscience with respect to empathy, tiers of emotion, and how we process other people's points of view.

The final section of the book looks at the next state of awareness and offers a glimpse of where it hides in plain sight. The chapters in this section allow readers to engage the next state and experience it if they so choose. They describe how various transformational paths and New Age approaches have led us astray in our quest for the next state, and how easily we can falter even once we find the next state in ourselves.

An entire chapter in Section Three is devoted to imagining what help may look like in the next state of awareness; the factors that will shape it, how we shift in our experience of differences, and what really matters when we offer help. Special attention is paid to both, the professional helper and what the next state means for everyday helpers: the tools we use, our demeanor and role, and the process and product of help. This section also describes the progression from our current state to what comes next, and answers questions that might arise as we proceed.

In reading this book, certain items are in italics for emphasis. Those in italics and underlined have relevance throughout the book, while those in bold summarize key points and concepts. Infused throughout the book are the teachings of Eckhart Tolle and others, to whom this author is forever indebted. Without Tolle's insights about conflict and the ongoing shift in awareness, this book would have never been possible.

Most importantly, to avoid any confusion, let it be said at the onset, *nothing in this book is meant to offend or discourage those who help or those who seek it.* This book uses help as a prism through which to examine the human condition. It does so because help is special. What we currently call "help" reinforces the deep mental constructs that create both help and the conflict that drives us to seek help in the first place. And yet, this is a breakthrough moment in human evolution and help is pointing the way. The purpose of this book is to offer each of us a chance to consider how we help and why; to question the underpinnings of our collective definition of what it means to help; and most essentially, to consider what we are truly capable of as human beings in the area of help and beyond. But first, we have to understand the symbiotic relationship between conflict and help as it exists today.

Section One

1   A Thinking Self

We live in a constant state of conflict with ourselves, with others, and with what is. We don't see it because it feels normal; we've grown accustom to it. We wake up, weigh-in, check for wrinkles or gray hairs, and our spirit sinks. Or we recall the argument from last night; the things we didn't mean but said with gusto. Or we remember it's Monday and we have to go to work; it's cold and grey outside, and need to hit the gym before dinner…

Worse still, our world is nestled in a much larger one that seems to be running amuck. Law-abiding citizens are finding it makes more sense to walk away from a mortgage contract then to pay it. Adult children are flocking home because they simply cannot make it on their own. Entire states are thinking about filing for bankruptcy. Global warming, long term health insurance, and spending cuts have become everyday topics of conversation…just as our commitment to civil discourse has all but disappeared. And we haven't even touched on world affairs.

We blame this condition on all sorts of things: bad parenting, a lackluster education system, the erosion of moral values; fewer people attending church, a rise in violence, the decline of the family unit, an unrestrained media. At times, it can feel like we're beyond help. But this is a hopeful sign: the fact that so many structures are crumbling is pointing to what's wrong *and* to the way out. We only have to look at the situation more deeply…

In our heart of hearts, we each think we're *somebody* -- and therein lies the problem.

════════════ Contracting Into a "Me"

Most of us were taught we *evolve* as human beings. We start with certain personal aptitudes and universal capacities, innate abilities and gifts, a given temperament, and we grow from there. We acquire language and, to a lesser or greater extent, the skills to communicate. We learn to navigate a family situation and over time, increasingly larger and more complex social settings. We accumulate knowledge and experience, to varying degrees and over differing lengths of time. We learn to maneuver in a society of expectations and a culture of rules and opportunities.

There is however, another point of view. We can be seen as *condensing* into our present form: from a state of pure energy which contains all possible configurations, we shrink down into *this* body and *this* mind. From there, the contraction continues: from the full breadth of all the possible ways we *could* be, we condense down into this *particular* person with its own thoughts, emotions, fears, and desires (See Yogic Sciences, Kashmir Shaivism; See also Shantananda, Easwaran, and Frawley).

You can imagine pure energy as infinite potential, brimming with every conceivable outcome, capable of manifesting any shape, form, thought, or entity. Then it contracts into a particular body and a particular mind. A body that loves to run, makes varsity track, has no sense of rhythm and consequently, can't dance, has a weakness in its back muscles which slowly becomes chronic...maybe condensing further to a body that used to run, grows heavy and lethargic, and tires on an up-hill climb.

The mind follows a similar contracting pattern. We start as an open slate of abundant possibilities and step-by-step, we create a self...a person-self. The person-self is our slice of the infinite breadth of possibilities...the one that's known as "me". It's comprised of all the thoughts, associated emotional states and behavioral patterns we repeat most frequently, the ones we *identify* with. It embodies our temperament, moods, beliefs, values, opinions, needs, feelings, mannerisms and reactions. We also share a set of deeply conditioned collective patterns with our fellow beings; among them,

- An underlying feeling of uncertainty;
- The tendency to compare people and things;
- A viewpoint that tends to be dualistic; and,
- A nagging sense of discontent.

This person-self has a voice. It's the voice in our head and a tool for expression. The voice speaks the mind. It interprets our external experience and narrates our moment-to-moment inner world. It tells us what we think and often conveys that thought out-loud, and gives expression to the repetitive ways we think, feel, and behave. But it also talks *to* us: reaffirming, rationalizing, analyzing, explaining, labeling, questioning, and reiterating our reality. The once abounding pure energy is more limited now: it's compressed into a distinct being where experience is processed in a very personal way.

From this point of view, we live life as *a person-self, a mental image of who we think we are*. Our patterned ways of being harden down from use and become automatic; or as some say, as we grow, we grow more so. The future becomes defined by what has come before. We anticipate, experience, and react to life in a fixed way, shaped by the past. So "I" am as I've always been...which leads to such comments as, "Well, you know me," "That's just how I am," "I have to be true to myself," or "I'm standing on principle here." It's all a process of contraction.

These two points of view are not contradictory. When we live as a person-self, we still continue to accumulate knowledge, only of a more limited kind: book knowledge, individualized experience, relational skills, and navigational tools. What distinguishes the two views is the sense of direction: one sees the person-self as an expanding experience, the other as a condensing one. The former sees the person-self as the goal; the latter sees it as a step. Yet even while we're condensing, we still have pure energy, the supply of infinite potential, at our disposal:

> [We have] the whole room, and we limit ourselves to the one tiny portion of it where we have "spun" our own creation....We perceive some objects and not others...make associations with our past experiences, and so we invest our perceptions with our own meanings...This, then, becomes our world...We have no other (Shantananda, 2003, p. 76).

Of all the possible realities, we shrink down to one – mine -- and a habituated collection of thoughts, feelings, and actions we repeat over and over again.

══════ We Each Have a Story to Tell

Every person-self has a story to tell. It's the story of "me". Our story is the running narrative in our head. You can compare it to a news story: a certain event happens and the news industry goes to work. It investigates and asks questions: What really happened? When did they know? What should have happened? Could it happen again? And, who's to blame? The result is a *story*. The same is true for the person-self.

We each have a story we repeat to ourselves and tell others about "my life"; how we see the world and other people. Our story is both self-defining and self-fulfilling. In my story, "I" play the leading role because everything in the mind is processed from the vantage point of "I". My likes and dislikes, preferences and prejudices, dreams and expectations, all play an integral part in my story. And my story evolves over time, complete with plots and subplots.

Our stories are grounded in the past and anxiety over the future: what happened to me, what might happen, the dilemmas I face, what I have to look forward to, what I've gained, lost, need, and worry about. Our stories embody the sum total of all the experiences we have processed to date. Whatever we choose to take in from the outside world is incorporated into our story. If it doesn't quite fit, we adjust it.

Our stories shape and confirm our sense of identity. Many people, for example, identify with their jobs and that becomes their story: "I'm a teacher, so I value education. I always put the children's studies first and tell them…." If you were to tell this person otherwise, he would take offense and get defensive because you'd be attacking how he sees himself.

People love to tell their story and will often do so unsolicited:

- "I was an only child. My parents were very busy, so I never gained the self confidence I needed to…"
- "I've been fat all my life. It's in the genes. I've tried every…"
- "I made lots of money but I blew it. I had a really good time but now, looking back, I should have…"
- "Everyone abandons me. It's happened all my life. I'm afraid to trust anyone. I just can't depend on…"
- "I love doing for other people. I've always been that way, every since I was a child. I've always been there for others…"
- "My mother raised a strong woman. I can do this job – degree or no degree. That's not the issue. What's important is…"
- "I keep choosing the wrong person. They just don't make me happy. In my next relationship, I'll be sure to…"

We may have a complaining story, a procrastinating story, or a story of poor health. We may be a victim, feel unworthy or taken for granted; feel superior, better educated or spiritually advanced. We may be overachievers; carry a story full of rotten relationships and unfulfilled dreams, or of abuse, poverty and missed opportunities.

Our story lines are endless. We can whip up a story about a single event or issue: the man who describes himself as an "avid listener, a fierce defender, and a staunch supporter" of his local public radio station – that's a big piece of his story. Or we can weave a story into a full-blown life style: the environmentally enlightened woman, complete with a license plate that proclaims her to be "vegan", who feels very strongly that everyone should follow her lead.

Once our stories firm up, they become a kind of emotional script. We tend to see events and circumstances through our story. We also use our stories to justify or explain ourselves: "Well, you know, I've never been very good at intimacy. I always…" Yet every story is a contracted point of view. It's a way of reminding ourselves and shouting out to the world -- "This is who/what/how I am."

Me or Mind?

The person-self is immersed in the mind, just as the mind is in the person-self. They feed off one another. When we speak of mind, we're doing so as in neuroscience: "as an 'emergent' property of neurons when they are assembled" (Lewis, 2009, personal papers). In other words, the mind "emerges spontaneously from the assemblage of neurons that make up the brain" (ibid.). By brain, we mean all of the brain's inputs, including our interactions with other people and their brains, as well as the social environment.

The person-self is made up entirely of thoughts; it is wholly mind-*made*. Our stories, principles, past and future – these are thoughts too. As a person-self, we are both created and controlled by the mind; a mind conditioned by the past, communicated and reaffirmed by a voice, and that imprisons the future; a mind that shapes how we see out and what we let in and in time, grows indistinguishable from who we are. As a person-self, the mind produces thoughts and chatters away. This constant thinking, what Eckhart Tolle calls "compulsive thinking", is a deeply ingrained, collective human trait. We are forever analyzing, dissecting, interpreting, planning, questioning, justifying, and configuring…thinking.

If you don't believe this, watch your mind for a moment. It tells you what's happening and what to do next. You are constantly thinking: What did he mean by that? Where is she going? Why did she do that? Try as you may, within a moment's time, you've forgotten what it was you meant to remember because another thought has taken its place. Our senses act as the mind's gathering tools. Even our emotions are slaves to it: emotions are mental perceptions that take place in the body; which is to say, we react physiologically to what the mind is thinking.

But why is this so? Why are we so addicted to the mind? It's because *the person-self is never okay as it is*. Its entire existence is haunted by fear and desire. So the person-self makes it its mission to avoid anything it finds threatening and attain whatever it desires. Unfortunately for the person-self, it doesn't rule the world – it needs the mind to help out. The mind's job is simple: make everything okay. The person-self relies on the mind to make sure everything goes according to plan; to keep us happy and shield us from pain, to make sure people like us and don't hurt us… in other words, to "create a semblance of control" (Singer, 2007, pp. 91; 13). This is, of course, an impossible task which keeps the mind constantly engaged and the person-self fully absorbed in it.

As a result, we live in our heads. We spend our entire lives lost in, deep in, mired in thought. We label every item, classify each event, and reflect on every situation. The mind creates our agendas and to-do lists; it generates our reactions, opinions, solutions, and actions. We become transfixed with problems: figuring them out, weighing our options, and trying to fix things; explaining how things work and why people behave as they do; strategizing what to do and anticipating off into the future. We are dominated by thoughts, inundated by them, driven by them. And in time *we become them*.

We become this person-self. We accept it *as* our self. We go by a given name, are a man or woman; a gay man, a businesswoman. We identify with a career: we're managers or care takers, plumbers, secretaries, stay-at-home Dads, mail carriers, or restaurateurs. We're blond or brunette, young or youthful, Democrat or Republican. We're contemplative, jealous, gentle, practical, joyful, serious or carefree. We contract down to a mental image of who we think we are; a descriptive set of characteristics that get woven into our stories…thoughts we make *real*.

What was once a mental construct is now "me", and "I" and "mine". **We live life as a person-self with "Mind" in charge.** We believe in the story. We obey the voice. We mis-take Mind and its thoughts for who we are and spend the rest of our lives attending to, improving, adding to, and maintaining that person-self. From that point forward, "We derive our sense of self from the content and activity of our mind" (Tolle, 1999, p.

18). And everybody does it, so we hardly ever notice (Tolle, *The Doorway into Now Intensive*, 2008).

=============== I Know, and I Know I'm Right

The person-self is a collection of thoughts we've grown attached to: it is our self, it's *me*. Of course, we could be anyone. In fact in some schools of thought, we could choose to be anyone at any point in time. There's no reason we have to be who we were yesterday.

Similarly, we don't have to believe what Mind tells us or do as it says. It's Mind that tells us that it's Monday, and cold and dreary outside. We could just as easily look outside and dress accordingly, without the mental commentary or dampened spirits. Periodically, we try to do just that: we make resolutions and vow, "From now on, I'll _____" -- lose weight, be more sensitive, listen to my kids, whatever. But very quickly, we slip back into our old established ways. There's a reason for this, yet it doesn't have to be so.

Nevertheless, once we accept this person-self as our self, it becomes our sole frame of reference. We see our self in a certain light and like to project and present that portrait to others. But because this person-self is not *some thing* we can touch or point to – because it's a collection of thoughts -- it needs constant reinforcement. So everything we think, do, and say is aimed at bolstering the person-self...at propping it up. Everything happens from the vantage point of "I":

- "Hi, *I'm* _____"
- "*I* need to _____"
- "This is important to *me*"
- "*I* love _____"
- "This is *my* family"
- "*I* have a degree in _____"
- "*I'm* in charge here"
- "This is *my* new _____."

Given the alliance between "me" and Mind, it's not surprising we put a lot of stock in *the content* of Mind. Mind processes information from our inner world and the world around us. It thinks and perceives. The way we think and perceive is unique to us: no-one else does it exactly as we do. Thinking and perceiving is central to who we think we are. It's how *we know*:

The act of perceiving and knowing is at the very root of our existence as individuals…[It's how we understand and give] personal meaning to everything around us. [It's what] distinguishes us as a separate, experiencing entity (Shantananda, 2003, p. 133).

Knowing is what makes us a *particular* person-self, distinct from everyone else…a "some" body. Who and how and what we know allows us to feel special, one-of-a-kind. In fact, as a person-self, **we _need_ to know**: it's how the person-self exerts influence, asserts itself, and confirms its existence.

And of course, what we know is *right*. We all assume our beliefs and opinions, values and morals, wants and needs are certain and irrefutable. But to the person-self, being right means something more than just being factual: it means being true, virtuous, and just. Being right gives us integrity and a sense of honor. As a person-self, **we _need_ to be right** because being right makes us "good". After all, since me and my thoughts are the same, if my thoughts are wrong…what does that say about *me*?

Knowing and being right are two of the essential ways we prop up the person-self. Doing so validates "me". It helps fortify and solidify who we think we are; our sense of self. In our search for constant reinforcement, we look to others to acknowledge and confirm "me" and "my thoughts" as well. So we spew them out as fact…when they're only thoughts. And we protect and defend them…as if *I* was threatened. I agree with everything that agrees with "me" and join up with others who share my views because it makes me feel good…it strengthens *me*.

======== The One That Knows

The person-self that knows is at the heart of all our difficulties. Thanks to Mind, we have an image to uphold and a perspective to defend. We need to appear in control and attempt to control all things. Along with knowing comes assumptions and the need to fix things; prejudice, jealousy, and division. And with needing to be right comes competition and winning. We end up fighting with everything – with our self, with others, and with what is.

Moreover, we tend to grow *more* Mind-dominated rather than less. Most of us think continuously. We thrive on distraction and noise; on drama, words, movement, and action. Our fascination with gadgets and devices has driven us even further into our heads. We spend entire days glued to the computer, thinking our thoughts and having them reflected back to us; "communicating" through chat rooms and blogs, never seeing another human being; absorbed in our own little worlds on cell phones and video games.

We build our lives around the person-self and the belief that it is who we are. And we've built an entire social structure around that. We see others as separate and distinct, in terms of how they compare to "me", my likes, and my needs. We gather as groups of person-selves and form fraternities over beliefs we hold in common. We interact according to concepts that order and direct us: rules, traditions, rituals, organizations, methods, and systems. All of these are thoughts. All are Mind-made. And all are predicated on a person-self that thinks and knows.

=============== ## A Person-ized Reality

As a person-self, we rarely consider *not* thinking. In fact, we tend to believe whatever Mind tells us. Through Mind, we create an individualized experience of reality based on thoughts, which is told and re-told through our stories and our internal running dialogue. That reality "becomes our world...We have no other" (Shantananda, 2003, p. 76). And it all seems *so real*.

Just consider for a moment the many conventions we accept as real: time, dates and calendars, numbers and words. We assume this tall, strong, leafy green entity that is flowing in the wind is a tree when "tree" is just a label we've given it. We have crime and justice, agreements and contracts, glamour and celebrity, money, credit, and means of exchange; language, books, and measures; work weeks, holidays, hierarchies, groups, and life stages; news and politics; governments, countries, tribes, and unions, all of which we accept as real. These are cultural conventions -- social *constructions* -- yet we accept them as real. Our daily life is circumscribed by these conventions and our reality is bound by them.

Within these walls, we live a life that feels incredibly real. We have a family to worry about, health problems and aging parents, kids who live in what can be a pretty scary place. We have jobs and timetables, competing demands, and people who need our skills. We have responsibilities to fulfill and expectations to meet; memories and hurts, worries and hopes for the future. Life feels profoundly serious, "immensely real, almost physically palpable" (Hofstadter, 2007, p. 180).

And yet, this is a surface view; our "life situation", as Eckhart Tolle likes to call it. It's the conditions and circumstances the make up our life; where "I" spend my time and Mind, and where the person-self lives. That's not to say that what we see isn't real. Rather, it's real *to me*. Our reality is a view of the surface of life from a viewpoint that is highly *person*alized – it's an "I-view". It's reflected through our deeply ingrained collective patterns, our personal history and experience, our strongly held values, our assumptions and needs. It's part of Mind's ongoing effort to create some semblance of control: to "bring the infinite…down to the finite" and make the "unknown known" (Singer, 2007, p. 20). It's a contracted point of view that's only real to me.

From this personal reality, we lock into a worldview. In time, it grows hard to even imagine another perspective. Meanwhile, Mind grows all the more crowded, noisy and full of information as the voice rages on. Even if the entire rug gets pulled out from under us, the person-self quickly recovers as Mind seeks to set things right again. But it's never enough… because we're never satisfied.

═══════════ ## How We Help

The person-self that knows affects every aspect of our life situation, including how we help. Why we help, how we view others, and what we do when we help are all influenced by the nature of the person-self; by:

- The process of contraction;
- Our deeply conditioned collective patterns;
- Our personal beliefs and stories that solidify;
- The unique way we think and perceive;
- The constant need to think;
- The becoming Mind and thoughts, and living in our heads;
- Our individualized experience of reality;
- The belief that it's all real; and,
- The feeling that it's never enough.

Looking at this list, it's shouldn't be a surprise that how we "help" separates and classifies people; that it feels intensely real and serious, addresses an inner lack or need, and involves repeating our stories; that it is referred to professionals who are expected to fix us and relies on thinking, analyzing, and figuring things out; and that it seeks to validate us as individuated persons. This kind of "help" props up the person-self…*both of them*. At least for now, help is Mind-made too.

2 The One That Knows *and* Needs

The person-self is not entirely a bad thing. It's just over-rated and outmoded. But why create a self in the first place? Why bother?

The fact is no-one knows for sure. Perhaps the power of the thinking brain just takes over and the self is an attempt to balance the thinking and experiential parts of our existence. Perhaps it's the momentum of millennia: in the Vedic sciences, it's said that Consciousness takes form in order to experience itself. We may be following suit, creating a self as an instrument through which to experience reality. Or maybe it's hard-wired. At birth, we're each given a "neurobiological chassis" complete with all the capacities evolution has decided are most valuable. Perhaps the self is among them…or at least it's been replicated so many times, the self is now an automatic fixture that becomes our organizing principle.

In his book, *I am a Strange Loop*, Douglas Hofstadter examines the idea of a self, exploring whether it is a "mysterious abstraction" or a "convenient fiction" (2007). He suggests that the creation of a self as a distinct entity is not really *that* extraordinary:

> Once the ability to sense external goings-on has developed…
> this ability…flips around and endows the being with the ability
> to sense certain aspects of *itself*…That this flipping around takes
> place…is a quite unremarkable, indeed trivial, consequence of the
> being's ability to perceive (2007, pp. 73-74).

So possibly one answer to why we create a self is because we can.

But maybe it's something more. Certainly a self serves a unique function for human beings because dogs don't seem to have one. It's hard to imagine a dog who has just missed catching a mole reflecting back on why she failed; whether her mother is somehow responsible, how it looked to the other dogs, whether her owner will be disappointed in her, and what it says about her future success as a dog. A dog has *being* but no self; Consciousness but no self.

One possibility is that human beings have a self is to feel safe. Perhaps Mind creates a self as a way *to last* – to counter our fears, realize our desires, and feel safe, solid and secure. For certain, once we adopt this person-self as our self, it takes on a life force of its own. The person-self, Mind, voice, story -- all collude as aspects of the same construction, driving us on. The self becomes an emblem of sorts, something we search for, as "I'm looking for myself". It's also something we can lose, as the divorced partner who claims, "I don't know who I am without him."

And the person-self is not just a personal matter. We identify equally and often more strongly with our <u>*collective selves*</u>: the associations we form around religion, academic institutions, football teams, professional organizations, political parties, countries, and causes. Consider the casual swimmer at the local recreation center who wants to be known as "Pastor Jim" at the pool. Our identities are *very* important to us, and in the case of our collective selves, they are all the more emboldened by the constant confirmation of others.

But regardless of our mix of collective and personal selves, as determined as Mind is, Mind has very little control over what actually happens. Anyone who has had their life turned upside-down by an illness, an accident, or the sudden death of a loved one knows this fact all too well. We each live with a subtle, underlying sense of insecurity; a feeling that things are never quite right. We never feel complete, or satisfied, or perfected. We're never truly whole. And even if we are for a moment, the feeling never lasts. We're always searching, looking for the next thing.

As a person-self, we live our thoughts. We're not automatons, just well-rehearsed. We still have a full array of choices at our disposal; we just tend to rely on a set of conditioned ways of thinking, feeling, and being. Nor are we passive and inert: we are actively engaged in our thoughts, our stories, and our life situations. We could choose to be anyone at any point in time, but we live as a contracted "me". And we do so in the hopes of feeling safe and secure...

As a person-self, **we _need_ to last**. It gives us a sense of purpose, a meaning for existence. It invests us in the future and gives us faith. It also drives us to grasp at and cling to people, thoughts, and things. Taken together, the need to know, the need to be right, and the need to last comprise the person-self's **core needs** (See Figure 2.1). The core needs are three essential ways we prop up the person-self. Through them, we can believe we are a special person, a good one; someone leading a purposeful life, with a promising future. Or to put it another way, the core needs help the person-self pretend…that it's *real*.

Figure 2.1

The Person-Self's Core Needs		
Need	Purpose Served	Related Tendencies
To Know	To feel special, exert influence, and confirm itself	To make assumptions; a need to fix things; prejudice and division
To Be Right	To feel true, virtuous and good	To compete and a desire to win
To Last	To have a sense of purpose and meaning, future and faith	To grasp and cling at people, thoughts, and things

Needs-Based Consciousness

It's important to remember our relationship to the person-self. The person-self is not some foreign entity that invades our body and takes over. It's who we think we are; it's how we see our self. If asked who we are, we'd describe the person-self…for each of us, it's *me*.

As a person-self, we relate to our self, to others, and to the world around us through our needs. Needs are part of the structure of Mind. When we talk about Mind, we're talking about the *conditioned mind* – the mind conditioned by the past, by life's events, experience and culture, by collective patterns and individual circumstances. Our thoughts are dominated by needs, beginning with the core ones from which all other needs flow. Needs serve many purposes: they feed our personal dramas and add to our stories; they keep us entertained and distracted; and they allow us to feel important, worthwhile, useful, and in control. Needs are one of the key ways we feel alive *as a person-self.* In other words, when Mind creates a self, it creates one that thinks compulsively *and* needs...one that knows and needs.

We live in a state of Needs-based Consciousness, meaning we relate to the world through our needs. Except for a handful of people, what we're calling **Needs-based Consciousness is the current state of human awareness**. Needs-based Consciousness (NBC) strengthens the person-self. It engages Mind's innate tendencies to analyze, judge, contrast, seek, label and justify. It keeps us fixated on our thoughts and stuck in our heads. Through our needs and their pursuit, it feels like we will last forever. NBC temporarily relieves our feeling of dissatisfaction, as we quickly replace one need with the next.

NBC also separates and hardens us. It leaves us deep in thought and focused on "me". If, as Einstein said, we can't solve our problems from the same consciousness that created them, NBC was what he was talking about: NBC has, and continues to be, the consciousness that creates our problems. It has produced an entire planet of "me's", each fully intent on pursuing its needs. As seen in Figure 2.2, NBC is a critical link in the person-self cycle:

<u>Figure 2-2</u>
The Person-Self Cycle

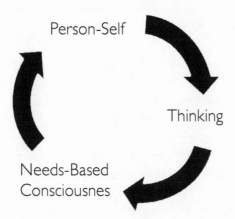

Person-Self

Thinking

Needs-Based
Consciousnes

A. What We Mean By "Needs"

By needs, we're not just talking about the obvious: more, bigger, and better "stuff". At some point, the Volvo doesn't thrill. And you can only redo your kitchen so many times. Even the latest gadgets become rapidly obsolete. Nor are we talking about being entirely selfish, just _self_-serving.

Our needs are props: they support and enhance who we think we are. They give us a direction, a drive, something to strive for. Needs include the expectations others have of us, the obligations we make, and the to-do lists of things we _need_ to get done. They include the promises we make, our aspirations and goals, logistical considerations, and the rituals, traditions, and conventions we abide by:

- I need to get this project done, always be on time, and be there for my sister;
- I need to learn to talk to my baby's Mom, feel more a part of this community, help build houses in Belize;
- I need to be recognized and valued, respected and appreciated;
- I need to motivate my employees, be a better leader, and realize my full potential;
- I need to spread the word of God, stand up for what's right, be admired by my fellow team members;
- I need to support my kids, downsize my lifestyle, and recommit to my family;
- I need to get in shape, be more health conscious, learn to relax and express my anger more responsibly;
- I need to start with a perfectly clean desk in the morning, always dress the part, and prove my worth to this company;
- I need some time to process my feelings, consider my options, make a decision;
- I need to get back at him for what he did, talk to her about getting back together, understand why she left me;
- I need to focus on what I do well, inspire others through my work, and lead by example;
- I need to minister to the needy, do a family intervention, get him to counseling.

Not only do we deal with our initial needs, but the standard to which we try to meet them – the _level_ of appreciation, the _degree_ of admiration, the _amount_ of time, etc. – generates additional needs. So we don't just want to support our kids, we need to give them more than what we had;

we don't just want to be a successful lawyer, we need to be a partner in the firm. We also "own" the needs we impose on others: to the extent we need him "to change", or "clean up his room", or "get some help", these needs belong to us and *not* the person we're imploring to act.

The main point is this: we're all about needs. We may call them desires or demands or necessities, but needs dominate our thoughts and our lives. Endemic to NBC are such thoughts as achievement, success, performance, productivity, fulfillment, progress, prosperity, security, and winning. And equally, failure, suffering, shame, disappointment, deficient, imperfection, incomplete, and losing. Another word comes to Mind as well: *contentious.* Conflict is an inevitable part of the NBC state of awareness: we fight with our self, we fight with others, and we fight with what is…and oftentimes, it has a lot to do with our needs.

B. The Tripod of Needs-Based Consciousness

NBC keeps us living on the surface, operating from the vantage point of "I" and "me" and "mine". When my needs aren't met, *I* often blame the situation on others or circumstances beyond my control. When bad things happen to *me*, I feel as though someone or something did them *to* me. When things don't go my way -- the way *I need* them to go -- I rant and rave, or rationalize it away and quickly forget what went wrong and why.

There's nothing wrong with NBC, it's just one dimensional. It's based on a tripod of assumptions:

Figure 2-3
The NBC Tripod of Assumptions

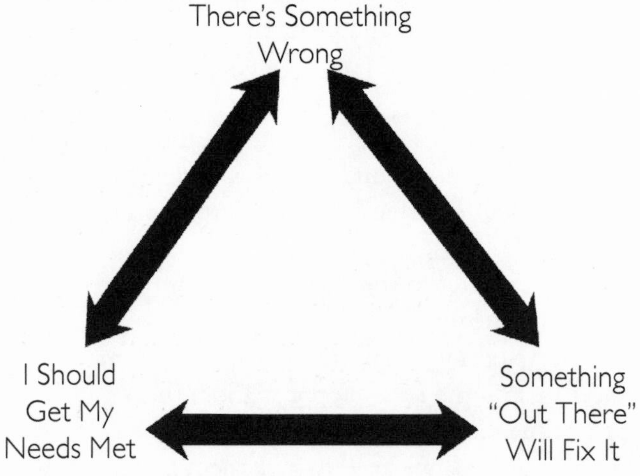

There's Something
Wrong

I Should
Get My
Needs Met

Something
"Out There"
Will Fix It

The first is we assume there's something wrong with the way we are, here and now. As we've said, the person-self is never okay as it is. There's always some problem, an obstacle or challenge that must be met; something that's not quite right, not perfect. We accept as truth what Don Miguel Ruiz calls the Lie of Imperfection:

> [You believe] you *are not* the way you should be, you *are not* good enough, you *are not* perfect…So you start to search for an *image* of perfection that you can never become…[that] you will never reach…because that image is false (2004, p. 20).

The Lie can apply to our self or our life situation: our income, living arrangement, relationships, etc. Regardless, things are not okay…life is not going according to plan.

The second is we look outward for satisfaction. We're convinced that something "out there" will make everything better. So we go looking for some thing that will make us okay, complete, and perfect; that will set things right in our world. Life becomes, as a result, a succession of very serious choices in which we must, we *need* to make the right one…as if we've only one chance and there's only one correct choice.

For some people satisfaction rests with a job, an engagement ring, or a new home; the perfect body, the most beautiful clothes, or extreme sports. For others, it's better health or greater security. Some people try to complete their self through what they know: they're constantly interjecting some tidbit of knowledge or piece of trivia that they think sets them apart from everyone else. Still others see yoga, meditation, religious devotion, or their "special gift" as the means to fulfillment. Unfortunately, "out there" is just another collection of thoughts and the satisfaction never lasts.

The third assumption of NBC is that we expect the world to deliver: we expect our needs to be met. When they're not, we're surprised, frustrated, and angry because we operate under the false assumption that _the world is here to make us happy_. We sincerely believe that life should go smoothly and we must get what we want. The disappointing results feed our stories and fill our surface lives with drama: "I'll never love again," "My career is ruined," "There's no point in going on."

The NBC tripod is an illusion through which we relate to the world. It's a trick that we fall for time and time again. **All needs are a form of resistance**. They are energy fighting against or for something to happen in a particular way; a contraction emanating from a contracted place.

C. The Nature of Needs

Needs are simply thoughts and most are quickly replaced. When one need fails to satisfy or is temporarily met, we quickly find another to take its place. Along the way, we compare our self to others and often compete with one another to get our needs met. Needs can also prey on our feeling of insecurity and give others the chance to judge and define us. Worse still, needs are self-seeding -- they proliferate. So the woman who is hovering over us at a restaurant, waiting to grab our table, who gets annoyed when we don't know to bus our own dishes and grows angry when the person she's telling this to is not responding to her liking, she's a profusion of needs! At first it's just our table she wants, but in very short order she needs cleanliness and order, recognition and respect, and for us to meet *her* standards…and this was just one minor event in her day.

While NBC engages all three core needs, it especially appeals to the need to last, as we search for something "out there" to make us feel safe, solid, and secure. Whereas most needs are temporary, some take on a more lasting nature. We call them issues, or "buttons", or attachments; they're the things we cling to. These deeper needs are often a projection of our own fears: we either fear something won't happen or fear it will. The more we fear, the more these attachments start to "run our lives" (Singer, 2007, p. 53). Moreover, the same energy we expend to meet our needs comes back to us *in kind*. So in the case of an attachment, if our deepest need is to protect a loved one because we know we could not bear to live without her, our own life situation becomes awash in over-cautious behavior, missed opportunities, and rigidity.

One final point about the nature of needs deserves mention. Needs generate *more* thinking. Through our needs we compile a catalog of unenforceable rules – a list of all the "should's, must's, and ought to's", depicting how we feel the world is meant to be. When events fail to conform, we mull them over in our head again and again. We think about "what if": what could have happened, what might have made the difference, what we should have said. We have so much faith in the power of our thoughts, we believe that with enough repetition, Mind will force things to change; it will set things right again (See Singer, 2007). Why else would we bother thinking them?

D. The Trouble with Needs

In NBC, our needs lie at the heart of every thought, feeling, and action. For many of us, this is hard to admit and even harder to accept. Oftentimes we *identify* with being a particular way: "I'm a great communicator", "a gifted teacher", "an anonymous donor", "a good provider" -- and we can't see beneath our identification. We're also trained to couch our behavior in good intentions such that the underlying needs never have a chance to surface and be examined.

To pull the veil back on our needs, we have to ask our self a question: *What is it we get out of* _____? Out of being a leader, standing in front of a group teaching, offering advice, keeping things perfectly clean and organized, letting others take control, tending to an elderly parent? It can run from pride to security to a general sense of satisfaction; or be as simple as doing so makes us feel good. Nevertheless, it's a need.

One way of answering this question is to stop doing what we're doing and see what needs arise (Singer, 2007, p. 121). Let's say someone is *the* premier local trainer on a given topic. She believes in her mission, gets all the best gigs, is nominated trainer of the year, is admired by her peers and sought after for events. If she's forced to stop, she'll notice what she misses: perhaps training is a chance to talk about her self and tell her story; she may miss the attention, the opportunity to feel important and discuss her ideas. Training may make her feel like a better person, that she's helping others, she's someone special. She may well find training meets quite a few of her needs.

When we pursue this line of questioning, the real needs that lie beneath the rationales are revealed:

- "Being a home health care aide is a noble pursuit" becomes, "I get a lot out of being a home health care aide. I've gained a real appreciation for life";
- "I serve my country because it's the right thing to do" translates into, "I do it because I believe in freedom and I'm afraid we'll lose it if we don't fight for it"; and,
- "I love her because she's wonderful" turns into, "Well, at the heart of it, she makes me feel good...*about me.*"

Living as a person-self in the current state of NBC awareness, everything can be traced back to an *"I"-need*. I-needs prop up and sustain the person-self in each of us. We define who we are, assert our self image, and assert our sense of self through our passions, our seeking, our yearnings...our needs. I-needs are also a prime contributor to much of the conflict in the world: they spur competition, sow ethnic tension and fuel unbridgeable divisions; they are the reasons we deplete natural resources, exploit peoples, and drive species and materials to extinction. Again, our needs are not necessarily selfish, although they very often are. They are always *self-serving.*

====== The Voice That Won't Stop Talking

Needs-based Consciousness is the glue that holds the person-self together. It is expressed through a voice, the same voice that tells our story. The Voice is the product of many conversations. It is conditioned by the past, our relationships with others, the media, and the culture. The Voice is commanded by Mind and as a result, talks all the time. It is Mind-made and very powerful. Don Miguel Ruiz calls the Voice, The Voice of Knowledge:

> When we are born, we don't have that voice. The voice...comes after we learn...language...different points of view, then all the judgments and lies...Little by little the whole Tree of Knowledge is programmed into our head...and eventually takes over (2004, p. 11).

Like the person-self, our needs, and compulsive thinking, The Voice is a deeply ingrained collective habit: *everyone* has a voice in the head. The Voice provides our internal running dialogue. It offers us non-stop commentary on the status of our inner world and how the outer world looks and feels to us. The Voice talks to us and keeps us company. It judges, consoles, and directs us: it tells us everything is okay, or what we should do to fix the situation, or how things will get better in the future. The Voice asks its own questions and then gives us the answer. It repeats events which have long since passed and if that doesn't satisfy, starts imagining tomorrow. The Voice feeds our stories and of course, keeps us stuck in our heads, mired in thought.

The Voice speaks the Mind and it *sounds like it knows.* Through it, we articulate and crystallize our I-needs. The Voice enforces the Tripod of Assumptions, reciting our numerous desires and deficiencies, conjecturing where we might go to find satisfaction, and then prodding us on. It ordains our unenforceable rules – the should's, must's, and ought to's – making us believe that someday, all our needs will be met. Generally, we live by The

Voice. We grow so accustom to it, it becomes background noise. If it ever went silent, we'd notice *that*.

The Voice is a driving force in the conflict that is an inevitable part of NBC. Internally and aloud, The Voice recites our frustrations and tallies our complaints. It tells us when we've been wronged and what to do next. It rationalizes our culpability and points the finger of blame. Whether fighting with our self, with others, or with what is, The Voice is a key player in the constant state of conflict we live in.

A Brain
That Fights with Itself

Everyday we make hundreds of decisions aimed at meeting our I-needs. In fact, the very nature of the human brain ensures we regularly face many competing needs.

Humans have what's called a triune brain. It's comprised of three sub-brains, each of which has survived because of its evolutionary value (Lewis, Lecture Series, 2009, citing the work of P.D. Maclean's *The Triune Brain*). The reptilian sub-brain is the oldest structure and houses the involuntary control centers such as heartbeat, breathing, and other physiological reflexes. It is generally considered the reward or "repetitive" center. It ascribes to the notion, "if it feels good, it must be good (evolutionally speaking), so do it again." Activities such as the need to eat, make money, seek revenge, have sex, and win are activated in this area of the brain.

The limbic sub-brain is the seat of our emotions, our small group/sociology centers. The limbic brain bridges the internal and the external world. It takes in sensory data, filters it, and then sends out directives. It is the limbic brain that gives us the experience of what someone else is feeling. Whereas reptilian brain emotions protect a single entity – say, a lizard -- through the experience of fear, limbic brain emotions protect small groups through such feelings as love and caring. It's been said that absent the limbic brain, we are little more than "angry reptiles" (Lewis, Lecture Series, 2009).

The neocortical is the newest and most recent brain, giving humans the skill of abstraction, the ability to work with and through symbols. This area of the brain allows us to create hypothetical events, strategize, and visualize "what-if" scenarios (Lewis et al., 2000, pp. 30-31). It's because of our vast repertoire of symbols -- predicated on our capacity to remember, categorize, and extract similarities -- that we are able to perceive, label, and provide commentary about our experiences; narrated by none other than The Voice. The neocortical brain is the source of our ultra-social desires and behavior: the capacity to cooperate, the idea of fairness and punishment, the desire for social cohesion, etc. Because of the neocortex, we are able to network, reason, plan, and execute as teams, for the good of "the many".

Not surprisingly, given these very different functions, the human brain is bombarded with many distinct and competing interests. Minimally, there are three different areas of the brain expressing different needs at the same time. Even when they agree on a specific need, they do so for different reasons! Say, for example, there's a candy bar in the freezer. The reptilian brain is saying: "Eat it. Eat it now. Then eat another one." The limbic brain may be whining: "I really want that candy bar but I know it's not mine. If I eat my kid's candy bar, he'll be so disappointed and I'll feel like a heel". And the neocortical brain may be cogitating: "If I eat it now, I'll spoil my dinner. I'll have an apple instead, it's a healthier choice. Besides, stealing is stealing, those are the rules. There, it's settled. On the other hand…"

The net result is *a brain that fights with itself*. In his book, *How We Decide,* Jonah Lehrer devotes an entire chapter to how "the brain *is* an argument" (emphasis added). Lehrer states:

> Conclusions are actually reached only after a series of sharp internal disagreements… Regardless of which areas [of the brain] are doing the arguing…the mind is an extended argument. And it is arguing with itself (2009, pp. 198-199).

With all this inner turmoil, Lehrer asks, how is it possible for us to finally decide? One might assume that logic wins out but "words, good ideas, and logic mean nothing to at least two brains out of three" (Lewis et al., 2000, p. 33). Instead, we often decide by overlooking, ignoring, or avoiding some often critical piece of information (Lehrer, 2009, p. 203). In effect, we take in what we pay attention to and disregard the rest.

The fighting nature of the brain explains in part why there are often *multiple* Voices in our head, each arguing with the other and scrambling for our attention. From the standpoint of Needs-based Consciousness, the process inside the brain might look something like this:

> The Voice describes a problem, an I-need → The need triggers *self*-serving behavior to make the person-self feel safe → The neocortical brain details a plan for meeting the need → The limbic

brain provides emotional support and ongoing critique → And when things don't go as planned, the reptilian brain gets angry!

When this scenario is repeated enough times, the circuitry of the brain forms a well-worn pattern – *a mental rut*. According to neural network theory, the neurons in the circuit fire in a particular sequence and become wired together from repeated use, creating a pattern that ultimately becomes automatic (Siegel, 2010, pp. 40-42). The net result is that we repeat the same thoughts, feelings, and behavior over and over again. This point was discussed earlier in Chapter 1, only now we have a scientific explanation for it. Rather than take action, **we re-act**: we act out the same time-worn patterns again and again.

Neuroscience verifies another point made earlier as well, about reality. Working together (to the best of their ability), the sub-brains create our reality, not as a direct experience but as a virtual one (Lewis, Lecture Series, 2009). Most of us assume that we see the world as it is; that we take what's there and "hold it" in the brain. This is called naïve realism. Naïve realism leads to the belief that there is one reality and we all see it the same way.

The fact is everyone's reality is different: it's personal. Referred to as neural realism, we take in sensory data and the brain compiles a virtual experience -- an indirect, *subjective* experience – of reality. We *person*-ize it, based on our physiology, individual experience, the culture we live in, etc. We in turn, live in and through that "I-view" of reality and assume others share our same view. When we try to force or impose our perception on them, we're surprised when they *re-act* as though it's foreign to them.

We could say everything we perceive is *a projection of our self.* Every problem we struggle with, every experience we find worrisome, every interaction that's uncomfortable or consoling – everything is processed through our history, memory and past experience, genetic make-up, etc. And normally, we act on these projections from a place of re-activity, a pool of repetitive, automatic responses that have become hard-wired in the brain.

To be sure, evolution provides us with the neurological base we need to survive and what we do with it – the skills we develop, the capacities we hone, etc. -- is up to us. But to make the hundreds of decisions we tackle each day to meet our needs, the brain relies on a contracted set of mental ruts and fights with itself, while absorbed in a reality "that's only true for you, the one who creates it" (Ruiz, 2004, p. 51). And that's just the beginning of the conflict.

===================== When We Fight with Our Self

Not only does the brain fight with itself, but we fight with our self over I-needs as well. In case you're not inclined to believe this, consider our collective addiction to *self* improvement. The reptilian brain is the source of addiction; recall its motto: "if it feels good, do it again". As in the case of many addictions, when it comes to self improvement, it's enough to *believe* it will feel good to keep us coming back for more.

According to a Market Data Enterprises report, the self improvement industry is worth more than $9.6 billion (2005). Most of us will spend whatever it takes, or whatever we have, to fill some inner lack or satisfy some inner need. We invest hundreds of millions of dollars each year in self help books; take every kind of gym or fitness class known to person-kind; and acquire each and every new gadget that comes on the market. We sign up for courses, conventions, inspirational talks, and seminars that will make us healthier, stronger, richer, firmer, independent, less stressed, more creative, less cluttered, and more intuitive; a better spouse, a more efficient Mom, a valuable employee, a solid leader, or a more astute care giver.

Few self improvement ventures are more seductive than the anti-aging boon. What started with Grecian Formula and Ponds has ballooned into a multi-billion dollar industry of creams, serums, nips and tucks, tighter eyelids, fat-free bellies, and whiter teeth. Each year, Americans spend $12.5 billion on cosmetics alone, making it one of the largest industries in the US (Medscape.com). In 2005, more than 3.5 million botox treatments were performed, costing an estimated $1.4 billion; for a treatment that needs to be done every 3-4 months (ibid.). And the number of new treatments, buffers, deep wrinkle therapies, vitamins, herbal supplements, and related paraphernalia weighing down the shelves is unprecedented.

But the fight with our self can be more insidious as well, especially when it involves one of our deeply held attachments. Any time we become attached to a fear or a desire – any person, thing, or thought – it seeps into every aspect of our lives. Our fight with weight and food can be just such an attachment. For many of us, the scale sets the tone for our day. It decides what we can wear, how much we can eat of what, how hard or long we work out at the gym. A whopping 70%+ of "normal-weight women over thirty are dissatisfied with their weight" (Lui, 2007, pp. 234-235). And the incidence of obesity in this country clearly attests to the fact that eating disorders come in all shapes and sizes.

Beneath this obsession:

We are longing for control of ourselves and our lives. We want to ensure that people will love, respect, appreciate, and hear us...We are longing for satisfaction and fulfillment (Kano, 1989, p. 123).

In other words, *we need*. In a society possessed with the perfect shape, our battle with food often starts anew every morning and can lead to some pretty destructive behavior and disordered thinking. Just consider the following:

In a large nationwide poll conducted in 1997, an astonishing 39 percent of normal-weight women said they would willingly *die* three years early if it meant they could reach their desired weight now (Liu, 2007, p. 235).

What's worse, none of our efforts or antics gets at the real problem... which isn't weight. It's the person-self that knows and needs. Instead we allow our fight with our self to run our life, everyday, from morning to night (Singer, 2007, p. 53).

Besides aging and thinness, we try to meet a lot of I-needs through self-improvement: controlling anger, learning to communicate, managing money, building self esteem, finding a mate, improving longevity, coping with grief, becoming more spiritual, etc. We fight with time, gravity, and nature. We fight with images of who/what we should be, and create stories about it whether we succeed or fail. We fight just to keep up...as The Voice rehashes our experience, blow by blow. It's the Lie of Imperfection at work again.

Self improvement is all about I-needs. It embodies all three assumptions of the NBC Tripod: it assumes that something is wrong with us here and now, that some thing "out there" will fix it, and that we will be successful. It's very enticing and can keep us hooked for a lifetime. Self improvement epitomizes living life on the surface, often literally. To the extent that we *identify* with our bodies and faces, the natural aging process becomes a living hell.

=========== Fighting to Help

Self improvement is Needs-based Consciousness in action. It gives The Voice plenty of new material, devours our attention, and spawns multiple new needs. It can give us a momentary sense of purpose and feeling of control that makes us believe Mind really is in charge. In time it becomes a mental rut: we're so convinced it will feel good, we try again and again... hoping it will *help*.

Self improvement is a form of conflict – inner conflict. We think we're helping but we're not, we're hurting. It survives and thrives because it props up the person-self and helps it feel real. The person-self is always on the lookout for more and better props, but it's never enough. We're never satisfied. We constantly look to reaffirm our self in our own eyes and find validation in the eyes of others. In NBC, we live with frustration because the world simply does not deliver. It can't; it's that way for a reason.

NBC is a powerful force and yet, as we can see from the "self improvement" kind of help, cracks are beginning to show. Cracks are beginning to show in many other areas as well. That's because NBC is predicated on a huge assumption: it's rooted in *more*. It assumes there will always be more resources to use, more cheap stuff to consume, more money to spend; more people, more thoughts, *more needs*. It's not sustainable, which is a good thing. But for now, we just keep setting our self up for more conflict…on an even grander scale.

3 Needing Conflict to Survive

Once we adopt this person-self as our self, we relate to the world through Needs-based Consciousness and get locked in the Person-Self Cycle. It's a cycle that cannot be changed from within it. While we begin as infinite potential -- as pure energy -- in effect, we contract into and settle for what feels like a manageable world where *self*-serving through NBC becomes the norm. And it's such a deeply ingrained collective habit, it's almost impossible to see.

The problem is we get stuck there. We get stuck as a person-self, directed by Mind, pursuing our I-needs...living on a planet full of person-selves doing exactly the same thing. The net result is conflict. It's inevitable. **Because of the NBC/Person-Self/Thinking link, we live in a constant state of conflict**. Caught up in the Cycle, there seems to be little choice but to fight to survive.

Self Proving

When we relate through our needs, we're doing what we call "self proving" (Thomas, 2007, pp. 48-49). Self proving refers to the myriad ways we prop up the person-self every day. In our life situation, it's the ways we try to prove we exist, that we're here and okay; that we know, we're right, and we'll last. As we've said, in the current state of NBC awareness, everything we think, do, and say is an effort to validate the person-self. We call that "self-proving". So the waiter who needs to say, "It's pronounced 'Reesling' and not, 'Riesling'" is self proving. The person who needs to get attention by having a screaming match on her cell phone in the shopping mall is self proving. So, too, the supervisor who simply must make his mark on completed staff work by changing *something*...he's self proving.

When we assume we're better informed or more cultured than others; when we put someone down, rally co-workers to our defense, or need to "set things right"; when we have to make a good impression, wear special attire to indicate our position, or attach a string of letters to our name; when we keep company with certain folks and not others, feel compelled to twitter our daily whereabouts (or write a book); when we need to tell others what to do or are driven to offer our opinion -- in other words, whenever we deal with I-need -- we're self-proving.

Of course, our style of self-proving can be highly unique. We may interrupt others when they're speaking, fiercely debate our beliefs, walk away with head-held-high, quietly seek revenge, or strive to be a better person. But most self proving is pretty obvious and rarely novel. Moreover, the satisfaction that comes from self proving is momentary at best; it often lasts only a second. So to get anything out of it, we have to self prove all the time. It's another form of need.

The Many Reasons for Conflict

Self proving, however, is not the source of conflict. It's more like an attitude we project when we try to get our needs met. We do, however, often re-act to the ways other people self prove which can be very irritating. Consider the coffee-crazed morning commuter who's careening down the middle turning lane. He *needs* to go faster. He's also self-proving: he is proving he's here and *he's* first. When the average Joe pulls out ahead of him in the turning lane *to turn*, the coffee-crazed commuter erupts in a violent rage – he becomes the angry reptile. Again, the coffee-crazed commuter is self-proving. Self proving makes the person-self in each of us feel more alive. But it's not the source of conflict.

On the surface, many factors contribute to the constant state of conflict: insensitivity, miscommunication, accusations, stereotypes, blame, rehashing the past, etc. Some people avoid conflict like the plague, become obstinate and immobilized by it; they slowly stew their way to conflict. Others complain continuously until things finally ignite. Factors such as these can be said to trigger conflict. They often serve as justification and explanations for why conflict happens.

To the casual observer, conflict looks like a problem of skills: we have difficulty communicating or relating to others and need a class in communications skills, anger management, or sensitivity training. It's interesting to note that "skills training" is traditionally expressed in terms of needs: we are deficient in some area and assume that the right training – "out there" -- will "fix" us. Training of this sort is a form of self improvement. It appeals to the neocortical brain, our rational brain. It requires that we recall specific tools and techniques in the middle of a highly volatile, limbic-reptilian-brain-type argument, which is very difficult. It requires that we:

First, stop and catch ourselves…; second, think about how to do it differently; and third, actually do it (Ellison, 1998, p. 216).

In other words, it creates yet another set of needs. When we fail, it adds to our story and gives The Voice something new to talk about; as Mind cogitates over how and why we failed and what skill we might employ for better results next time. It produces more needs, and even more thinking.

From a slightly deeper view, the fact that we live in a constant state of conflict shouldn't come as a surprise at all. Consider for a moment what "me" spends most of its time doing:

- Striving to get its needs met;
- Fighting with its self;
- Comparing its self to others;
- Stirring up drama for its story;
- Craving approval;
- Knowing with certainty what's real;
- Needing to prove it's here and important; and,
- Assuming it is right.

Put a couple of these folks together in a room and conflict seems pretty certain. As we've said, every step in the creation of the self can be seen as a contraction. Every principle, belief system, opinion -- every thought -- we embrace is a further defining, solidifying, and condensing of "me". And while the person-self is just an assemblage of thoughts, we readily forget that fact. Instead, we accept it as our self…it's *a fiction we live.*

To sustain and reinforce that fiction, the person-self is *always ready to fight to protect and defend itself.* We've already seen how we fight with our self. We also fight with others. And when we do, we fight over thoughts; thoughts that make up who we think we are and therefore feel worth fighting for. Our needs collide, our realities collide, our unique ways of thinking and perceiving collide, our personalized set of convictions and creeds collide, our re-actions collide; even the ways we self prove collide. It is differences run amok.

Oddly, we rarely anticipate the collision. Instead, we assume. We assume others share our opinions and see the world as we do. We assume we agree over what's important and why. We assume we share the same *meanings*...of respect, parenting, commitment, ethical behavior, and love. We try to invoke one of our most unenforceable rules: the belief that others will meet our needs and validate us. When they don't, we fight. It's a conditioned, re-active pattern; a form of self-proving. And we all do it.

============== When We Fight with Others

Needs underlie all conflict, but like self proving, needs are not the source of conflict. By conflict, we're obviously talking about a very broad definition: from an inner angst we feel over some condition in our life, a misunderstanding among friends, something said out of anger between spouses and the rush of hurt feelings that follow, a disagreement with a colleague who embarrasses us in front of staff; to an all-out battle between ex's, neighbors, communities, and countries over something else that really matters.

Conflict is the experience of differences. Two or more people have different views -- different thoughts -- and they argue over them. The specific content doesn't matter: differences are always over something that feels important at that moment. Conflict comes from resistance within our self and creates resistance in others. It can be over minor opinion or a major belief, a problem to be solved or a decision to be made, the color of a bedroom or how to manage money in a marriage. It can be loud and intense, or sullen and quiet. The intensity of conflict may vary over the importance of what's being discussed, but not always. Some people with more to prove are quick to argue; some argue better in front of an audience; still others feel they are above it all. The silent treatment can be just as vicious as an all-out war of words. In the current state of NBC awareness, conflict is inevitable and normal. *It is not however, natural.*

Authors Friedman and Himmelstein speak of conflict as a trap we get locked into (2008, pp. 10-12). They suggest that the ways we deal with conflict keep us trapped within it:

A conflict trap is a set of mutually reinforcing responses...that keeps the parties locked in battle…These interlocking actions and reactions are in turn supported by any number of underlying… premises and assumptions the parties have about one another and about conflict (ibid., p.11).

One could say that today, the conflict trap, or its potential, frames most human interactions. Certainly, we each have a tendency to oversimplify and re-tell events from our own perspective with the flair of a controversy in the making. Similarly, we seem to intrinsically divide an issue into two views, each opposed to the other. Moreover, as evidenced by our ready reliance on litigation, the conflict trap has become an American institution: in almost any setting, we re-act by threatening to go to court. Even our most intimate family matters get played out in front of the entire family court system.

Let's return for a moment to the scenarios presented in the Introduction:

Sibling 1: "It's time. You know it's time. I've been here from the beginning and I can't take the full burden. It's too much for me to continue to care for her. I need a break. I simply don't know how to make you two understand what I've been through. The doctors, the meds, dealing with Medicaid, the home health aides…it's just too-"

Sibling 2: "Good God, can you give it a rest? This is a serious time. This isn't about you. There are major financial issues here to consider. How can we afford the care she needs?"

Sibling 1: "How can you talk about money at a time like this? You've never been there for her and you know it. We're talking about hospice and you're talking about cash. How typical of you."

Sibling 3: "You know, I've said all along, she would be better off in a setting that could watch over her 24/7."

Sibling 1: "So you're saying I've not been there for her. That's what you think, right? You're saying I haven't done more than my fair share. I've been the one…"

Sibling 3: "I'm saying we need to all calm down and think this through logically. We need to do some research, talk with the doctors, project out a timeline, analyze the different options, review the costs. We need to approach this with compassion, yes, but with foresight and planning."

Sibling 2: "She is on death's door for Christ's sake and you're doing a Gant chart. Are you out of your mind? You've got a lot of nerve falling back on your 'I can handle everything routine' when the time for that was months ago, not today. I am so sick of your attitude, I could just-."

Sibling 1: "This is so sad. Not one of you is thinking of her. I know what she wants, she's confided in me. She trusts me; she always has. I know she wants a DNR order, what dress she wants to be buried in. I have a handle on this stuff because I've always been there…"

In this scenario, everyone wants (needs) to help Mom. On the surface, the siblings differ over what's important. They feel misunderstood and misinterpreted. Yet the discussion is also laden with old emotional scripts: chances are they've fought for years over who's the better care giver, the more dutiful son or daughter, etc., and each feels wholly justified in his/her position.

From a slightly deeper view, Sibling 1 may identify with being a victim. He *needs* to take care of Mom because it makes him feel better about his self. It also feeds his story, how no-one ever appreciates all his hard work. While we don't know for sure, Sibling 2 may have fought with her self many times over Mom's care. She may feel guilty when she compares her self to Sibling 1's seeming self-less generosity. Sibling 3, on the other hand, may see himself as the practical one, the peace maker. He sees how the other two re-act in the old family dance and knows he's beyond that point. In any event, desire and fear, pride and judgment are all at work in this scenario.

The conflict trap is also evident in the second scenario:

Contractor: "We have a contract. You signed the contract. I did the work to spec. Now you need to pay. That's how it's done in the business world…I assume you know that."

Home Owner: "Look. I contracted with you to get my backyard resurfaced and to bury the debris. You may think the work has been done to spec but it's not what we agreed to in the contract.

There's crap all over the yard. What little may have been buried is still showing up through the dirt and if that is level, I need to take up drinking."

Contractor: "Oh, so now you're the authority on level! That yard is level and far better off than it's ever been. We actually did *more* work than what the contract called for and we're waiting – patiently, I might add – for payment."

Home Owner: "Well it might have helped if you'd returned my calls. I've been trying to talk to you for weeks."

Contractor: "Look. I agreed to meet with you to settle this thing. I am trying to help here. We can litigate this but it's going to cost a lot of money and lost time. I suggest you make a list of what you think needs to be done and I'll have my attorney look at it."

Home Owner: "I can make a list until the cows come home but it won't make a bit of difference. You are not going to fulfill the contract and I am not going to pay for shoddy workmanship; I don't care what your attorney thinks. I suggest we both go over there right now and I will show you the deficiencies directly. Then you can tell me how you are going to straighten out this mess."

Contractor: "You're cheap. That's your problem. I know folks like you. They just grind you down. You'll never fulfill your –"

Home Owner: "You don't know me at all. I'm not cheap and never have been. And when I make a contract, I fulfill it…unlike some of the stories I've heard about you."

Contractor: "You little weasel. I do a good business. People know me as a quality businessman who keeps his word. You just want to weasel your way out of paying. You've probably got some short man complex or something. You can't admit when you're wrong and you won't live up to your obligations."

On the surface, both parties are making accusations, falling back on stereotypes, and even resorting to name-calling. From a slightly deeper view however, each is self proving with gusto. The contractor is showing what a reasonable person and good businessman he is, while the home owner is proving he won't be bullied by this guy, that he's not one to be messed with. What's more, their realities are colliding: each has a fundamentally different perspective of what he knows is real; from the specific work to be done, the timetable and payment schedule, to the expected outcome.

In both situations, the participants are locked in the conflict trap. Conflict is a reflection of the frustration in our lives. Consistent with the NBC tripod, we see differences as a problem, we look outward for resolution, and we expect the world to deliver. The nature of conflict has a cumulative quality: surface-level triggers and slightly deeper factors meld together until the scale finally tips, and conflict erupts. There are also deeper causes of conflict, the ones we don't notice…like our obsessive thinking, our needs-driven awareness, and the core needs that drive us. Figure 3-1 depicts the many layers and reasons for conflict. Taken together, they form a pattern we repeat over and over again…with the same disappointing results.

═══════════The Ultimate Source of Conflict

Conflict is a symptom, as is the conflict trap. We attack it in the same way we attack other symptoms: as needing *more* Mind. We look for a solution, see is as a problem of tools or will power, and analyze it from a surface level view. Whether it's a lover's spat, a disagreement, an argument, a dispute, a battle or call it what you may, the ultimate source of conflict is the person-self: **being a person-self lies at the heart of all conflict**. When we fight with others, it takes two person-selves to show up to make a conflict. And it takes one to step outside its self for the conflict to be resolved; absent, and often with, judicial intervention. As long as we live as a person-self, stuck in our heads, addicted to thinking and needing, there will always be constant conflict.

In conflict, we assume we know. We know what the other person said, what they meant, and what they will say. We know what they need and what they need to change. We know what they did, should have done, and have yet to do. We know their intentions, how they feel, what they're thinking, and what they want. We compare our selves and on every score, we come up better. Most importantly, we know we're right and the other person is wrong. And we tell them. In fact, we're so convinced that we know we often express our opinions as fact, as *the truth*. And if by chance, someone disagrees with us, we also know how to convince them otherwise. What's more, we *need* to know; so even when we don't, it's important to appear as though we know.

Figure 3-1

The Many Layers and Reasons for Conflict		
Surface-Level Triggers	Slightly Deeper Factors	Even Deeper Causes
Insensitivity and Accusations	Having to Defend "My" Thoughts	Compulsive Thinking
Feeling Misunderstood or Not Heard	Believing My Story	NBC
Having Different Views or Competing Needs	Obeying The Voice	Feelings of Frustration
Being Obstinate, Avoiding, or Complaining	Individual Habits And The Pool of Re-activity	Core Needs: To be Right, to Last, and to Know
Being Locked in the Conflict Trap	Deeply Ingrained Collective Patterns	
Confusing Issues with Needs or Carrying the Past	A Surface-Level "I-View" of Reality	
Needing to Seek Revenge or Retaliate	Fixed Values, Beliefs, and Points of View	
Either/Or Thinking	Self Proving	
Blaming, Judging, and Stereotyping		
Stating Opinion as Fact, Struggling Over Power, Etc.		

Conflict feeds the person-self, the one that needs and knows: it makes it stronger. Conflict strengthens our self image and our belief in our self. It affirms our sense of rightness and gives us a feeling of control. It keeps things interesting, gives us something new to talk about, and temporarily makes us feel more alive. In other words, conflict is *self*-serving. But it runs deeper than that: **the person-self needs conflict *to survive*** (Tolle, In the Presence of a Great Mystery CD, 2002). Conflict *adds to* our sense of who we are. It consolidates our belief systems and crystallizes what's important. Once we adopt this person-self as our self, we are always ready to fight and fight back because *through conflict, the person-self defines its self.*

Conflict tells us who and what we are. Of equal import, it tells us who and what we're *not*. Conflict is one of the easiest ways we have to compare and contrast our self with others and declare unequivocally: "I am this and I'm certainly not that." As Eckhart Tolle tells us:

> Every [self] is continuously struggling for survival…The conceptual "I" cannot survive without the conceptual "other." [And] the others are most other when I see them as my enemies (2005, p. 60).

This explains why conflict feels like such a threat: to the person-self made up entirely of thoughts, to be wrong means *"I", myself, might not be real*. It throws the whole fiction we live open to question. The entire house of cards begins to topple: if my thoughts are wrong, then maybe "I" am wrong…if "I" am wrong, then maybe "I" really don't know…or worse… maybe "I" won't last…

In the extreme, every question, every difference of opinion, every disagreement or disappointment becomes a potential threat to who we think we are. And yet, conflict has a seductive quality because it's a chance to win: to bolster and embolden the person-self and prove it exists. So oftentimes we take the bait, growing even more invested in our thoughts and thinking, living life on the defensive. Conflict may make us distinctive, but it isolates us as well: soon everyone looks like the enemy…even those we love or once loved.

══════ Conflict: Inevitable, But Not Natural

Not surprisingly, when two person-selves try to have a conversation about anything that matters, conflict often results. Meet Jordan (J) and Ashley (A):

Jordan: "So, I guess we're trying to work things out. Right? I mean, you agree with me, right? That's what we need to do."

Ashley: "Jordan, I don't know. I've told you, I'm confused. I had to-"

J: "But things have changed right, I mean after the other night."

A: "I said I was confused. Look, we had six years together and half of them were horrible. You were never there for me and the kids and now, we have one good night and you want me to give everything up, move back in and try again. I've told you, no. I am not interested. I know you feel bad and everything, but, no, you're not going to change."

J: "You don't really mean that. You know what your problem is? You're scared. You said it yourself – I can read you. That's why you're having so much trouble looking at me. You're afraid you love me so much that you *have* to try again. And it scares you."

A: Jordan, I said I don't feel comfortable talking with you right now because you hurt me so much. The casinos, the other women, the…"

J: "There were no other women. Except that one. And that was a special case. And talk about who hurt who – the night I find out I can't get into the Marines, that very same night, you say you're leaving? Well, you're right, I got in the car and went looking for some -"

A: "Jordan, I don't need to hear this story again, for God's sake. Shut up, will you? There were many other women besides that one at the rest-stop. But the gambling and the insecurity you caused me and the kids – it hurt a lot. I just can't put up with it any more. I am finished with this. I just want to move on."

J: "You're a liar. I was always there for the kids. I took care of them when you went back to school. Some Dads aren't there for their kids, you know. But I've been there for them. *And* I've been there for you."

A: "You have got to get some counseling. You're sick."

J: "Then what was the other night? What was that all about? That was something, right? We made a big turn there. You know it. "

A: "Jordan, I had too much to drink. And you were pushing, pushing as usual. You think once you've made a decision we all need to fall in line. The other night meant something to you, I just don't know. I'm-"

J: "See, it's just like I told you. You want this to work. You want me. You want me to be your husband and if you just-"

A: "Jordan, it would be easier. I'll give you that. And I think the kids deserve both parents. But the husband I want has to be someone I can rely on -- someone who doesn't stay out all night, and sleep around, and spend the mortgage money when he's feeling bad about himself."

J: "I told you, I never slept around-"

A: "Oh Jordan, shut up. What about the woman at the gym, and Linda, and the girl at the bar, and-"

J: "Those were years ago – and that woman at the rest-stop was your fault. You weren't there for me. You're never there for me. We get into a fight and you kick me out. What am I supposed to do all night? Sit around? No way. I go out and I take care of myself. You set yourself up for this."

A: "Jordan, I can't stand this. I need to move on. I need you to stop calling me, stop pushing me. If we need to talk about the kids, fine. Otherwise, no more please."

J: "You don't mean that. I was moving on too, you know. A lot of women gave me their phone numbers over the past months since you broke us up…"

A: "Why do I need to hear this? You have told me this story a hundred times…"

J: "Look, I have an idea. I have something to say."

A: "Just fulfill your responsibility as a Dad and leave it at-"

J: "I can be the man you want – stable, predictable, whatever. I have no problem giving up the all night binges. I can be that man you need but first, you have to learn to communicate. When you do, this marriage will work fine. Once I see some progress on your part to communicate, I am more than willing to make this work."

A: "How many times have you promised to give that stuff up? How many times? It never lasts. I don't talk to you because you're never there. And when you are, you don't listen. You just tell me what you think. Well I need to move on. I need to find out who I am, and get my self respect back."

J: "Deep down, you want this to work. You need it to."

A: "Jordan, it would be easier, financially. I'll admit that. And maybe better for the kids. But I have to weigh-"

J: "You know I'm moving on too. I gained a lot of self respect from being out there on the circuit these last few weeks. Those women found me attractive. They gave me their phone numbers. They-"

A: "Is that what 'finding yourself' means to you? Through what some woman says in a bar? I'm not talking about that at all. This simply won't work, Jordan. We are in two completely different places. Please, stop call-"

J: "I've told you what it will take for this to work. You have to learn to communicate. If you can't then this is on you. "

[Some time passes.]

J: "So the other night, you were just, what, meeting your female needs?"

All conflict is difficult to listen to, but it's especially so when we can see the person-self in action. Conflict is all about being a person-self that needs and knows. That's why traditional communications training places such a heavy emphasis on *listening*: if only we could listen, so the thinking goes, we could know the other person's needs as well as our own. The problem is, as we've said before, this assumes we're able to put these skills into action. Moreover, it assumes that our failure to listen won't simply be replaced by one of the many other surface-level triggers or deeper factors that cause conflict.

In an argument, viewpoints quickly harden down into positions. We judge and blame one another. We're intent on proving who we are and what we're not. It's my way or yours, and we both can't win. And even when all evidence is to the contrary, we believe what we want to believe. To that end, the brain supports us.

═══════════ ## You're a Liar #1

We've already seen that we don't experience what's "out there" directly. Instead, the brain creates a virtual reality we live in and through. Our reality is *person*-ized: we stamp it with our physiology, our past, our knowledge and culture. In a conversation, we may think we're seeing the same problem, recalling the same events, acknowledging the same set of circumstances, and envisioning the same way out of a dilemma, but we're not. Our different realities – what author Dr. Lewis calls our "mockups of unparalleled persuasive power" (2000, p. 119) – collide. And when they do, our retort is simple: "You're a liar!" Since I need to be right and we don't see things the same way, *you* must be lying.

The brain can't pay attention to everything. By necessity, it focuses on some factors and filters out a great deal of other, seemingly extraneous information. Otherwise, we would be on perpetual overload. But this can work to our disadvantage as well. To manage the world, the brain simplifies what's "out there" by "Photoshopping" things in and out of our experience. What the brain "sees" is a function of what has served us well from an evolutionary standpoint. So the brain deletes some things and aggrandizes others; it experiences what it pays attention to and ignores the rest. It also fills in any gaps that might exist with our own assumptions and works to make sense of whatever it sees (Lewis, 2009, Lecture Series). Many of us have had this experience when we witness something illogical: we see a rabbit dancing across a road and immediately the brain tries to make sense of it -- it's not a rabbit, it's a dog; it's not dancing, the dog's foot is broken, etc. As Dr. Lewis suggests: "We need to have a healthy skepticism of what we think we know is real" (ibid.).

But the brain has certain tendencies that make hearing and communicating with a fellow human being even more complicated than we might anticipate. The brain adds more of what it already knows and can effectively block out what doesn't fit with its present understanding. Jonah Lehrer, author of *How We Decide*, describes a study of potential voters designed to determine why additional, but contrary, information didn't change their point of view on given candidates. The researchers found:

The voters weren't using their reasoning faculties to analyze the facts…[but] to preserve their partisan certainty…[they found] that voters tend to assimilate only those facts that confirm what they already believe (Lehrer, 2009, pp. 205; 206).

Dr. Lewis makes a similar point. Citing how unreliable our memory can be, he explains that the brain's circuitry – our mental ruts – shifts over time making it impossible to remember precisely what happened (Lewis et al., 2000, pp. 130-134). And it does so in such a way that it "register[s] novel sensory information *as if it conformed to past experience*" (ibid., p. 138). The net result is that we only hear what confirms a past memory which has already been distorted in some fashion. When we add to this the very real problem of translating into words what we *think* we *feel*, having a conversation – let alone discussing differences that are important to us – becomes incredibly difficult.

========= Conflict and "Truth"

As we said before, everything we perceive is a projection of "me". So in the above example, Jordan *really did* want to get back together. And he may have believed he was only unfaithful once and rationalized the rest away. Similarly, Ashley *was* confused: on some level she knew it would be easier financially to stay together as a couple and yet, she wanted the relationship over and done with. Regardless, there was nothing either of them could say or do to make the other believe what he/she already knew was true; especially when it came to how they perceived their self.

In sum, conflict is Mind-made. It is two self images living distinct realities debating different sets of thoughts, each believing his/her thoughts to be true. In addition, we come to the conversation with a fixed image of the other person; an image that may have been formed in our brain's memory decades earlier. Yet when someone doesn't conform to our image, we're more apt to change what we see than to change the image. That's one reason why families and intimate partners tend to repeat the same arguments from the same positions. When presented with an old image, we simply fall back into our old patterns, culminating in the same disappointing results.

Both the individual and the collective person-selves thrive on conflict. It's the ideal setting for self proving. We even try to prove what we think we know about conflict, that:

- Conflict drives out the truth;
- There are two sides to every story;

- Honesty is the best policy;
- The person who's at fault is responsible;
- When wronged, someone needs to be punished; and,
- Every problem has a solution.

Once we collapse into a thinking person-self and contract further into one that needs, conflict and frustration are the end-result. We could thus add to our original Person-Self Cycle, the inevitability of conflict and frustration:

Figure 3.2
The Person-Self Cycle II

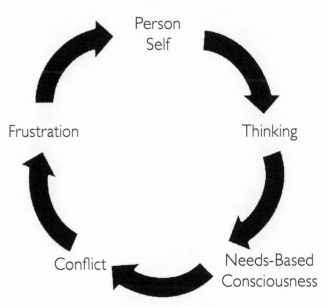

The Person-Self Cycle affects everything. We can't think, or feel, or do anything without its influence; even the things we hold dear…like how we help.

Section Two

4 How Conflict and Help…are the same

Conflict is about being a person-self that knows and needs, but it's also about helping. Entire industries have grown up to help people through a difficult time; to help resolve a problem or decide what to do. We now turn to an examination of how we help. How we help is a daily reminder of the extent to which the Person-Self Cycle has come to dominate our lives. It's something we all do, everyday and in a variety of setting. Helping appeals to the better part of us. It engages our ultra-social leanings and our desire to support and coordinate with one another. It's something we hold dear; part of the human experience.

More often than not, help is genuinely offered, well-intended, and meant to serve. But help is Mind-made. It's a reflection of where we have evolved to as human beings: it comes from the same Needs-based Consciousness, the same thoughts and compulsive thinking, and the same person-self we've been talking about. How we help should be the very best part of who we are and yet, at this moment in time, it's broken: it actually *adds* to the constant state of conflict we live in. What's worse, the kind of help we really need is in critically short supply.

This chapter examines how help is broken, both the help we offer in our everyday lives and the help we provide as professionals. In chapter 5, we will consider how the broken nature of help has seeped into one helping profession in particular, that of mediation, which *should be* immune from its influence.

================ When the Person-Self "Helps"

In conflict, we assume we know. It's a chance to prove our self; to show that we're right and the other person's wrong. Helping shares that very same assumption – namely, that we know. It can start very innocently: we offer assistance to someone, share an idea, or recommend a particular course of action. As a person-self, we assume every problem needs a solution and that people recite their problems to us because they want our help. We see our help as valued and desired, and most of all, correct. We're also convinced we're acting from the best of intentions; that our only desire is to minimize suffering and relieve emotional pain. In fact, it feels rude to just sit there while someone tells us their story and *not* offer our advice and counsel.

But the person-self always does something for a reason, the core of which is to prop itself up. To our surprise, the other person rejects our assistance. He re-acts and resists. He may get defensive and angry, or rebuff us in more subtle ways. He may say he's already tried our suggestion, that it won't work or it's stupid. He may question our intentions or doubt our credibility. And we thought we were helping!

When we help, we assume we know. We know precisely what the problem is or how to figure it out. We know what the other person needs to do and how they need to do it. We know what they should think and how they should be; the best advice to give, the exact time and way to intervene, and the perfect course of action. Whereas in conflict we know we're right and they're wrong, in helping we know what the problem is and what they need to do to fix it. Figure 4.1 contrasts the different ways we assume we know in conflict and in help. Often it's hard to know where one leaves off and the other begins.

When we help, we know *the one truth*. We know that we both can't be right, and the steps are often as important as the outcome. Take, for example, the father who wants to help his kids with their homework. He dictates the single, best way to study, sets the goal of getting an academic scholarship into college, and criticizes, cajoles, and blames the kids when they resent his study tactics and regimentation. He thinks he's helping… just as his Mom once helped him.

When the self that knows, helps, we're talking about help from a broad perspective. We're trying to help someone accept what we have to say, understand and act on things from our perspective, or convince them of the best way to proceed. We're trying to ensure they "do the right thing" for the right reason, or avoid getting hurt. We're trying to get them to live up to the person, partner, employee, or parent we know they can be! We may even think we're helping to make the world a better place. But we're also looking to get our needs met: we're trying to get what we want. When the person-self helps, **we help by *doing*:** we do to or for someone else based on what *we know* is best.

Figure 4.1

How We Assume We Know In Conflict and In Help	
In Conflict, We Know	In Help, We Know
• What they said, what they meant, and what they will say • What they need and need to change • What they did, should have done, and have yet to do • What their intentions are, how they feel, what they're thinking, and what they want • How we're right and they're wrong	• What the problem is or how to figure it out • What they need to do and how they should do it • What they should think and how they should be • The best advice, how to intervene, the perfect course of action • What they need to do to solve the problem

Everyday Help

Like conflict, help is a product of the conditioned Mind and constant thinking. Mind generates problems, drama, and conflict because they serve a purpose: they're a chance to shore up the person-self and reinforce who we think we are. While we think these events happen *to* us, it's actually what we bring to the situation that makes it problematic. Mind also generates how we help. When we help, we're trying to make *the other person* see things *our way*. We know the One Right Way…it's our way.

Everyday, we each "help" in myriad ways; as friends, lovers, parents, bosses, spouses, elders, colleagues, mentors, care givers, etc. Let's look at a couple of examples. Take the simple case of two friends having a conversation about snow shoveling:

Friend 1: "I am so exhausted. I've been out shoveling snow for hours! I even had to take a nap!"

Friend 2: "You know, it's probably unwise to have snow shoveling as your sole source of exercise."

Friend 1: "Well, I don't do it all at once. I take breaks and do a little at a time. It's just so tiring."

Friend 2: "Why don't you get your snow-blower fixed? It would be so much easier."

Friend 1: "Yeah, I know. But you know me...I just didn't get around to it last summer. There was so much going on."

Friend 2: "You should join a gym or something. You're body is so tight. You're going to kill yourself out there shoveling. That's just crazy. And there's no-one there to even call an ambulance. Maybe a strengthening class or swimming. But something!"

Or consider this casual conversation between two seniors about a daughter-in-law:

Senior 1: "I'm so worried about my Jenny. She just doesn't get it. She's not maternal, or nurturing. I don't know how my son stands it. She still can't even cook!"

Senior 2: "Well you need to take her under your wing. You're a wonderful cook. Just–"

Senior 1: "Oh God, I've tried all that. I've invited her to dinner to show her how it's done. I've offered to have her cook with me. I've invited her to bring dishes to supper. I've asked her what she wants to learn to cook. I've even written down recipes I think she likes, step-by-step-by-step."

Senior 2: "Well what happens when the two of you are together?"

Senior 1: "She talks about work! Her responsibilities, how hard her job is, whether she'll get some promotion or other. How will she ever make a house for my son? And what about grand-kids? I'm just not sure how to get through to her..."

When the person-self helps, *we know*. We talk back-and-forth, come up with options, and voice our opinion; we tell people what we think and tell them what to do. We say things like, "Well if I were you, I'd _____", or "You know what I'd do, I'd _____."

Sometimes our help comes in clever disguises. We think we're taking care of someone by sparing their feelings or protecting them from an unpleasant event. Or we talk around and over an issue in the hopes the other person picks up on what we're saying without a long, drawn out discussion or argument. Sometimes we try to control people for their own good, or believe we're saving them from themselves, or feel we need to intervene on their behalf. We also divine our experience as truth; we say: "You need to understand that _____", "A professional never _____", "Based on my experience, what's best is _____." When we, as person-selves, help, we get caught in *the need to know*: we substitute our views for someone else's and expect them to follow our lead.

However we express our "help", doing so meets our own needs. Helping makes us feel good: it strengthens our sense of self. We feel capable and kind, giving, compassionate, and useful. We know what to do and are sought after by others; we're the go-to person at work, the uncle the kids turn to, the wise elder at church. Helping feeds our self image and makes us feel more alive. It confirms our personal reality, gives us a sense of purpose, and fulfills our I-needs. When we help, we feel rewarded, gratified, and proud. Helping is *self*-serving.

Often when we help, what we really want is for the other person to change. We believe "if only he/she would" talk to me, stop this or that, respect my boundaries, see how hard I'm working, be more caring, courteous, civil, faithful, sincere, etc. – then everything would be okay. So we counsel, direct, advise, warn, demand, and threaten, and we call it help. Then helping becomes a not-so-subtle form of manipulation, as we "help" the other person be what we *need*.

In NBC, when the person-self that knows, helps, we actually stir *more* conflict. Instead of being welcomed, our "help" triggers a reciprocal need to know in the other person that ping-pongs back-and-forth. We've all had the experience: we suggest a great idea at work, tell someone the easiest way to move heavy furniture, or suggest the kids need fewer scheduled activities, and bam, the other person re-acts. And we act right back from the same pool of re-activity. Our "help" gets mixed up with our own personal needs, with issues and memories from the past; our buttons get pushed and core needs get aroused. In no time at all, we're fighting.

================ Prescriptive and Directive "Help"

Let's look at another scenario of everyday help in slightly more detail. An employee has been working on a new service for her clients and decides to present the idea to her boss:

Employee: "I've been working on this great new idea and I really think you'll like it. My clients-"

Boss: "It won't work."

Employee: "But…you haven't even heard it yet. I've worked on this for months and I'd at least like the chance to-"

Boss: "I know, I don't mean to be rude but I heard about it already and it won't work. Not with this population. They can't handle it; they're not ready."

Employee: "Yes, but, we have to offer them something. They're leaving us and going nowhere. There's nothing out there to back them up. They're just floundering…"

Boss: "Well, find some funding and we can talk, but these folks need something far more tailored to their needs than what you're proposing. It has to be on highly graduated or they'll never get it."

The employee leaves, dumbfounded.

Chances are, the employee left feeling a lot more than dumbfounded. She probably felt angry and resentful; not to mention betrayed and embarrassed. The boss thought she was doing the employee and the agency a favor: she was using her wealth of experience to prevent a potential disaster. She knew the program wouldn't work and didn't want to waste time or money on something the clients wouldn't benefit from and the board of directors would be furious about. *She was helping.*

But the employee didn't see it that way at all. To her, the boss was disrespectful, condescending, and heavy-handed. The employee re-acted and got defensive; she hadn't even been given a chance to explain her idea. This exchange may well have been a turning point for her: she just learned she couldn't trust her boss to support her. From that point forward, she may decide to toughen up and go on the offensive. The next time she comes up with a suggestion, she'll come loaded for bear, ready to defend her self.

The point is this: in the current state of NBC awareness, "helping" means substituting our views for someone else's. We impose our "solution" on their "problem". Whenever the self that knows, helps, we override the other person's judgment, *even when they ask for it.* We devalue and disempower the seeker.

Instead of helping, we provoke conflict because people don't want to be told what to do, or how to think, or why they're not okay. They resist and re-act, and resort to old mental ruts. They get frustrated and angry, combative and confrontational, and before long, we're locked in a battle of wills, each trying to protect and defend our self...*which is precisely what the person-self wants!* As a person-self, we're compelled to fight and fight back: we need to prove our self, defend our thoughts and ideas, and protect our image because our very "I" feels under threat. And yet by doing so, we generate more tension, more stress, more hostility and dissent. We add to the constant state of conflict we live in.

When the self that knows, helps, our help is prescriptive and directive: we know what to do and how to do it *for someone else*. We're attached to our one way of doing things, a particular or "right" outcome, sometimes to helping itself. Helping of this sort is a contraction: it comes from a narrowed point of view and limits the range of possibilities. It puts people on the defensive and feels like a competition. It shrinks the likelihood of there ever being an alternative solution, other than yours or mine.

Prescriptive and directive help also contracts how we see one another. We "totalize" others: we brand them based on this one particular subject or event, and write them off as liberals or fanatics or losers. We forget that other people are the sum of many, and often conflicting, views, life experiences, circumstances, and deep feelings...just as we are. We get wrapped up in the drama, in thinking and conjecturing, totally stuck in the head. Worse yet, we miss the possibility that there might be an option, another way to be...or another way to help.

=========== The Professional Side of Help

Professional help shares many of the same characteristics and problems of everyday help. We are a society of fixers living in a culture of "helping".

But the problem is not the helpers or those who seek help. The problem is how we help, how we're trained to "do" help.

Help begins with a need – an "I" is *in need*. Something is wrong that needs fixing; some one is in some kind of conflict. It may be an immediate, "hot" issue or the residual effects of a long ago battle. "I" may be fighting with my partner, my kids, or at work. "I" may be at war with my self, my attitude, or my past. "I" may be wrestling with worry, grieving a loss, or angry at the world. I may feel totally overwhelmed by my obligations. Maybe "I" am struggling to help someone else and can't understand why she's closed herself off to me or is leaning on me so heavily. Whatever the problem is, it's all-consuming: we think about it, talk about it, mull it over, compare it with the past, and try to figure it out. Sometimes we seek help; other times help finds us. In a very real sense, help is an attempt to feel safe, solid, and secure; or make someone else feel that way.

Help-*ing* begins with a professional, some one who's thought *to know*. The very essence of the helping relationship begins with a distinction between the helped and the helper: the one who's broken and the one who fixes. There's a division, a separation. And the problems with professional help unfold from there.

=============== Broken Help

Let's begin with several examples. Counseling is a good place to start identifying some of the ways in which professional help is broken. In counseling, there is a "seeker" and a professional, and an appropriate distance between the two. The seeker is suffering from some kind of problem, an inner need or lack. She's looking for answers and the professional is there to offer his/her thoughts on the matter.

The counseling process is often intensely serious. The client is asked to recount her personal story, replay the past, and reveal her inner-most thoughts and yearnings. She is describing her reality, seeking approval, and hoping to have her needs met, all at the same time. The professional operates from a major frame of reference (a particular school of psychology, for example) that's been studied, researched, homogenized, and credentialed. The client's life situation – her "I view" -- is analyzed, questions are asked, explanations are proffered, and causes are uncovered. There's a lot of mental work going on.

The focus is on helping the client grow and change. The professional makes a diagnosis and proceeds with the client to "fix" the problem. During the sessions, the client may re-act to what's said or feel badly about herself. She may fight to change herself, her feelings or behavior, or object in some other way: to the label, the approach, or the work being done. For both parties, helping creates yet another set of needs: the professional needs to stay on top of his/her field; the client has a list of things to work to change.

In many respects, certain kinds of teaching and doctoring, spiritual work and ministering share these same features. There is a professional who defines the problem, deciphers its causes, and helps fix it in a preordained manner. There's a knower and a seeker, a problem or inner lack, a primary frame of reference, the retelling of stories, a "diagnosis," and a recommended path towards resolution. There's often a considerable amount of inner conflict and mental work involved as well.

The court system is another example of how help is broken. At court, there's one way of doing business -- the court's way. The court divides, separates, and classifies people: there are plaintiffs and defendants, hearings and trials; those with authority and everyone else. Among the various professionals in the courtroom, attorneys, family service workers, substance abuse counselors, etc., all speak on behalf of their clients. At court, the judge is the ultimate authority in charge; the one that knows. Everything is executed according to rules and regulations, calendars and dockets, and for reasons and rationales unbeknown to most people.

People come to court to solve some problem or need. It's also a chance to self prove: they want to tell their stories, preferably directly to the judge and in lurid detail. The parties see the judge as the final arbiter: the one who will establish once and for all which party is right, honest, and good, and which is the liar. But the judge isn't there to cast blame. He/she doesn't care about the absentee landlord, who slept with whom or spent the rent money at the track, or how often the contractor failed to show up. Nor is the judge there to spend a lot of time discerning "the truth". The judge wants to get the case settled; fairly, if possible.

At court, *everyone* knows: from the file clerk to the parties themselves, the attorneys, the judge's chief assistant, and the judge. The experience is never as portrayed on TV: the parties spend most of their time waiting and filling out forms, and their moment of glory is often brief and unsatisfying. Typically, there's no trial, no impassioned statements, and no deliberating jury. The problem is known, the facts are discerned, and the judge decides and tells the parties what to do. The balance of the system then enforces what the judge "prescribes".

Traditional government-sponsored help can be even more rigid. In the case of "problem families", social workers do inspections and develop case histories. They interview neighbors and other family members. They conduct initial screenings, assessments, and evaluations. Case managers, mental health specialists, and educators are enlisted to help identify problems and decide what's to be done. All of this is done in a fixed sequence, using obligatory forms and formats, and in accordance with detailed rules and procedures. The process is a huge intrusion into family life, putting everyone on the defensive and family members at odds with one another. Once the analysis is complete, the family is red-flagged as failing to meet what the government defines as a proper family setting. The professionals know, the family does not.

The professionals write their reports, stipulate needs, specify remedial actions, establish timetables and milestones, and monitor and measure results. The parents need child development classes, marriage counseling, communications and dispute resolution skills. The mother needs job training and time management, and the father, computer skills and stress reduction. The children need tutoring, ongoing counseling, impulse control and executive function therapy, and perhaps, medication. Everyone needs fixing in prescribed ways, everyone's told what to do. And once on the government's radar screen, it's nearly impossible to break free.

Finally, let's consider the relatively new area of Collaborative Law. These are the new evangelists among lawyers: they have seen their way clear of 19th century jurisprudence and its "gladiator" tactics, and are ready to start their practice anew. Collaborative lawyers agree in advance to negotiate in good faith and if by chance negotiations break down, neither will be retained or profit from subsequent litigation. It is a profound paradigm shift. In the case of divorce, for example, adversarial lawyers "focus on legal issues" while collaborative lawyers attend to "what the client requires to make a healthy transition". Adversarial lawyers "align with the client's views" while collaborative lawyers act as "wise counselor...advisor, negotiator [and] conflict manager". Similarly, adversarial lawyers "insist on control" while collaborative lawyers "value a team approach" (Tesler, 2008, pp. 27-31).

Collaborative divorce lawyers often work with a group of professionals, each with a designated focus and expertise: the two lawyers "guide negotiations and manage conflict," coaches and a child development expert deal with clients' "shadow emotional states" and educational needs, while a financial consultant is present to "educate the less-knowledgeable spouse in basic money-management skills" (ibid., pp. 31-32). While collaborative lawyers emphasize the importance of client participation, as one author puts it:

> Apart from the financial cost of so many professionals…[the] underlying message [is] that two divorcing adults are incapable of doing anything…without massive and continual professional assistance…They are "victims" of emotions, requiring ongoing assistance and hand-holding (Zaidel, 2008, p. 5).

In other words, like their more traditional counterparts, collaborative lawyers and their fellow experts assume *they know,* and their clients are on the receiving end of that knowing. The net result can be an air of superiority that can feel at odds with Collaborative Law's expressed intent.

=========== ## The Professional "I Know"

In all of the above examples, the work is valuable, necessary, and essential in many instances. People can do horrible, irreparable damage to one another and especially to their kids. The problem isn't the helpers, it's how we help: it's done by one person to another. We *know* what *they* need to do and how *they* need to do it. We're attached to our one way of doing things, a particular or "right" outcome, sometimes to helping itself. Our help is Mind-driven, dominated by thoughts and thinking. It's **prescriptive and directive**: "I know what you need" is the professional equivalent of "I know".

When we help as professionals, we create a division between us and them, between those who help and those seeking it. We reaffirm the NBC Tripod: people come to believe they are somehow broken or deficient, and that the fix is "out there". This belief can set in motion a cycle of dependency that lasts well into the next generation; a dependency that can manifest, oddly enough, as a sense of entitlement…to services, to intervention, to help. Put another way, given enough time, people begin to believe they need help. They *expect* someone else will be in charge, intervene on their behalf, or take care of them. It becomes part of a Mindset. We inadvertently confirm a view that some people or certain groups are not as capable as others, and all the stereotypes that go along with it. We dis-empower and devalue the seeker, and instill a feeling of helplessness long into the future.

As professionals, we believe there is One Right Way to help. We may follow a pre-scripted way of diagnosing a problem, doing our work, or deciding what needs to be done. We may be militant about our field; believing that everyone needs therapy, all men commit some form of domestic abuse, or abstinence is the only way to create responsible attitudes towards sex. As clinicians, we "treat" a problem one way; as pastors, we "minister" to it another way; as consultants, we approach problems in an altogether different manner. And in all cases, we believe our help works. When it doesn't, we claim that more help is needed or more money is needed to do help. We affirm the status quo and generate yet another set of needs.

For the sake of clarity, One Right Way does not mean one type of service. In many cases, we "pile on" services in the hopes of resolving the many causes of conflict and with each service, spawn another set of needs to be met. The Sieve Model, for example, suggests a graduated scale of services for divorcing parents (Silver and Silver, 2009). Most people can be helped by "less invasive elements" such as parenting consensus surveys, expanded parent education, and mental health coaching. More "mediative and therapeutic" interventions follow, such as therapeutic dispute resolution, court-based reality training, and serial mental health consultants. Especially high conflict parents might additionally appear before a court-based parenting tribunal; receive a preliminary opinion from a panel of experts; undergo a focused parenting evaluation, custody screening, and finally, a comprehensive custody evaluation (ibid., pp. 338-339). We "tailor" services to meet the needs we identify.

Now at this point you might be thinking, "Hold it. I'm a professional. I'm paid to know. People come to me for help. I'm trained and I've got the credentials to prove it. I know where the client starts and I end. If they accept my help, fine. If not, it's their choice." To say it again, *it's not the helpers.* Consciously or not, we each subscribe to a deeply conditioned collective definition of what it means to help. That definition is embedded in our education system and reinforced through our training. It's the foundation of many of our most revered institutions and organizations. **In the current state of NBC awareness, we "help" by doing, one person-self to another;** by one that knows to one that needs. We substitute our views for another person's. We impose our "solution" on their "problem" – or we highly recommend it with the full force and authority of our position behind it. And we expect them to follow our advice.

Regardless of our particular field of "help", helping meets our own needs. Helping props up the person-self and strengthens who we think we are. Through helping, we find, add to, or confirm some piece of our self and fulfill our core needs. Our sense of self may be enhanced by knowing what to do, having *the* answer, or giving advice; we may identify with being a helper, a professional, or a supervisor; we may feel empowered by the profession, or take pride in our education or credentials. We may love working with people because it makes us feel good, needed, useful, and productive; it makes us feel special in a way that's meaningful to us. In fact, helping props up the person-self in *both* people: while the professional feels detached and competent, the person on the receiving end is temporarily at the center of attention. He/she is amidst plenty of drama and conflict, and both have plenty to think about.

But prescriptive and directive help stirs conflict. Sometimes the help itself is a form of aggression, when people are forced or coerced to take part. Regardless, in time, the client re-acts and resists. They stop coming, grow frustrated with the process or make themselves scarce; or worse, they acquiesce and become unwilling to make a decision without us. They resist in more subtle ways as well, ways we professionals seldom see. They fight back: they find a place where *they too can know* and feel safe and secure, strong and competent. They have to...we all do.

Whenever the person-self feels threatened, it fights back. So whenever we feel incapable or beaten down too long, discounted or disrespected, we need to find a way to build our self back up. Often we take it out on someone else, someone with less clout, or someone smaller; a child, a staff person, a pet. We erupt without warning and push back in any way we can. Whether we're helping or being helped, we're always self proving.

=================== When Helping Hurts

How we help validates the deeply ingrained mental constructs that create conflict in the first place: it props up the person-self, stems from Needs-based Consciousness, and is vested in continuous thinking. It creates frustration for both the helper and those seeking help, and causes more conflict. How we help shows just how much the Person-Self Cycle has come to dominate our lives, and how it perpetuates the status quo. Figure 4.2 summarizes the features of our broken help:

Figure 4.2

How Everyday and Professional Help are Broken and Stir Conflict
We:
• Assume we know what to do and how to do it *for someone else*
• Help by doing, to or for another person
• Know the One Right Way and substitute our views for someone else's, expecting them to follow our lead
• Create a professional distance or an environment that separates "us" from "them"
• Dis-empower the seeker, reinforcing the belief that he/she is deficient or in need, and set in motion a cycle of dependency
• Find, add to, or confirm some piece of our self and fulfill our core needs through helping
• Uphold the view that the world is here to meet our needs and other unenforceable rules
• Divine our experience, both personal and professional, as truth
• Try to control people for their own good, change them into what we need, or mis-take them for their "problem"
• Grow attached to our one way of doing things, a particular or right outcome, or helping itself
• Generate a continuous stream of needs and reaffirm the power of Mind – of thoughts and thinking -- to set things right again
• Regard the "seeker" as the one who grows and changes

To put it succinctly, how we help is broken because we steer people in the direction we want them to go: **we need "to get them to _____".** Then helping hurts because it's our way and their situation, our solution and their reality. "They" become separate and other.

5 Is All Help Broken?

So we're left with a question or two. First, isn't there such a thing as *genuine* help? And second, can't we do help without feeding our egos or meeting our own needs? The answer to the first question is yes, absolutely. The answer to the second is no, sorry. And the two are not internally inconsistent.

Help can be offered in a deeply caring, authentic, and giving way. Obviously, the degree to which help is prescriptive and directive differs across fields: some professions are far more prescriptive and directive than others. Similarly, whether we're helping in a professional role or at home, work, church, little league, or in some other setting, some people are more prescriptive and directive than others. Nor does everyone or every field exhibit all of the features of broken help depicted in Figure 4.2: certain features may be displayed and not others, and to varying degrees. Moreover, some conditions demand that help be prescriptive and directive – *but not as a general rule.*

There are, also, occasional self-less acts of help. But that's the point: they're rare and the exception…so much so that we notice them. In the current state of NBC awareness, we "help" by doing, one person-self to another. It can come "from the heart", but it still meets our own needs and props up the person-self. Having said this, someone might protest: "You are absolutely mistaken. I've done this kind of work for twenty years and

I do it totally out of the goodness of my heart." No-one is denying that. Only this person-self is attached to having a good heart. That's how she sees her self; it's her self image, a key part of her story, The Voice tells her so repeatedly. As we've already said, not all needs are entirely selfish, just *self*-serving.

It should be noted, we're *not* saying that how we help is imperfect and doesn't help everyone. That's a given. We're saying something deeper: **the very concept of help – the deeply conditioned collective definition of what it means to help – is broken.** It's governed by the Person-Self Cycle. It's prescriptive and directive. It creates resistance in others and adds to the constant state of conflict we live in.

Once again, the problem is not the helpers. Nothing in this book is meant to offend or discourage those who help. It's to offer each of us a chance to consider how we help and why, and to question the underpinnings of our collective definition of what it means to help. There are many wonderful people who lovingly give of themselves, but so long as the person-self that knows and needs, helps, our help will never be as vast, or as deep, or as open as it can be. In other words, how we help can be other than prescriptive and directive, but not without moving beyond the same consciousness that creates the help we offer and the conflict we live with, in the first place.

Mediation: An Exception to the Rule?

A group of students sit in a circle preparing to answer an instructor's question: "So you're all here at Basic Mediation Training. What brought you here?" The students respond one by one: "Well, I really like helping other people"; "People are always coming to me with their problems and appreciate my ideas, so I thought I should come"; "Well, I don't want to brag but I think I have pretty good suggestions. People come back to me and tell me, 'Yeah, it worked pretty well.'" The instructor turns to the group and takes a deep breath: "Well, a mediator never offers solutions." Everyone sits quietly, anxiously, with the same question stirring in their heads: What the hell do they do then?

For a relationship between two or more people to work, at a minimum it needs a way to safely raise issues; to say what needs to be said; to address feelings where appropriate; to decide on a solution or course of action; and to change direction. When this is not present, people often turn to the Alternative Dispute Resolution (ADR) field for help. Mediation is one component of ADR, along with arbitration and others, and has been found to have application from criminal justice cases, divorce, co-parenting, family problems, business transactions, neighbor disputes, and landlord/tenant problems; to issues of public policy, of a commercial and corporate nature, as well as national and international conflict.

If ever there was a field which *should be* the exception to prescriptive and directive help, mediation is it. The entire field literally pivots on a single premise, that of **self determination**; so much so that students are told early and often that a mediator does not give advice or offer solutions. Unfortunately, that's about where the agreement ends. Mediation is a field full of differing opinions. So everything that follows is meant to describe the field *in general*.

To be safe, we'll begin with a well-known author's definition of mediation. According to Christopher Moore, mediation is:

> *Generally* defined as the intervention in a negotiation or a conflict of an acceptable third party who has limited or no authoritative decision-making power, who assists the involved parties to voluntarily reach a mutually acceptable settlement of the issues in dispute (2003, p. 15).

Generally speaking, the purpose of mediation is to provide parties with a safe place to have a conversation. The mediator is a neutral third party who is impartial to the parties, the issue being discussed, and any outcome that may result from the discussion. The entire exchange is confidential, meaning the mediator does not discuss the case with anyone, although the parties are free to talk about it as they please.

Like all forms of professional help, mediation reflects the current state of NBC awareness. Mediators deal with needs that come in all shapes and sizes. Figure 4.3 considers some of the many needs the participants, and the mediator, bring to the table:

Figure 4.3
(Extrapolated in part from Coleman et al., 2008, pp. 20-21)

The Many Needs at the Mediation Table	
Participants' Needs	Mediator Needs
To be able to express views and feel understood	To allow both parties to feel heard
To be respected	To provide a feeling of safety
To maintain relationships	To enable exploration beyond black & white thinking
To avoid embarrassment	To avoid domination by one party
To feel in control	To feel, be, and appear impartial
To feel legitimate or legitimized	To avoid zero-sum framing
To gain greater clarity and feel less stressed	To allow fixed worldviews to be examined
To have the process be fair	To enable new alternatives and ideas to surface
To get the matter resolved and save face	To create conditions for decision-making and solution seeking

Compared to other helping professions, mediation has certain inherent limitations or unique qualities depending on where one sits. It:
- Deals with one problem at a time;
- Can take one session or involve multiple sessions;
- Doesn't diagnose the problem or the people involved, or look for causes or reasons;
- Doesn't assign blame or try to prove what did or didn't happen; and,
- Doesn't try to change or transform the participants.

Mediation is a process for resolving conflict and making decisions, one issue at a time.

As a field, mediation is committed to thinking; especially when it comes to defining and re-defining, scrutinizing and clarifying, making and re-making the field itself! Even for mediators, many questions remain.

For example, there is disagreement over what mediators do: Are we settling disputes or conflict which "denotes an understanding of the problem in a broader or deeper sense" (Alexander, 2008, p. 102)? Mediators disagree over what it means to be impartial: Does that mean both parties get equal time? Should there be rigid rules governing what's fair? Should a mediator be the one who applies those rules? We also disagree over how to be neutral. Is it possible, for example, to be neutral to the parties and their conflict, and yet cringe every time a voice is raised, emotions get hot, or people make inflammatory statements or venomous accusations? In other words, does being neutral extend *to conflict itself* and the ways people interact with one another? There's a lot of mental work going on in the ADR field.

A Field Full of Controversy

One area of considerable debate is the number and nature of the major schools or styles of mediation. While each mediator fervently believes his/her style is best, there is very little information by way of a standard definition of each, and even less about which style works best when. Again, generally speaking:

Facilitative mediators see their role as facilitating a conversation between the parties. They do not offer solutions but they control the process of mediation: they decide when to take a break, whether and when to caucus separately with each party, and the generic road-map of the mediation. Facilitative mediators look for "interests" or needs to be met, and frame issues into "mediate-able" problems. Some also see it as part of their job to keep a lid on any overt expression of emotions. The "goal is an agreement negotiated by the clients that satisfies the needs of all involved" (Bannick, 2007, p. 176).

Transformative Mediators control neither the process nor the outcome of mediation. They regard conflict as a crisis of interaction (See Bush and Folger, 2005), and "help the parties to (1) clarify their own goals...; and (2) consider and better understand the perspective of the other party, *if* they decide to do so" (Folger and Bush, 1996, p. 266). Transformative mediators follow the parties' lead and lean into emotions when they are present. More than reaching an agreement, Transformative mediators focus on the long term relationship and each person's perception of his/her own competence.

Evaluative mediators "take an interest in both the content and the process of the dispute" and "exert a considerable degree of influence over both in pursuit of a settlement" (Della Noce, 2009, p. 194). They assess the "strengths and weaknesses" of the dispute (ibid., citing Riskin), offer "judgments about the content [of the dispute] that are seen as useful to achieving a settlement" (ibid., citing Lowry), and "as long as people are represented by lawyers… freely discuss the law…and…give their assessment of what a judge might do," all towards the goal of settling the dispute (ibid., p. 198).

Narrative mediators emphasize the stories people tell themselves and one another, and how parties transition from a conflict-laden story to a new, alternative one. The Narrative mediator helps build an "externalizing conversation" in which *the conflict* is a third party (Winslade and Monk, 2008, p. 13). He/she maintains a stance of "naïve inquiry" to respectfully examine the meaning behind what's said, helps deconstruct assumptions or underlying obstacles, and seeks to identify openings for a new story which is not a blending of the two, but a fresh future that enables the parties to go on (ibid., pp. 66-97).

In mediation, participants are especially vulnerable to "hearing with their brains". They try to make sense of what's said based on their own reality, hear strictly what conforms to what they already know, and force new information to fit into established memory. Since mediators cannot offer suggestions, solutions, or advice, they need a different set of tools to help make conversation possible. Tools are a good way to contrast the various styles of mediation because different styles use different tools, and some use the same tools for different reasons. For example, some mediators establish ground rules and regularly caucus alone with each party; other mediators do neither.

To examine mediation tools, let's consider another scenario. Two co-parents sit down with a mediator to discuss parenting time:

Husband: "This will be a really short discussion because you've left me with no alternative. You simply won't abide by the agreement you signed. You agreed to one week on/one week off and now you're saying you get eight days and I get six, or something screwy like that. This is more of the same and it's not going to-"

Wife: "That is not what I am saying at all. I simply said it was taking Samantha a longer time to adapt and we should ease-"

Husband: "We've been *easing* for months. You need to-"

Wife: "Don't you dare tell me what I need. I'm trying to do what's right for our daughter. You haven't abided by a lot of provisions in this agreement either. We're supposed to discuss decisions beforehand and I can't even get you on the phone."

[There's a pause.]

Mediator, to the Wife: "So you feel that no-one has fully abided by the provisions of the last agreement and part of the reason there's a problem is because you can't get him on the phone. Is that right?"

This is called *reflecting*: the mediator reflects back what was said to the speaking party. Facilitative mediators use reflection to ensure both parties hear what was said. Transformative mediators rely heavily on reflection to give the speaking party an opportunity to change or clarify what he/she said, and the receiving party a chance to process it, especially if it differs from his/her current understanding.

After considerable back-and-forth, the following exchange takes place:

Husband: "Look you're just carrying on here. I've agreed to Sundays but you just keep pushing, pushing. It's always been your way or the highway. I'm so sick and tired of this crap." Raising his voice, "I hate the way you behave. No, I hate you. You have ruined our daughter's life. You're a control freak and a pain in the ass," getting louder still, "If I could undo one thing in my life, I-"

Mediator, interrupting: "When you started today, you both agreed to certain ground rules. I'm wondering whether continuing in this manner is helpful to either of you."

[A moment passes.]

Wife: "Look, just hear me out, for a moment. Wednesdays are no good. Not every week. She has obligations. She's got band practice and if she gets behind on her homework, she's done for. I just want what's bes-"

Husband, having calmed down: "Why is it, you just can't accept that I may be as good and as thorough of a parent as you are? What is it with you? This isn't a competition. I-"

Wife: "I didn't say that at all. I said I am concerned about her homework."

Husband: "And who isn't?"

Mediator: "So, you've both stated that the long-term goal for your parenting schedule is one week on/one week off and on an interim basis, Samantha will spend an extra day, that of Sunday, with her Mom. It also sounds like you both see one another as capable parents and place special emphasis on getting homework done. Does that fit with your thinking?"

After reaffirming the ground rules agreed to earlier, the mediator *summarizes* what's been discussed. Many mediators summarize the areas in which participants agree in order to move the deliberations along. Transformative mediators summarize where they *disagree* to emphasize the opportunities parties have to decide what to do. In addition, many mediators ask *questions* to draw out information and generate ideas. Transformative mediators do not generally use questions and instead let the participants decide, based on what they say, what the mediator needs to know.

After lengthy discussion:

Husband: "You know things have never been this bad."

Mediator, reflecting: "So, the relationship has never been this difficult between the two of you."

Husband: "No, it hasn't. It's depressingly hard to raise a kid with this kind of crap."

Wife: "You know all this takes is a little communication on your part. You are so dead-set on keeping me out of your life. You've made this almost unbearable. If you could just see your way clear to --- oh, what difference does it make."

Mediator: "So far this discussion has been about parenting time.

But I'm hearing you would both like to work on building a better relationship, maybe seeing a future where communication was smoother and you could both enjoy watching your daughter grow up. Is that right?"

This is called *reframing*. It's used to re-cast a given issue or discussion in a new light in order to change tracks or open up new options. Often the future is referenced as a way to encourage participants to think about how the relationship or situation *could* be. Transformative mediators do not generally use reframing.

=============== Mind-Made Mediation

Mediation is predicated on self-determination, meaning participants must be able to make their own decisions. Participants should, for example, decide:

- Whether to participate in mediation;
- When and why to terminate a session;
- What and how much they choose to divulge;
- Whether they feel heard;
- Whether to enter into an agreement; and,
- What that agreement entails.

While different styles of mediation adhere to varying degrees of self determination, with that as its cornerstone, it seems counterintuitive that mediation should suffer from the same prescriptive and directive bias present in other helping professions. But it does, in at least several significant respects.

A. Steering Participants

Mediators often "steer" participants towards a particular outcome or towards reaching an agreement. In effect, the mediator *knows*.

Short of offering a solution, mediators can easily use the tools at their disposal to "direct" the parties towards a solution the mediator believes is best. While frowned upon in professional circles, in a session mediators can ask questions that lead parties in a particular direction; emphasize certain options over others in their summary statements or simply fail to mention those the mediator disagrees with; or point out common ground that doesn't exist or that the parties prefer remains unexamined, now or indefinitely. Similarly, a mediator can refer to his/her own past experience, advocating a particular solution that has worked in the past and will, in the mediator's opinion, work in this case.

Sometimes mediators are not so subtle. They view reaching an agreement as *the goal* of mediation; or worse, see agreements as a measure of *their* ability and performance. Then mediators push parties to settle. They may speak at length about what happens if the parties fail to reach an agreement; draw attention to the mediator's track record of resolved cases; or comment on how decent people cooperate, work together, and solve problems without court intervention. The mediator may also make special reference to the time people waste in court, the cost of hiring attorneys, or the civility mediation affords "mature, responsible parties".

Again, the mediator does not have to outright offer a solution to steer participants. While the technique may be less overt than in other helping professions, the results are the same: the professional does the deciding and expects the parties to follow, while the parties can feel forced to take action they might otherwise not take.

B. Controlling Participants

When a mediator asserts control over the process or the participants, he/she is attached to One Right Way. It may be as simple as sitting at the head of the table. Doing so immediately conveys the importance of the mediator and the power he/she has over the participants. It takes away the participants' right to decide, even over where they sit.

There are many ways mediators assert control. A sampling includes:

- Actively enforcing ground rules, telling parties when they are not adhering to the rules, or that they are out of line;
- Redefining the problem as described by the parties into one the mediator prefers;
- Using facial expressions, body language, sighs, grunts, etc. to communicate the mediator's disappointment with something that's been said, how a solution is taking shape, or how a party is behaving;
- Second-guessing the participant's viewpoints, recollections, or choices;
- Aggressively overseeing the expression of emotions, suggesting that emotionality is somehow inappropriate or a distraction to the task at hand;
- Encouraging parties to defer to the mediator's knowledge and experience by responding to such questions as: "What would

you do?" or "Do you think she's being reasonable?" or "Didn't you just hear him say that?"

Some mediators might argue this kind of control is necessary in order to reach an agreement, a.k.a. to "steer" the conversation. They might claim that it helps them manage the process; which is another way of saying, creating the kind of mediation process *the mediator* prefers, whereby parties:

> Find alternative ways to express their anger; describe the problem and their feelings using "I" messages, without blaming or name-calling; express how they themselves are responsible for the problem; brainstorm solutions that satisfy both parties and achieve a win-win; and forgive and thank one another (from a Basic Mediation handout).

Of course this assumes the mediator is capable of forcing a highly volatile, limbic-reptilian brain-type argument into a rational box, which is not likely to happen. But more importantly, when a mediator controls the process or the participants, the mediator substitutes his/her views and needs for those of the participants. Whether done directly or indirectly, intentionally or not, the mediator superimposes his/her idea of what a reasonable conflict, a productive conversation, or a respectful conversation looks like on the participants.

When this happens, the mediator knows what the parties need to do and how *they* need to do it. He/she knows how to best describe the problem, when emotions are appropriate and to what degree, which solutions "have legs", and what it takes to "close the deal". The mediator is the one that knows and helps, and as such, overrides the participants' judgment, and devalues and dis-empowers those who seek help.

C. Self Proving

Mediation's prescriptive and directive bias also stems from how mediators use mediation to self prove and meet I-needs. Sometimes we silently judge the parties as broken, deficient or needy, to feel better about our self. Sometimes we ask too many questions or do too much of the talking. Sometimes we re-act when parties push back and threaten us: when they question our authority, disagree with something we've said, or resist our "guidance". Sometimes we identify with doing this kind of work: we feel special that we can do the kind of work so few people can tolerate; or we see our selves as peace makers and therefore, peaceful; or we like being in charge, being seen as a "solver". When we use mediation to self prove, we're looking for a win-win-*win* -- where the mediator needs to win too.

Prescriptive and directive mediation is Mind-dominated. There's a distinct separation between those who help and those who seek it. As professionals, we assume we know what the problem is and how *they* need to fix it. We're attached to our one way of doing things: to who sits where, who speaks first, whether there are ground rules, how loud the conversation gets, and how deliberations progress. In other words, we need "to get them to _____": to see the obvious solution, learn to listen to one another, make the right choice, be more reasonable, stop repeating old destructive patterns, learn to compromise…even reach a settlement.

This kind of help is *self*-serving. It bolsters the person-self. It strengthens who we think we are, and allows us to find, add, or confirm some piece of our self. It preserves the fiction…the fiction that we live.

Broken Mediation

Just to drive the message home, let's look at an example. The case involves a father and daughter, and a dentist who has provided the young girl with implants one year ago. The mediator has already seated the parties and reviewed the ground rules. The mediator's comments are notated with (S) for steering, (C) for control, and (SP) for self proving:

> Mediator: "Well I want to thank you coming today. It's good of you to try to resolve this in a rational and calm manner. Yes, good you – all of you! (C) So you know the ground rules and now each of you may have some uninterrupted time to explain how you see the problem (C). Perhaps the dentist should go first (C)."

> Dentist: "Could I please have a piece of paper. I would like to take notes."

> Mediator: "Of course. I don't like to put paper out because I want parties to focus on the mediation (C)."

> Dentist, sarcastically: "Thanks. I think I can handle it." To the Mediator, "Well, as a fellow professional, you know how difficult some clients can be." The mediator tips his head (S) and the Dentist continues: "Well, I put in some perfectly good implants a year ago and now, after a year of no problems, these folks are crying foul and want their money back. It's that simple."

Father: "You can come off as arrogant and high and mighty as you want but that's not what happen-"

Mediator: "I'm wondering if you would refrain from name-calling as discussed in the ground rules (C). It really doesn't help move the conversation along (S). Forgive me for interrupting, you were saying?"

Father: "Um, oh yes. The implants were put in last year and from the very start, there were problems. Your records, Mr. MD, should indicate we were back in your office within two weeks of the surgery. And more recently, they've starting shifting in her mouth. They are literally moving! You said they would last for at least ten years. Now she has to have the work totally redone and I need my money back to pay for at least a piece of it."

Mediator: "So the work was done a year ago and you had problems from the get-go. More recently, the implants have starting moving around in your daughter's mouth and you want your money back. So the purpose of today's conversation is to agree on a reasonable price to help offset the cost of additional surgery (S and C). Is that right?"

Father: "No, that's not right. I want this guy to understand the pain my daughter has gone through and the suffer-"

Dentist: "Oh, please, you're not going to use the old pain and suffering argument are you? I'm not paying you a red cent. Forget it. You don't have a case at all."

Father: "She has suffered. She's suffering now."

Daughter: "You know, Dad, I can speak for myself."

Mediator, to the Daughter: "It's probably not helpful to interrupt your Dad (C). Respect is a key part of mediation (C)."

Father: "I need that money."

Dentist: "No way buddy."

Mediator: "So while you may not agree on the specifics, certainly you both agree something needs to be done here to resol-(S)"

Dentist: "Can't you hear? I said he doesn't have a case. Those are perfectly good implants installed by me – a professional dentist with thousands of satisfied customers."

Father: "She's had numerous second opinions. Everyone agrees you did a shoddy job and they think-"

Mediator, interrupting: "Yes, I can hear, thank you (SP), but the goal here is to find a resolution acceptable to both parties (S and C). What I'm hearing (SP) is you both agree something needs to be done so at a minimum, this issue doesn't end up in court (C)."

Dentist: "Let it go to court. Who cares? I told you when I did the surgery, outcomes will vary. The amount of time an implant lasts depends on a whole variety of factors. You knew that at the time."

Father: "But not less than a year. You never said anything about-"

Mediator, interrupting: "So you both agree there was some discussion over the fact that the implants may not last forever (C). I'm wondering what your relationship was like before when you got along (S)?"

Father, distracted: "I guess it was fine but that's not the point. The point is I need that money to pay for the surgery my daughter has to go through in order to replace the shoddy work this guy-"

Dentist, interrupting: "My work was not shoddy. What, you had a couple of amateur dentists look into her mou-"

Mediator: "Please remember you agreed not to interrupt (C). Now you've both been at this for sometime now. I know, as reasonable people (S), you'd prefer to settle this matter here rather than have to pay attorneys and the like (C). This is about compromising (S and C). So what alternatives do you have in mind (S)?"

Father: "I'm not ready to compromise at all. My daughter is suffering. I want him to acknowledge that this is his fault. I want him to recognize what he's done."

Mediator: "So what you really want is for him to admit his wrongdoing (S). Do you think that's realistic(C)?"

Dentist: "I'm not admitting crap. I just want to get out of here."

Mediator, to the Father: "So you said you're not ready to compromise. It sounds like you might need some time to think about your options (SP and C). This is really a problem of fairness and deciding what each of you means by that word (S and C). Of course, you know --" The Daughter begins to interrupt and the Mediator glares at her (SP and C), and continues: "You can choose to take this to court but you won't be satisfied with the outcome (C and S). It really sounds like what you both want is a fair and prompt resolution to this matter (S). How do you think that can be achieved (S)?"

Mediation always involves a lot of mental work. But prescriptive and directive mediation antagonizes and alienates the parties and leaves them feeling angry, manipulated, and disrespected. It also makes a mockery of self-determination. Even calling it self determination puts the power in the hands of the mediator to decide whether the parties feel self-determined, as opposed to having the mediator monitor his/her own directive-ness. While as mediators, we may stop short of imposing our solution on the parties' problem, we nonetheless take away the parties' right to decide by imposing our views on their situation, our way on their reality. Although mediation was never intended to change the participants, participants do learn an important lesson from this experience: they learn not to come back, not to use mediation again.

A Rare Truth

In sum, even the best of help is broken. *It has to be*:
- It comes from the same Mind that generates conflict; that thinks compulsively, rationalizes some things and filters out others; is prone to mental ruts and charged with the impossible task of creating some semblance of control.
- It is rooted in needs; in a traditional approach to problem solving which focuses on what's wrong, on the problems and deficiencies of others, as we grow more separate and isolated. And,
- It presupposes a person-self, the one that needs and knows.

Help is done to and by two mental images, each with a unique way of thinking and perceiving, their own virtual "I-view" of reality, an underlying feeling of insecurity, and core needs to be met.

Irrespective of the setting, when we "help" we reaffirm both the Person-Self Cycle and the status quo. We also get something out of being the helper...and whatever that may be, it takes something away from the person seeking help. In the end, helping adds to the constant state of conflict we live in.

When we, as person-selves, "help", we forget a rare truth: we can't possibly know the experience of another. Our "solution" is just a personalized bundle of thoughts; it's one of many, including the option of doing nothing. Our ideas are fine *for us*. But **we can't solve another person's problems** because we can't possibly know their Mind, their experience, their reality. When we think we can, we do them a dis-service: we overreach and override. We force our self, our needs, and our thoughts onto others. It's never enough, nor is it really what anybody wants or needs.

If we can stand back for a moment and breathe, how we help is sending us a message. It's asking us to begin to notice how help is broken...and that it's a reflection of how we live.

6 "Help" On a Social Scale

When we move up to a social scale, everything is magnified: there are many more person-selves, doing much more thinking, with scores of needs and a lot more to prove. When multiple person-selves live life on the surface, both frustration and conflict are plentiful. Not surprisingly, blame plays a big part in how we try to make sense of our experience. In the media, our life situations, and society-at-large, it's almost a knee-jerk re-action to look outward and find someone to blame. Normally, we blame the individual for his/her problem: we see it as a character flaw or the result of poor upbringing. But there are other perspectives as well.

Not only are there more person-selves knowing and needing, but on a societal level the *collective* person-self assumes an increasing role. The groups we join and the collective selves we form give us an even greater reason to fight and fight back. Oftentimes we identify with our collective self more strongly than the personal one – with the bonds we form around religious affiliations, academic institutions, sports teams, activities, professional associations, political parties, and causes – in our roles as coach, deacon, committee chair, caucus leader, treasurer, etc. The collective person-self needs protecting and defending too. Only now we stand with the power of the entire group behind us.

So, too, "help" moves to a larger venue: it's done by organizations, corporations, non-governmental and not-for-profit groups, and massive institutional infrastructures. For our purposes, we'll call this social help

– help done on a social scale. Social help is cast in the same broken mold as other forms of help but as the scale increases, the lines start to blur between the help it provides and the conflict it causes. Social help continues to be prescriptive and directive but it's also competitive, defensive, and at times, very hurtful. The net result can be a culture we're not very proud of.

And yet, all of this is pointing somewhere – being stuck in a mental image of who we think we are, the entrenched cycle of NBC, the conflict and frustration we live with, the broken nature of help. How we help is an example of the cracks that are appearing in many of our institutions and systems; in the problems we face, and the solutions we advance. But first we have to see it: we have to notice that when everything is a projection of "me", everyone suffers…

This chapter will briefly examine who is to blame for this, the human condition. While it may be an interesting mental exercise, our interest lies with what the various explanations have to say about our present-day culture; about where we've evolved to as human beings. We will then turn our attention to social help, which both reflects and reinforces that culture.

I. Who Can We Blame?

So, who *is* to blame for the human condition -- for this collection of person-selves that think and need, and are destined to live, at least for now, in a state of perpetual conflict? Traditional explanations place blame squarely with the individual.

A. Rugged Individualism

According to the Liberal-Humanist view, individualism reigns supreme. Individuals as seen as "rational, independent, unitary beings" (Winslade and Monk, 2008, p. 100); they are responsible for their own lives and their own life situations. Individuals act based on self interests and are "morally responsible" for their decisions and actions (ibid.).

While the "primacy of this individual cognitive universe" is a relatively new concept, the Liberal-Humanist view was dominant during the formative years of the major social science disciplines and hence, extremely influential in shaping Western culture (ibid., p. 101). As a result, when we visit a psychologist or counselor, for instance, the focus is on our *personal* past: our family and relationships, upbringing and personal experiences. Psychological "success" includes having a strong sense of self, a healthy dose of self esteem, and a belief in one's capabilities, steadfast convictions and the capacity to effectively navigate life's hurdles.

Equally, in the West, when we face a problem – an addiction, a unruly child, trouble with a neighbor, the death of a spouse, etc. – it's seen as a *personal* problem, one the individual needs to overcome. Individuals are expected to cope, transcend, and change in response to life's many challenges and when they can't, don't, or won't, they're seen as weak, lacking in will power, or somehow at fault.

According to this perspective, "power" is attached to the person via his/her status, wealth, position, etc. (ibid., pp. 109-110); of course, what we do with it is up to us. Likewise, conflict is blamed on the individual: it's endemic to his/her nature. So we say, "She's always been argumentative", or "He just doesn't know when to quit", or "She has trouble walking away and turning the other cheek". In fact, some of these concepts are hardwired into the brain. For example, the brain has an innate sense of individual rank and dominance; it "enjoys" punishing wrongdoers and has an internal preference for fairness (Lewis, 2009, Lecture Series). This explains in part, why many people cringe at the idea of punishing parents for a child's wrong-doings: "How can I control what my kid does every moment of the day?" a parent might ask, and we can "feel the fairness" of such a claim.

"Culture" under the Liberal-Humanist view, refers to a collection of traits attached to individuals of a specific group, all of whom share these same characteristics (Winslade and Monk, 2008, pp. 102-103). So we speak of the Hispanic, Chinese or Indian culture, or the culture of Hasidic Jews, Mormons, or Quakers. As such, culture is something that can be *taught*: it's considered "an additional level of sophistication and expertise" that supplements one's initial training (Lederach, 1995, p. 51). As professionals, we use this idea of culture to tailor our "help" to the needs of a particular group: we might ask, "How can we adapt our service model to accommodate the needs of the Latino community?"

The Liberal-Humanist view permeates our society: we value individual rights and freedoms, liberty and free will, personal respect and integrity, and the right to control one's destiny. Plus we see our self in that same light: as autonomous, separate beings with all the chances to make the most of, or waste, our individual lives. It therefore makes sense that when something goes wrong or someone offends us, we take it *personally*. But that doesn't necessarily make it "a personal problem", one only *we* experience. Rather, we all share roughly the same set of personal problems, to varying degrees, and in some measure, it's the luck of the draw.

There is another explanation beyond the Liberal-Humanistic one that addresses an Eckhart Tolle concept alluded to earlier: that events are neutral and it's what we bring to the situation that makes it problematic (The Secret of Self Realization Intensive, 2008). What we bring is culture: language, meaning, understanding…everything.

B. The Cultural Mind

While not as familiar as the Liberal-Humanist view, the "Constructionist" perspective emphasizes the importance of culture in producing the human condition.

According to this view, everything we know, say, think, do, and feel is given to us by our culture; we literally absorb the world around us and fashion it into our self. As opposed to "rational, independent, unitary beings," we are the product of the culture we live in: our identity, beliefs, ideas, behaviors…even our "very language and patterns of thinking" all come from our culture (Winslade and Monk, 2008, p. 103). Culture in this case, does not refer to a collection of traits attached to a group of individuals. Rather, it is our "socio-historical context", the culmination of all humans who have come before us and those who are here now (ibid.). Culture is at the very core of who we are, how we understand, and how we relate to others.

The Constructionist perspective places particular emphasis on the use of language and how humans form meaning. Under this view, power is derived from what's called "discourse", a concept taken from the work of philosopher Michel Foucault. A discourse is a "cultural idea" of sorts (ibid., p. 118). Discourses reflect the beliefs, fore-drawn conclusions, biases, stereotypes, and "certainties" embedded in our language. They tend to be accepted and adopted without question, and subsequently inform our thoughts, feelings, behavior, mannerisms and actions. As a result, discourses circumscribe the choices we believe we have and the subsequent decisions we make. If we listen, we can hear the discourses woven into our conversations:

- "Our pensions should be equal" pertains to the discourse that in a divorce as in a marriage, everything should be split 50/50;
- "This is an emotional time. He needs his Mother" speaks to the judgment that mothers are the more nurturing parent;
- "Smoking will get you cancer" reflects the tenet that we each

are responsible for our own condition of health or disease, and/ or that we get what we deserve;

- "Whatever you do, just finish your degree" reflects the conviction that to get a good job, one needs a good education; and,

- "You need to get a second opinion" suggests that there are always two opinions, as well as the certainty that two concurring opinions count as truth.

The notion of cultural discourse offers some insight into what we mean when we talk about *social* conditioning -- how deeply conditioned collective patterns are formed and particular beliefs become absolute. Every culture has a worldview which embodies certain built-in assumptions. This worldview is conveyed to us through language which in turn, molds how we think and lend meaning to our experience. Repeated enough times, what's said becomes "true" and with continued repetition, we grow conditioned to believe such "truisms". In effect, we *internalize external* patterns: we adopt the values of those around us, and the wants and needs reflected in our culture; they become hard-wired into the brain. As a result, we know what it means to "be a good Catholic"; we recognize "appropriate gender roles"; we understand what "it takes to get ahead" – from *our* cultural vantage point. Similarly, we internalize that some people are less capable than others; that we act in a particular way when we've been betrayed or offended; and that some folks are like "me" and others are not.

From a Constructionist perspective, conflict is not the fault of the individual. Instead, conflict erupts as a result of the discourses internalized over a lifetime (ibid., p. 21). Constructionists see individuals as made up of many different viewpoints, the product of a lifetime's worth of conversations, who are able to know themselves only in relation to others. This view is not meant to excuse the individual, but rather to emphasize the role external influences play in shaping human nature.

C. The Collective Spirit

Another perspective, closely related to the Constructionists, describes certain human tendencies to which we are especially prone when we gather as groups, tribes, or other collectives. These Postmodern constructs may also account for the human condition.

For example, Postmodernists speak of "grand narratives", large scale explanations or utopian views advanced by one group as to how the world is or should be. Grand narratives are much like unenforceable rules, lists of "should's, must's, and ought to's, only on a social scale. Grand narratives are forced on others, often at the expense of alternative viewpoints. Postmodern theorists suggest that rather than a single grand narrative, there are many "micro-narratives", called "heterotopias", meaning that we are a pluralistic society with many voices (Powell, 1998, pp. 148-150). For those who were once part of a bygone grand narrative, this can be very threatening because these new voices, referred to as "the Other", infringe upon what was thought of as "private space" (ibid., p. 150). We are cautioned though, "Our world resists grand narratives as much as individuals and groups crave them" (ibid., pp. 150-151).

Postmodernists also point out that "all Western thought is based on a center – an origin, a Truth, an Ideal Form...or God" (ibid., quoting philosopher Jacques Derrida, p. 100). Centering strengthens the power of some groups while marginalizing others; it creates "in-groups" and "out-groups". Taking the thought a bit further, one might argue that by marginalizing some groups over an extended period of time, their numbers grow until they feel sufficiently empowered to fight back, as is the case in citizens' rights groups of all stripes.

Similarly, we tend towards binary choices, binary regulation, and binary opposites (Powell, 1998, pp. 52-53, 101-103, 105-107). Binary choices pertain to how culture limits us to yes or no answers, to binary choices, such as in a political survey which asks if we agree or disagree with a given policy or will vote or not vote for a given candidate. Binary choices restrict the range of options available to us. They also contract how we think, which is called binary regulation. Because we innately prefer a "center" – a single Truth, the One Right Way, *the* answer – we tend to see the world in terms of binary opposites: others are either with us or against us; choices are either-or, black or white, all or nothing.

What Postmodernists and Constructionists scrutinize most, though, is our use of language and how language shapes our reality and relationships. Language is verbalized thought. It is:

A window into how people organize both their understanding and expression of conflict, often in keeping with cultural patterns (Lederach, 1995, p. 76).

Language is self-reinforcing: we use it to formulate ideas and then, confirm our point of view; to give expression to a feeling and then, cement that feeling in our memory; to judge others and then, blame them for their shortcomings; to foment conflict and then, rationalize our part in it; to figure out what others need and then, tell them what to do…to "help".

Just consider the role language plays in the mass media; how it sets the tone and shapes impressions, and what our use of language says about our culture. Postmodern theorists emphasize the importance of "deconstructing" language as a way of reading or listening for the assumptions – the discourses – that are embedded in a conversation, as well as in our thoughts, behavior, and feelings (Powell, 1998, pp. 100-105; See also Winslade and Monk, 2008, pp. 115-118). When we listen in this fashion, we look for the prejudices, religious dogmas, stories, judgments, etc. that are hidden beneath the words; especially the ones we hold on to even tighter when we feel threatened.

Language penetrates every aspect of our lives, so much so that we're not even aware of it. As a result, we don't tax people, we soak the middle class; we don't ignore criticism, we dismiss it; we don't control others, we lord over them; we don't vote "social issues", we see them as our moral fiber; we don't lack name recognition, we're politically handicapped; we don't have resentments, we nurse them. All of this conditioning creates the deeply ingrained collective beliefs we fight for and fight over. It also produces a lot of mental noise.

II. The Present-Day Experience of Culture

Present-day culture is the setting in which social help takes place. It is also a reflection of where we have evolved to as human beings. It's therefore useful to examine present-day culture; how we shape it and it, in turn, shapes us, especially how we help and fight. We could pose the question this way: What does a culture of person-selves look like – one that has evolved, say, since the time the Buddha first declared that suffering is part of every human life? Surely, rugged individualism, the cultural Mind, and our collective spirit all play a decisive part.

=========== A Daily Dose of Discord

It's been more than a decade since Deborah Tannen wrote her book, *The Argument Culture*. At the time she summarized the situation this way:

> At the heart of the argument culture is our habit of seeing issues and ideas as absolute and irreconcilable principles continually at war (1998, p. 284).

In keeping with the analogy, since then conditions on the ground have gotten worse. We live in a culture defined by rapid-fire talk shows, competitive events and contests, showmanship, spin-doctoring, and reality TV. It's no wonder people are so easily sucked into the virtual realities of computer games, we live it everyday on a personal and cultural level.

We are a culture of rugged individuals, and as such we are forever upping the ante: trying to be louder, more hostile, and more outrageous than the last contestant...or energy executive, or politician-turned-philanderer; in other words, the last person-self. As in Tannen's world, we remain characterized by "polarized debate" and a style of critique and criticism that is "deeply rooted" in our culture (ibid., p. 257). Only now, the tenor of the discussion, our language and demeanor, has turned violent...and it's become habitual.

This kind of "inflamed rant" has largely replaced normal discussion unless we're talking about the most mundane of issues. It is presumed that when someone disagrees with you -- *especially* in a public forum -- you will scream your position back at him until it devolves into battle of wills and the best person wins. As one psychologist put it: "Feelings come first, and the reasons are invented on the fly, to throw at one another" (Lehrer, 2009, quoting Jonathan Haidt speaking of moral arguments but it applies generally, p. 172). Power no longer rests with the persuasiveness of our argument, but rather with how abrasive we can be; with the cleverness of our retorts and our capacity to outlast our opponent.

This is the new conversation, the **Daily Dose of Discord**. It's the new normal. Several features set it apart from the "argument culture" of the past:

- It's aggressive and infectious. Many multiples of voices are all speaking at once, craving attention and trying to prove their version of the "grand narrative" is best. The Daily Discord is often laced with hate and violence. It is supported and pumped up by the incessant and fear-mongering voices of talk radio and television...all speaking with apocalyptic urgency.
- The debate is intensely dualistic and intractable. There are two polar views – two binary choices -- two opposite positions with no conceivable bridge. The people in the middle are silent or have been silenced. We are neatly divided into warring factions, reciting formulaic arguments, thinking our own thoughts and living our own version of reality.
- The Daily Discord is loud and directive. It's awash in self

proving and stoked by bad examples. It is aggravated by easy access to technological devices where information and misinformation abound. Its tone is shrill, forceful, and bombastic; and if that doesn't work, we litigate.

The Daily Discord is the same conflict trap we spoke of earlier, only amplified and institutionalized on a social scale. It is complete with multiple sets of "mutually reinforcing responses…that keep [people] locked in battle…supported by any number of underlying…assumptions [they] have about one another and conflict" (Friedman and Himmelstein, 2008, p.11). When deeply polarized debate becomes the norm, it can grow pretty tiring and there has been, in some circles, a public outcry for greater civility. But such calls rarely take root or have any lasting impact.

All of this should come as no surprise. We've already seen how the person-self is a contraction. Everything that comes from it is, by definition, a contraction as well. As a result, when we congregate in groups, the groups reflect the same *self*-serving tendencies, are incited by the same competing needs, and are obsessed with the same compulsive thinking as the person-selves that comprise them. Naturally, the energy we expend comes back to us in kind: just like the person-self, **we live in a culture that needs conflict to survive**…to protect and defend who we think we are and who we know we're not.

Since Tannen's book was written, the constant state of conflict we live in has grown even more pervasive and if possible, more diametrical. People are immediately classified as either "us" or "them", strengthening some groups while marginalizing others. As individuals, we are constantly asked to choose: "To side with the rich and hate mongers or align with working people and hope" (Gerard, Daily KOS, March 25, 2010); to vote for common sense or against America; to improve the lives of Americans or take the first step towards socialism. Everyone wants to be the group that owns the One Right Way, the truth. In such a world, we treat others based on where they stand on any given issue. They are either "Us or *NOT*": they're on our side or not worth our time…agree with us or not really *people*…not fully human.

We live in an Us or NOT culture; a culture that is always ready to fight and to fight back, to protect and defend the person-self and its collective counterpart. At best, it ratchets up the separation we feel and spurs a real sense of isolation that causes people to retreat into their homes and churches to try to feel safe. At worst, we throw acid, attack people with hypodermic needles, plant bombs by the roadside, build walls and fly drone operations to keep "the Other" out. From a cultural standpoint, we've taken the person-self that needs and knows to a whole new level.

=============== The Us or NOT Culture

There are many characteristics of the Us or NOT culture that are easy to recognize. Ours is a culture:

- *Obsessed with differences*. Differences are *the* defining quality of a fellow human being. Even in families we compare and contrast: "She's a lovely person. Just don't get her talking about the Methodists. You'll never get her to shut-up".
- With many diverse and *competing groups*, each pushing their own agenda, passion, or cause: from fathers' rights coalitions to carpenters' unions, organic growers to obesity defense groups. Each group is doing the same thing: dividing us into opposing camps based on our opinions and advocating One Right Way...expecting us to follow.
- That makes full use of the Daily Discord's *contentious tactics*; we speak in gross generalities, invoke absolute truths, and state opinions as fact. The goal is to destroy the opposition, score political points, and "go for the jugular"; we are forever upping the ante. Our language is littered with criticism: RINO's and DINO's, ditto-heads, hatriots, empty-headed hacks, establishment politicians, jihad chic.
- *Catalyzed by the media*. As opposed to having only a monetary interest in marketing hostility and people behaving badly, the media now *makes* news and incites others to act (Avlon, 2010, pp. 108-143). Techniques like the "split scream" and "echo chamber" intensify the media's impact, "condemning us to mutual incomprehensibility" (ibid., p. 142).
- Conditioned in the *"habit of hate"*. We re-actively hate anyone who has made a major or public mistake, especially if they're seen as better off or somehow more responsible than we are (NPR's *Morning Edition*, Renee Montagne interviewing Lucy Kellaway, July 7, 2010). As a result, Wall Street executives, the Chair of BP, CEO's of major institutions are the locus of our wrath: "Hating people...has become a global pastime...it unites people – and it's fun, too" (ibid.).
- That *preys on fear,* violence, and extremism, appealing to anyone and everyone who's angry about something. We're

especially afraid of the unknown, of change, and of people different from our self.

- Endowed with a *sense of entitlement*. Simply stated, we believe we have a right and whatever that entails; it's as if we've become our own "center". Add to this an unbridled set of core needs and we feel compelled to assert our influence, compete to win, and grasp at anything that seems meaningful.

- Where *nothing is ever enough*. Even the most right wing organizations regularly purge their ranks to ensure members are conservative *enough*. To meet such high standards of purity, our focus, by necessity, narrows: we become proficient in a contracting range of issues and spend Mind on more and more details. Even when we get what we want, we're not satisfied: after a lively campaign of "Drill, Baby Drill", when President Obama opened up the East Coast for offshore oil drilling, top Republicans were quick to criticize the action as insufficient (See NPR's *All Things Considered*, Scott Horsley reporting, March 31, 2010). Later, people on all sides attacked the government's effort to manage the offshore oil spill in the Gulf.

The Us or NOT culture is full of judgment and re-activity; it is *self*-absorbed and often, *self*-righteous. Blame plays a critical part: knowing who knew what when claims equal bragging rights as knowing who did it. Anyone who has worked in an office knows the more dysfunctional the workplace, the more blame gets spread around; even the Pope is not immune. The need to get even is also an essential ingredient. Getting even is a uniquely human desire: without a person-self to protect and defend, this need does not exist.

Most importantly, the Us or NOT culture is riddled with assumptions; with beliefs, fore-drawn conclusions, biases, stereotypes, and certainties, the discourses we've internalized over a lifetime. Cultural discourses are embedded in our thoughts and thinking, and pulse through our Daily Discord: we believe that our form of democracy is best, there's only one way to God, etc., etc. Discourses frame how we perceive and relate to one another. They shape the issues that are discussed and the policy decisions that are made. Cultural discourses circumscribe how we think, and how and when we act. As the product of centuries of social conditioning, these discourses have grown exceeding hard to identify, nearly impossible to notice, and even harder to untangle and examine dispassionately.

In sum, Tannen states:

The most grievous cost [of this culture] is the price paid in human spirit: contentious public discourse becomes a model for behavior (1998, p. 280).

And we teach that model to our kids. Phoebe Prince was a fifteen-year-old girl who had recently emigrated from Ireland to South Hadley, Massachusetts. As the "new kid", Phoebe became the subject of routine and aggressive bullying at school and through social media networks. She was called vulgar names, harassed and threatened, and had things thrown at her – all in an effort to force her to leave the small local high school. Phoebe's "crime" was that she was new, different, and had briefly dated a popular boy at school. Unable to face the continued abuse, humiliation, and embarrassment, Phoebe hanged herself on January 14, 2010. Nine Massachusetts teens were charged as a result, for crimes ranging from stalking to statutory rape. While the incident touched off an uproar in the small community and drew national attention, "cyber-bullying" and "bullysides" continue as kids would rather *die* than face the ruthless acts of children who have been indoctrinated early into our "habit of hate".

In an Us or NOT culture, it's as though we are unable to hold two opposing views in Mind simultaneously. Sometimes it's difficult to even imagine a point of view different from our own. It's much easier to totalize "the Other" and group them under a single header: socialist, baby killer, enemy...new, different, threatening. We never get beyond the words.

A Culture of Groups

The Us or NOT culture is a culture of groups, many diverse and competing groups. Individuals form groups for a variety of reasons, coalescing around common interests, causes, themes, and beliefs, etc.; from bridge clubs to church groups, professional associations, schools, issue-organizations, communities, tribes, nations, etc. We are indoctrinated into the ways of groups from a very early age: as members of girls and boys clubs, summer recreational programs, and scouts; complete with uniforms that set us apart, a pledge to profess our allegiance, badges to guide our activities, and dues for the honor of being a member.

We tend to join groups of like-minded people, with others who share our views; who look and think as we do and affirm what's important to us. In our groups, we form a collective sense of self. Like its counterpart, the collective person-self is a collection of thoughts we've grown attached to and identify with. We create collective stories, share dogmas, rituals, and beliefs. We have pot-luck diners, go to meetings, become blood-brothers, and "have each other's back". The group counteracts the isolation we feel. Better yet, it confirms what we knew was right all along.

Groups play an extremely important role in the Us or NOT culture because they fill a **need to belong**. Belonging is closely related to the core need to last and is a deeply conditioned collective pattern; it's an I-need we look to the group to satisfy. Recall that the person-self is never okay as it is. By belonging, the group props up the person-self of everyone involved, making us feel part of a bigger whole. It also instantly divides us in two: an in-group and an out-group. For every issue or cause, there are two sides, a "for" group and an "against" group, that see the matter from fundamentally different vantage points.

As our focus by necessity narrows, it's not unusual for those composing the "for" and "against" groups to have once been on the *same* side. Consider for example, the issue of Cape Wind, a wind farm in Nantucket Sound. Both the pro- and anti- groups cite environmental reasons for their position. The pro-side argues that wind energy will reduce reliance on foreign oil and decrease the use of coal which ruins landscapes and pollutes rivers and streams. The anti-group fears the wind farm will negatively impact marine life and birds (The Environmental Report, Curt Nickisch reporting, April 5, 2010). Under any other circumstances, these two opponents would be allies.

Group activities involve a lot of thinking and prescriptive rules. There is often a single leader or designated sub-group that speaks on behalf of the group; that establishes its policies and governs its operations. Members tend to assume they share the same views, not just on the group's mission but on all issues. Most groups embody their own collective assumptions and impose a new set of needs as a cost of belonging. In return, members have the full force and power of the group behind them: the group is committed to protecting and defending "its own" as well as the group as a whole; it's one of the privileges of membership.

When we belong to a group, we share a unifying sense of purpose. We belong because it makes us feel good. It increases our self esteem and expands our authority. Belonging appeals to the neocortical brain's ultra-social and ethnocentric leanings: we participate and cooperate together, believe our group is virtuous and superior, and will use any difference, no matter how superficial, to include some and exclude others from the group. Once a member, there's a strong incentive to keep the group together; to accomplish its mission, show solidarity, and maintain connections. And like the person-selves that comprise them, groups are stronger in the face of conflict and opposition. The threat doesn't have to be factual or even substantiated, just believed.

When We Fight Within and Among Groups

When we join a group, we do so *as a person-self*. That's why meetings are so difficult and group ventures are almost always problematic: we each come as a person-self. Surely, the group can impose rules of order or hire a facilitator or stipulate a code of conduct, but what makes this necessary is that we each show up as a person-self that needs and knows. Thus in addition to fighting with our self, with those we know and work with, we also fight in and as groups. In the current state of NBC awareness, groups fight for the same reason individuals do: they need conflict to survive.

Conflict boosts the collective sense of self. It's one of the key ways a group defines what it is and what it's not. Conflict fills many needs for the group: it attracts new members, motivates the base, solidifies alliances, weeds out the doubters, cements "group think", and kindles group spirit. In nations, it spurs patriotism and nationalism. Group conflict adds to our stories and gives The Voice something to talk about. It provides a chance for the group to show what it knows, compare and contrast its self with other groups, and prove it's on "the right side" of an issue. In effect, the more opportunities to engage opponents, the more empowered the group and the greater its solidarity.

When we fight in and as groups, we reflect the Daily Discord of our times: there are many voices, each aggressively asserting its view; we are divided into polar opposites; and the debate is loud, directive, and can be laced with violence. Groups are always ready to fight and fight back. The fact that an opposing viewpoint *might even exist* ignites a reciprocal need to defend and protect the integrity of the group. By facing down the opposition, a group asserts its dominance: it confirms its superiority, commands respect, and silences its critics...both the individual and collective self grow stronger.

Whether we're fighting over beliefs, policies, money, initiatives or who gets the church social hall on Saturday, we fight over thoughts. It's still entirely Mind-made...as is ideology, competition, contentious tactics, the media, extremism, belonging, and groups...Daily Discord, the Us or NOT culture – all of these are thoughts. But they can feel very real. They can feel worth fighting for. In the Us or NOT culture, when groups conflict, we:

- Perceive our side as virtuous and vilify "the Other";
- Magnify and embellish differences;
- Oversimplify the problem and its causes, the solution and its effects;
- Couch alternative viewpoints in apocalyptic language;
- Speak as one voice and see no gray areas;
- Have little regard for facts that contradict our position;
- Mind each other's business and totalize one another;
- Prey on fear, and hold on even tighter to what we believe; and,
- Band together as if we were fighting fear itself.

It's only thoughts; as we've said, language is just verbalized thoughts. But like the person-selves that comprise them, in groups we fight over *the thoughts that make up who we think we are.* "I", the group, even life as we know it can feel under threat.

Roused by our fellow members and with the full force of the group behind us, group conflict often has another feature: the **desire to hurt**. In the human brain, the amygdale promotes aggressive behavior. Interestingly, the amygdala also governs the fear response and the feeling of anxiety (Pfaff, 2007, p. 140). In addition, the hypothalamus is thought to be involved, which is related to pain (ibid., p. 141). So when we fight with the intent to hurt, the feelings of fear, anxiety and pain all come into play simultaneously. The fact that "the Other" is already dehumanized in an Us or NOT culture makes it that much easier to rationalize our behavior. Consider the case of a Suffolk County, New York hate crime where a group of local teenagers murdered Marsela Lousara, an illegal immigrant. At the time some residents wondered aloud: Who is really to blame for a crime when "illegal" is repeated enough times that these people are no longer human beings...and the kids do what the community supports and really *wants*?

Group conflict is a form of group proving. When we belong to a group, we can cease to believe there is any way other than our own. We impose our needs, our self, our collective assumptions, our way of life – our grand narrative -- on others and expect them to conform. We use the group to *self*-serve; to prop up the person-self, stay stuck in our heads, and focus on "me", "my kind", and what "I" need. And the greater the conflict, the more selves it serves.

III. "I Know" on a Social Level

When we fight as groups, we often do so over collective prescriptions; meaning, we fight over "help". Help on a social scale is done by groups, in organizations, non-profits, agencies, foundations, corporations, and institutions. Some examples of social help include the education and health systems, political groups, first responders, professional associations and unions, social service and many government organizations, environmental groups, missionary and relief organizations, the United Nations, and organized religion. Social help suffers from the same drawbacks as everyday and professional help, but it differs in one significant respect: it is steeped in the Us or NOT culture. As a result, the lines start to blur between the help it provides and the conflict it creates.

Social help begins with a problem -- many "I's" are in need; something is wrong that needs fixing. Social help is done to fill needs, including the core ones. Only on a social scale, our core needs are magnified and intensified; they warp into group, organizational, or institutional issues. The need to know, to be right, and to last transmute into prescriptive- and directive-ness, judgment and defensiveness, and competition and competitiveness.

The Social Side of Help

Social help can be described as any time one group seeks to impose its definition of what's good or right, needed or should be, on another. It's "I know" on a societal scale. It can, in some instances, be quite harmless such as between consenting adults who understand what's involved and expected of them; say a person wants to join a particular religious congregation and requests the minister help guide him/her in its teachings. There are many other instances however, when social help is not so innocuous.

Social help becomes a problem when as members of a group, we assume we know what to do and how to do it *for everyone else* -- be it another person, another group, or an entire country. We divide the world into two categories: us and them. Our group knows the One Right Way which we believe is not only best, but the only true way. We expect others to follow, willingly, and disparage anyone who objects or opposes us, fails to conform, or gets in our way. With the group behind us, it strengthens our convictions and resolve: our goal is "to get them to _____" -- to follow the law, conserve natural resources, fund morning kindergarten, stay in their own country, decrease the size of government…and to do so while maintaining our group as we know it.

Social help is about competing needs and interests, and the presumed supremacy of one point of view; one set of thoughts, one reality. Indoctrinated in the ways of the Us or NOT culture, there is rarely a middle ground, often little interest in cooperation and even less in collaboration; compromise means one group concedes that the other is right, and both groups can't win. Social help is also about power and money and to this end, social help groups make full use of the media: to publicize and defend their position, ostracize and undermine their opponent, strike fear in its listeners, and justify the group's continued existence.

In fact, social help groups are not above any of the Daily Discord's tactics. Divisions are often deeply dualistic and intractable, and debate is aggressive and contentious. People are blamed, judged, and leaned on. While the differences experienced are often among groups, the divisions that occur within institutions, among agencies or levels of government, and even within a small group can be just as disruptive, intense, and hurtful; sometimes more so. Former members can be banned, rejected, excluded, defrocked, or excommunicated. Everyone is under scrutiny, everyone's on the defensive.

All this is to say, social help is prescriptive and directive. It stirs competition and feeds on it, and creates an atmosphere of judgment and defensiveness. It is yet another reminder of the extent to which the Person-Self Cycle has penetrated our lives. What's more, it feels *completely normal* -- because we're lost in thought, dealing with our life situation. It's rare we even consider there might be another way to be…or another way to help. Figure 5.1 pulls it all together, from our discussion of individual, cultural and collective tendencies, to the Daily Discord, the Us or NOT Culture, and social help.

Figure 5.1

Pulling It All Together			
Contributing Factors	Daily Dose of Discord	The Us or NOT Culture	Social Help
Individualism, Many Disparate Voices, Grand Narratives	Language as Aggressive, Littered with Criticism	Multiple Voices Each with One Right Way/One Truth	Defensiveness and Judgment (Core Need: To Be Right)
Social Conditioning, Centering, Binary Choices	Deeply Polarized, Intractable Positions	Gross Generalities, Absolute Truths, Opinions as Facts	Competitive and Competition (Core Need: To Last)
Underlying Embedded Discourses, Fear of "the Other"	Conflict Trap on a Social Scale; Forceful and Shrill	Re-activity, Intent to Hurt, Growing Isolation, Hold on Tighter to Beliefs	Prescriptive and Directive (Core Need: To Know)

Social Help and Conflict

Like everyday and professional help, at the core of social help is the person-self, the one that needs and knows. Social help is done one group of person-selves to another. As part and parcel of the Us or NOT culture, it is no stranger to conflict. Social help groups and organizations are frequently embroiled in conflict of one form or another: a charter school is cited for closure; a policeman re-acts inappropriately; tuition hikes are proposed or service centers are put on reduced hours; a political body is charged with incompetence or corruption; an ambulance service is found to under-serve certain neighborhoods; a new site is chosen for a garbage dump; a public park is ruined by vandals.

As members of a group, when conflict erupts, we are often at our worst. We are outraged, damning, infuriated and sometimes violent. We think in terms of all or nothing and often, desire to hurt. And the intent to hurt isn't always simply in re-action to what's happening: social help *itself* can cause pain. We fight wars to spread our beliefs and protect our interests. We impose sanctions to force others to behave as we want. We prey on people's fears to gain support for unpopular initiatives or create a backlash against policies we don't like. We provide foreign aid "to get countries to _____"; from breaking up drug cartels to smoking out the Taliban. **In social help, the lines blur between help and conflict.** When this happens, we grow even more isolated, and feel surrounded by hate and extremism.

A. The Example of Education

Consider education, a form of social help. Education begins with a problem, a need to be filled. Among other reasons, we educate people to create an informed electorate, to ensure a civilized society, to enable individuals and the economy to prosper, and to help provide people the skills they need to navigate life. The educational system is highly prescriptive and directive, extremely competitive, and always ready to fight and fight back. If you don't believe that, just mention the word "consolidation". In no time signs will spring up demanding: "Cut Waste -- Save Our School." People will do just about anything to preserve an institution as they know it.

Like professional help, education has very defined ways of doing things; everyone is told what to do. There is a teacher and a seeker, in this case a student in search of knowledge. The student is in need, is deficient in some area. While teacher and student converse, and perhaps even share stories, there is a proper distance and deference between the two. The teacher has a particular frame of reference, an area of expertise – the teacher *knows*...as a result of once having been a student him/herself. This "cycle of dependency" can last for generations, through the student's children's children and beyond.

Education is help by doing: the teacher lectures, instructs, enlightens, guides, and informs the student, progressing through a set curriculum in a prescribed manner. And the student is expected to follow. The activity of learning is full of mental work: reading, memorizing, examining, investigating, and exploring what others have found to be factual. Ultimately, the goal is to help the student grow and change. The educational system is trying "to get the student to _____": to meet rigorous academic standards and achieve the credits or grades necessary to earn a degree or pass to the next level; all the while, maintaining and enhancing the institution.

The entire tradition of education is based on the assumption that the truth is gained through argument and debate, harkening back to Aristotle and ancient Greece (Tannen, 1998, p. 257; See also pp. 257-276). Even today, the debate format serves as a common teaching tool (ibid., p. 257). Such a format emphasizes black/white thinking, being correct, and participation over intuitive, non-conceptual insights, understanding meaning and nuance, and recognizing cultural discourses. It's easy to imagine how such a system might create Minds predisposed to "certainty over open-mindedness" (Burton, 2008, p. 99).

Education teaches students to think -- vertically. The system comes with its own set of hoops to jump through, and once engaged, you play by its rules. Students attend to certain matters and not others, a form of binary regulation. They are scrutinized, judged and sometimes publicly humiliated; tested, graded, compared, and indoctrinated. Likewise, teaching comes with its own set of needs in terms of additional training, certification, research, and publications. And the essence of the entire system is thoughts and thinking: it is predicated on gaining more and more knowledge, at the expense of either depth or breadth.

In the educational system, the teacher is the *knower*. If you're the student, you're looking for the answer outside yourself; you're looking outward for satisfaction. It's the tripod of NBC on a social level: there is a need or a problem and we look to the outside world for satisfaction, expecting it to make us happy. All forms of social help share that same characteristic; the same can be said of training, treating, healing, governing, preaching, legislating, consulting, etc. Social help is the institutionalization of NBC, taking a need and looking outward for "the answer". In fact, one could argue...that's what faith *is*.

B. The Example of Religion

Obviously, academe is not immune to conflict: campus shootings, student protests, teachers behaving badly, and professors going berserk over tenure decisions. But things get a little dicier when we consider organized religion, another form of social help.

Few institutions are as prescriptive and directive, and have created as much widespread competition and defensiveness as "the church". The church has all the trappings of a group. There are very strict lines between us and them: the church hierarchy, the clergy, and the congregants. There are rules to follow, confessions to be made, and the papacy or locus of power to obey. There are vestments, celibacy and penance, rules of worship, codes of Canon law, scriptures, commandments, and tithes. In fact, the history of the church is an illustrative example of how, on a social level, help and conflict blur.

Religion shapes our worldview. It is the source of much of our social conditioning and imbues many of our most deeply ingrained collective patterns. Obviously, the original teachings were meant to help: to help people live fuller lives and get outside themselves. The problems began when these teachings were analyzed, dissected, elaborated on, interpreted, and reconfigured with the intent of trying "to get people to _____." The teachings then became forceful collective prescriptions that inevitably engender conflict.

Let's take just one aspect of organized religion: the concept of eternity. It's difficult to name another *thought* which has, over the centuries, caused more pain and suffering, generated as much righteous indignation, and produced such outright fear and fighting as the notion of eternity. From a very early age, we're taught about right and wrong and wrong always comes at a price. When we misbehave as children, we sit in the corner alone or forfeit some treat or event. As God-fearing adults, we go to hell.

In his book, *A Very Brief History of Eternity*, Carlos Eire describes eternity as the desire for immortality, a "search for meaning and purpose or ultimate justice" (2010, p. 26); a conviction that in some way "proclaim(s) a higher transcendent reality" beyond space and time (ibid., p. 21). Eternity began in the Jewish tradition with Yahweh, a jealous and demanding eternal God that held "exclusive and superior oneness" and a monopoly on Truth (ibid., p. 35). Once the idea of a "single monolithic reality" was established, it was only a short time before the promise of an afterlife and salvation was born (ibid., pp. 36; 33-37). Almost single-handedly, the idea of eternity sparked the Crusades; created a schism in the Church and the subsequent secularization of society (ibid., pp. 119-131, 143-150); and sufficiently "scared the hell out of people" to make for a more docile and manageable populace (ibid., p. 160). Catholicism re-acted to the splitting off of Protestantism by "[holding] on even more tightly than before" to its beliefs and rituals (ibid., p. 130). At the time, the goal of eternity put everyone on the defensive, incited competition and contests, and was chockfull of rigid mandates.

Eternity planted the seeds for heaven, hell, and purgatory. It gave the Church a reward – a commodity, if you will -- over which it had exclusive control, to use to get people to be who and how the church wanted. The concept divided the masses into believers and non-believers, and relegated civil and more mundane power to government while retaining spiritual and eternal power for the Church (ibid., p. 94). Moreover, it instilled in people a sense of guilt, blame, and judgment that circumscribed generations of lives: faced with "certainty of moral failure in this life", eternity offered the "possibility of forgiveness" in the next; in return for abject obedience, the Church held out the promise of salvation and the "fear of eternal damnation" (ibid., p. 110). The Church has always made liberal use of fear in its "sale" of eternity...to get what it wants.

In the end, eternity stirred more problems than it ever resolved, producing a lot of thinking and "scholastic disputes" of little practical value (ibid., pp. 100-105). It thrust into question the idea of a soul and immortality; the meaning of faith and the role of doubt; and the relationship of God vis-à-vis "his creation". It has forced millions to grapple with the purpose of life, feeding the core need to last as well as the more practical matter of how to motivate people to behave in the absence of "reward and punishment in an eternal afterlife" (ibid., p. 178).

And the problems continue to this day. A recent book by Brian D. McLaren, *A New Kind of Christianity*, challenged organized religion by offering a fresh take on Jesus. Instead of the "one who saves us from hell," McLaren suggests that Jesus had more of a social agenda: he was pointing to a new "era," one beyond our current condition (McLaren, 2010, pp. 129-130). Instead of promising "life after death", Jesus was "promising a life that transcends 'life in the present age'...[which] is soon going to end..." (ibid.). And so it goes.

As part of the Us or NOT culture, and given its monopoly on eternity, the church is often the center of controversy. It is fully aware of the "unifying" value of conflict; how it props us and strengthens the collective self and preserves the institution. Today, perhaps more than ever, the church is awash in issues that stir conflict: the role of women, contraception and abortion, end of life issues, marrying gay couples, the rise of fundamentalism, etc. The discord surrounding these issues is one befitting an Us or NOT culture: the debate is highly polarized, emotionally charged, and hurtful; there are many competing voices, interests, and needs; people speak in terms of absolutes and generalities; and the entire affair is catalyzed by a media obsessed with scandal and intent on spreading fear.

As in the case of most social help organizations, once established, the institution takes on a life force of its own and with it, comes the *need to survive*. As of that moment, the institution can no longer serve as a neutral backdrop for the exploration of ideas or the examination of discourses; least of all, those that underpin the institution. It has its own survival to worry about. It begins to speak with one voice; rules proliferate and authority is increasingly centralized. The institution's survival becomes yet another cause to fight back and fight over. Any conflict it faces outside its walls or challenge it faces within, is used to bolster itself. It begins to see fellow institutions as competitors and potential threats, and looks to its entire membership to rise up and defend *the institution as we know it*...just as churches continue to do to this day.

When the lines between help and conflict blur, social help hurts. Unfortunately, the sexual misconduct of priests stands as an all too painful case-in-point. The problem of pedophile priests is estimated to have affected as many as 10,000 children and involved thousands of priests (NPR's *All Things Considered*, Daniel Schorr reporting, April 7, 2010). The children trusted these priests. They put their faith in them. The priests were the "*knowers*", ambassadors of God. They took advantage of their role as helpers, as holy men, and preyed on the children's faith to meet their own needs. Worse, the church kept it secret for decades; defending its actions on the grounds that it had to consider "the good of the universal church". In other words, it needed to **preserve the institution as they know it**. When the lines blur, help becomes secondary. Survival comes first.

C. Other Examples

There are numerous other examples of social help gone awry, when help and conflict overlap; examples of groups, craving their version of the grand narrative, trying to impose their collective prescription of what's right or good, needed or should be, on others in the name of help. Social help divides peoples; it propounds one truth. When, as members of a group we assume we know what to do and how to do it for everyone else, we all suffer because ultimately, the "everyone else" pushes back. They have to... they have their own collective self to protect and defend.

Social help is the Person-Self Cycle in action. It permeates the large and the very small acts of social help that pepper our lives:

Team v. Union. With its market share at an all-time low, management at General Motors sought the help of the Japanese team model to make the company more profitable and ultimately, save GM from financial ruin. They went to Japan and studied every feature of the model, seeking to replicate it in the U.S. down to the finest detail. They even took pictures of Japanese plants to re-create its "look and feel". Rules were changed, responsibilities were delineated, and "team" became the new rallying cry.

While the concept was predicated on mutual cooperation and interdependency, it wholly undermined the union/seniority system already in place. Instead of team spirit, the new model pitted worker against worker, a situation the union had worked for decades to avoid. Co-workers began snitching to management when a fellow worker was unable or unwilling to keep up, causing dissension and alienation among fellow employees. Advocates of the model blamed "insular, mini-empires" and those who had "privileges to protect." Despite their best effort to "help", the entire effort failed miserably and left both management and workers angry and resentful over the bungled attempt (NPR's *This American Life*, March 27, 2010).

Fur v. Hats. Animal-rights activists planned to make Israel the first country to make the use of animal fur illegal. A warm climate, Israel has a relatively small market for fur, totaling an estimated $1.5 million as compared to the billions spent in other countries. Additionally, under the Jewish faith, it's considered wrong to cause unnecessary suffering to animals. Activists believed that since the industry was so small, such a ban would be relatively easy.

That was until they met the shtreimel. The shtreimel is a velvet and sable "hat", designed to look like a crown, worn by some ultra-Orthodox married men on the Sabbath and on holidays. The proposed ban caused considerable uproar with opponents describing the shtreimel as a critical part of their history and tradition. As one woman said: "It signifies beauty and royalty...We *have to* wear our shtreimel. No, we're *going* to wear our shtreimel" (NPR's *Morning Edition*, Lourdes Garcia-Navarro reporting, April 7, 2010).

When we "help" on a social scale, we impose our "solution" on another group's reality. We are attached to our one way of doing things, a particular or "right" outcome, sometimes to helping itself. We expect people to follow...and we're surprised when they don't.

The growing rash of budget cuts is yet another example of broken social help. As is often the case in social help, *multiple* "sides" assume they know and think they're helping: one group wants to help preserve the social safety net as we know it; another wants to restore fiscal integrity and decrease the deficit; a third wants to reduce the intrusion of government in our lives. When budget cuts are involved, the full force of the Us or NOT culture comes to the fore: mutual blame, intractable positions, apocalyptic language, fear of the unknown, upping the ante, agitation by the media, and no chance of satisfaction. There's an all-around sense of entitlement: in effect, budget cuts are fine until they affect "me". It's a setting ripe for conflict.

The conflict caused by social help is more menacing than that stirred by everyday and professional help. It's different in several respects:

- First, it can happen on any scale: conflict can occur within a group, among groups, agencies or organizations, or take place on a community, institutional, national or international level;
- Second, its implications are often widespread and long term, as are the effects of its unanticipated consequences;
- Third, the cause is not always obvious. For example, groups may fight over the collective bargaining rights, but what's really at stake is union support for political parties and fear of a more general curtailment of basic rights;
- Fourth, the hurt social help causes can be committed by the helpers *them selves,* as in the case of priests, but also the rare group home administrator, teacher, home health aide, etc; and,
- Finally, the conflict and hurt social help causes can result from neglect, when the group, organization, institution, etc. puts its own needs and survival ahead of those it serves. It then becomes a guardian of the status quo, both organizationally and culturally.

When social help causes conflict, it intensifies our underlying feeling of uncertainty and isolation. With the full force of the group behind us, hearing another point of view becomes virtually impossible. In fact, the brain ensures it.

You're a Liar #2

Recall the "You're a Liar #1" discussion, it concerned virtual and absolute reality. In it, we discussed how we assume other people share our same experience of reality and when they don't – when they take issue with our "facts", recall an event differently, don't remember saying something, or contradict our position – we get indignant and shout, "You're a liar!"

We've already said that conflict is the experience of differences. Of course, people see things differently for many reasons: there are genetic predispositions, personal predilections, the effects of past experience, cultural influences, etc. Nevertheless, we tend to assume that given the same information, people will generally draw the same conclusion:

> We are raised believing that reasonable discourse can establish the superiority of one line of thought over another...that each of us has an innate faculty of reason that can overcome our perceptual differences and see a problem from the "optimal perspective" (Burton, 2008, p.103).

The fact is not even doctors do this. In a study dating back to 1949, 52 mental patients were seen by three nationally recognized psychiatrists. The psychiatrists reached the same diagnosis only 20% of the time, "and two were in agreement less the half the time" (Menand, 2010, p. 71).

We all have different points of view. Points of view harden down over time from repetition, and also as we age because the brain's plasticity declines and we tend to rely more on established patterns (Doidge, 2007, p. 304). But what's really interesting is what the brain *has to do* in order to hear another person's point of view.

Each of us has an inborn capacity to read the emotions of another human being. Facial expressions, for instance, have been shown to be universal -- irrespective of culture, the brain reads fear, happiness, etc. in the faces of people the same (Lewis et al., 2000, pp. 38-40). Reading emotions, however, is a skill that has to be honed. We take in sensory information and the brain gives us *our experience* of what the other person is feeling. Our accuracy depends on a host of factors, including the extent to which we practice reading emotions. In fact, there are "tiers of emotions" we must read: reptilian emotions include fear and anger; the more mammalian emotions include grief, love, and guilt; and the neocortical emotions cover such feelings as contempt, pride, shame, embarrassment, and other so-called "moral emotions" (Lewis, Lecture Series, 2009).

But to hear another person's point of view -- what neuroscientists call "empathy" – actually entails three separate steps (See Lewis, 2009, Self-Published Article). The first is involuntary: as we said, we're always modeling or "mirroring" what we see in others and simulating that experience in our self. As a result, emotions are contagious; through this kind of modeling, we spread them around. This can be easily experienced simply by sitting with someone who is profoundly depressed. Invariably, the same spell is cast over you. Of course our modeling can be wrong: the person may be sad or grief-stricken and not depressed. The degree of accuracy depends on how much we practice this skill.

The second step is called "self projection". Self projection is a voluntary activity. To hear another person's point of view, the brain must, in effect, ask, what does the world look like from this person's perspective? To imagine another person's perspective takes effort: the brain must compute and compile what such a view looks like. In the final step, the brain balances the two viewpoints: it alternates between self and other, and then decides how to proceed.

This means that the brain must *intentionally construct* another person's point of view. In contrast, the brain *feels* our personal opinions as *sensations*. That's why our opinions are so easy to believe: they literally *feel* right. Moreover, since the brain can only run one "emotional model" at a time, it may have to deliberately switch off one emotion and replace it with an altogether different one as part of the hearing process. Taken together, this makes hearing another person's point of view especially difficult.

Given what's been said thus far about the brain's circuitry and the formation of mental ruts, this also explains why *unlearning* something is so hard. "Certainties" and socially conditioned discourses die hard because to unlearn a certainty requires (a) translating a hard-wired sensation into an articulated position; (b) examining it dispassionately; and (c) possibly, constructing an alternative to contrast it against. It takes a lot of work! To make matters worse, if another person's perspective is not something we believe in, the brain experiences it as unpleasant. It activates the same part of the brain related to pain that the intent to hurt does. We end up unable to listen because we find it so offensive or hurtful...we re-act and shout: "You're a liar!"

Now it should be noted, "knowing" or thinking that we know how another person feels or that we understand their point of view – even if we're really good at it – is not the same as knowing what they need to do and how they need to do it. In other words, it doesn't give us permission to "fix them". It's not a license to impose our self, our needs, our remedies, and our thoughts onto others...to try "to get them to _____". That's a leap we make every time we do everyday, professional, and social help.

Given the complexities involved, this discussion suggests that it's unlikely that members of a group share the same views, either generally or on a particular issue. The Public Conversations Project, for example, uses special dialogue techniques to create a context for discussion among groups around deeply polarizing issues. They have found that when group members are asked to speak for themselves -- instead of a having a group leader speak for them – considerable differences arise among groups members, and there is far more gray area in the discussion than initially imagined (Public Conversations Project, Training Series 1, 2009).

Certainly, there was a time when we relied on one another more heavily and the ultra-social tendencies of the brain were more active. And since it takes such effort for the brain to consider another person's point of view, it makes sense that we prefer to take in more of what we already know and to be told it by people who look "just like me" (See Cultural Cognition Project). As Jonah Lehrer tells us, "fellow-feeling" is fragile and once people feel isolated, "they stop simulating the feelings of others" (2009, p. 187). When fear of "the Other" takes hold and our enemies are no longer human, only the worst can happen.

====== ## When We're At Our Worst

In the case of social help, when the lines between help and conflict blur completely, we are no longer able to tell who's trying to help or hurt whom. At that juncture, points of view are not even expressed, let alone heard. Opposing groups stand at the ready to defend and protect their beliefs without regard for who suffers. When this happens, the Us or NOT culture *its self* is propped up, along with every individual and collective person-self involved. This nation's re-action to health care reform legislation stands as a case-in-point.

There were, of course, the highly publicized town meetings which epitomized the Us or NOT culture: two opposing positions with no conceivable bridge; many multiples of voices shouting at once, vilifying one another; entire halls of people screaming, trying to impose their definition of what's good or right, needed or should be. While one could argue this is just democracy in action, the situation was in fact, worse than that:

- There were reports of bricks being thrown through windows at Democratic offices in New York, Arizona, and Kansas, and members of Congress receiving threatening phone calls, emails, and faxes (See NPR's *Morning Edition*, David Welna reporting, March 25, 2010);
- There were cries of socialism and communism, boos and jeers,

a swastika painted outside a Representative's office, racial epitaphs, wails of Armageddon, and laments that the Nazis had taken over (Avlon, 2010, pp. 31-36);

- With few people having read the bill, there was little regard for the facts, with talk of "death panels" and "killing granny" cluttering the airwaves and a media of "professional polarizers" galvanizing the crowds (ibid., pp. 35; 31);
- There were fistfights, brawls between activists, Congressmen were hanged in effigy, and one person had his finger bitten off (ibid., pp. 31; 36). A Representative from South Carolina even used the "You lie!" assault against the President when their opinions differed.

In the end, things got so bad – the lines between help and conflict became so blurred – a rift occurred where it was least expected: the anti-abortion block split in two, with anti-abortion Republicans on one side and anti-abortion Democrats on the other. In other words, everyone lost and people on all sides of the issue suffered. Typical of when social help and conflict merge, after all the shouting was over, the "best fix" was to split the difference; we then congratulated our selves on being able to have such a difficult and heated debate. But no-one was satisfied. The only matter resolved was that the dust of this issue would get kicked up again, in the not-too-distant future.

Health care is not the only place where we are at our worst. There has been a dramatic increase in militia and minute-men type groups, and other so-called "patriot groups". Members of such groups are anti-government, anti-immigration, anti-taxation, and anti-regulations. They have their own prescriptive thoughts on conformity, unable to see or hear anyone's point of view other than their own. Similarly, anti-Islamic sentiment and rhetoric has grown significantly. Sometimes referred to as "Islamophobia", supporters have called for a "burn the Quran" day, sponsored a referendum to prevent the use of Shairia, or Islamic, law in Oklahoma State courts, and staged protests across the country in opposition to a mosque/cultural center near Ground Zero. The person-selves that profess these views think they're helping. Meanwhile, they breathe new life into the Us or NOT culture.

At the core of such "activism" is fear: fear of "the Other". People are afraid of how the world is changing, who's in charge and what it means for them. Many are part of a bygone grand narrative. They are threatened by the new voices infringing on what was once thought of as "private space". Having seen what happens when a majority imposes its collective prescriptions on everyone else, they fear what being in the minority will mean. They're trying to preserve America…as they know it.

================ A Propped Up Civilization

Whenever we know what to do for everyone else; whenever we fight over One Right Way, impose our one truth, and expect others to follow; whenever we try to get other people to be as we want or preserve institutions as we know them – irrespective of whether we are fighting with our self, with others, or as groups, organizations, nations, etc. – we're fighting *what is*. **We're resisting what *is*** (Tolle, The Doorway into Now Intensive, 2008). We're assuming that "what is" is a mistake; that it's wrong and needs to be changed. That's not to say we should sit idly by and concede defeat. It's just to question the need to fight over something that *already is*.

When we fight, we forget this is Mind-made; it's based entirely on thoughts. It's a social construction: politics, the media, political parties, nations, gender roles, polarity, education, organized religion, knowledge – it's all thought. But the problem is more than simply propping up the person-self. We've built an entire social structure on the belief that we *are* a person-self. **When we create a person-self, we create a fiction. When we build a civilization around it, we *institutionalize that fiction*.** We make it nearly impossible to see…or see otherwise.

And yet, <u>*all of help is broken*</u>! We can literally dissolve into the very worst version of our self over policy issues – over ideas and concepts and labels. Moreover, the problems we face are increasingly complex and more interdependent than ever. Good ideas in one field cause big problems elsewhere: heart monitors in hospitals create alarm fatigue in nurses; ethanol in gasoline push food prices out of reach in Middle Eastern countries; postal rate savings for junk mail swamp an already over-flowing waste stream. And our traditional solutions aren't working: throwing money at our problems hasn't made us the best, applying more Mind hasn't delivered "the" answer, and engaging in more divisive conflict has yet to derive "the truth".

This is happening just as deep fissures are appearing in our financial and health care institutions, transportation networks, economic and employment systems; in our ideas about family and community support, and the role education and religion play in our lives; in the promise of pension and long-term financial security; in our relationship with the environment. These are more than just problems with how we help. **These are cracks in NBC *itself*.** As we've said, NBC is predicated on a huge assumption: it's rooted in *more*. At some point, it's simply unsustainable. That's why the public outcry for civility often rings hollow – it's going to take something far deeper than more Mind to make a difference. It's as though our entire society is falling apart…it's beyond "help".

***

We began this discussion wondering who's to blame for our human condition. As is turns out, it's not a matter of fault. It's not personal. It's not cultural or collective. It's structural: it's a function of the conditioned Mind…and it's habitual (Tolle, The Secret of Self Realization Intensive, 2008). It can't be helped, in either sense of the word. But it can be moved beyond.

Section Three

7 Right on the Cusp

How could so much be so wrong with how we help? With something we prize and value and hold dear? Better yet, how did we miss it?

How we help is sending us a message: it's telling us NBC has run its course. It's telling us that how we help is a reflection of where we have evolved to as human beings and as such, it fortifies the very mental constructs that *create* conflict: a deeply ingrained sense of self, a bottomless well of personal and collective needs and unenforceable rules, an addiction to thoughts and compulsive thinking. It's telling us that all our problems stem from the same source, the same cultural presupposition: that we *are* a person-self, the one that needs and knows.

NBC has run its course! Everything from here-on-in is just a variation on a theme: another issue, competing interests, binary choices, a daily dose of discord, more conflict – more Mind. What's important though, is not just that help is broken but *what it's pointing to*. As Einstein said, we can't resolve the problems of the world from the same level of consciousness that created those problems. That's why the issues we face are growing more numerous and widespread, increasingly complex and interdependent, and our traditional solutions aren't working. **To move beyond our present condition means moving beyond the current state of NBC awareness.** We've taken it as far as it can go. Naturally, we will transition to whatever is next.

Many people are coming to this same conclusion at this very moment,

111

acknowledging that what we're doing, clearly, isn't working; that we're evolving beyond a wholesale reliance on conceptual thought and all its trappings. So, too, numerous authors and spiritual teachers have pointed to it. Yet we're not looking to create some new form of consciousness to replace the old one. Nor are we looking for some "center" – a Truth, or God, or key we can turn to for hope, solace, and salvation. In fact, we're not *looking* for anything. We don't have to. The shift is already happening.

When we live as a person-self, we miss just about everything else. Stuck in our heads, ruled by The Voice, and locked in our own reality; subsisting in a culture of self proving, that feels on the brink of falling apart.... it doesn't leave much room for anything else. As a result, we miss the message, the simultaneity of it all. We also **miss the many signs pointing to the next state of awareness**. These signs are often hidden in plain sight. By noticing them, we gain a glimpse into the next state of awareness. They are "hidden" in the mystery; in the possibility and the stillness.

=========== Missing the Mystery

When we talk about the mystery, we're not talking about the unknown. Many people assume when we say the word "mystery", we're somehow looking for an explanation. That's the person-self at work again, anxious to prove what it knows. But that's not what we're talking about. We're talking about experiencing what happens in and around us, some of which is *unknowable*. The balance of which is known all too well and consequently, rarely seen, attended to, or reveled in.

It's important not to dismiss this out of hand as just another exercise to force us to stop and smell the roses. Cynicism is a natural outgrowth of the Us or NOT Culture. Likewise, the tendency to ignore possibilities is one of the re-active ways we cope; with the separation and isolation we feel, and the fact that the kind of help we need is in such critically short supply. Experiencing what we miss is an introduction to the state of awareness that succeeds NBC. Regardless, everything that follows is a choice: you can engage in the experience or choose not to. It's up to you.

A. The Outer Experience

Many signs of the next state of awareness lie in what happens around us. We don't notice them because we have our heads down, rushing to some place or fiddling with some thing in our hands. We're totally absorbed in our day: the e-mails, the week's events and meetings, appointments to keep. We're caught up in "me" and "mine," in "I" and "our". We forget to look up -- *without thinking.*

The earth and our solar system is a pretty amazing place. But we forget to be in awe of gravity, of DNA and the perfection of water. Occasionally, we wake up – when a baby is born, or a friend dies, or in some moment of special alertness -- but mostly, we miss it. We miss the *feeling of energy* circulating and vibrating around us. Every thing is energy vibrating at some frequency. Matter happens to have a very low frequency, but energy vibrates in sound, in people, and throughout nature. Surely you've had the experience of energy shifting in a room when someone walks in. Now extend that sensitivity to every *thing*: flowers, pets, colors, office space, food, rock walls, traffic, conversations. Can you remember the last time you listened to energy pulsating through a sound -- a bell ringing, a deep alto voice, a moment of silence?

Information has a certain energy vibration too: "Information organizes matter into form, [into] physical structures...[it] *in-forms*" (Wheatley, 1992, p. 104). All too often we miss that at its core, information is energy. Instead we "confuse the system's structure with its physical manifestation" (ibid.), putting our faith in what we see and neglecting what lies beneath. We try to manage and control it, force its flow in a particular direction, inhibit or widen its distribution, instead of standing back and watching how it moves naturally.

Thought is another form of energy. Thought vibrates in the body. According to some ancient teachers, everything we see and/or feel "leaves some imprint or residue" upon us (Frawley, 1996, p. 54). Emotions are where Mind and body meet; they vibrate at a higher energy frequency than thoughts. Oftentimes we unconsciously "tune into" the emotions of the people around us and adopt their emotions as our own. Neuroscientists say we change in the direction of those we are "mirroring". All of this happens largely outside our awareness.

So what else do we miss?

- We miss the fact that space is not empty, that it "seethes with almost unimaginable energy" (Lanza and Berman, 2009, p. 117). We also miss that we *see separation* between objects because we've been conditioned "through language and convention to draw boundaries" (ibid., p. 118).
- We miss the fact that the universe appears precisely built for life. In their book, *Biocentrism,* scientist Dr. Robert Lanza and astrologist Bob Berman point out that when we

get caught in the argument of evolution versus intelligent design – all Mind-made and thought-based – we miss the essence of the discussion: "If the Big Bang had been just one part in a million more powerful," *we* would not exist (ibid., p. 84)! Moreover, "the universe's four forces and all of its constants" are perfectly aligned "for atomic interactions… atoms, elements, planets, liquid water, and life" (ibid., pp. 84-85). These authors suggest that such a universe is not the result of some incredible coincidence that "popped out of absolute nothingness". Instead, the universe is *biocentric*: "Life creates the universe, not the other way around" (ibid., p. 93).

• We also miss the experience of the *qualities* of the world we live in. When we live in our heads, we relate to the world and our fellow human beings through *labels* as opposed to the actual object or being. So, blue is a concept, not a color with a particular feeling-state. A blue jay is a construct, not a spectacular looking, soft, fluffy, loud entity with rough little feet, bones as light as air, blue/gray and opaque white coloring, that has high energy and makes sharp, piercing, clear, whistling sounds. As scientists Lanza and Berman state: Mind's "habitual ways of branding creates a terrible experiential loss" (ibid., p. 114).

In his book, *The Way of the Explorer*, Apollo astronaut and one of a handful of people to have set foot on the moon, Dr. Edgar Mitchell takes this experience of energy and space one step further. Dr. Mitchell marvels that atomic matter is not "like tiny ping pong balls," but rather "a continuous flux of energy combining and splitting" (2008, p. 124). He is fascinated by the notion of non-local correlation: that in the quantum world, particles communicate instantly irrespective of distance. And that certain patterns in the universe seem to repeat over and over again (ibid., p. 160). He speaks of all matter, not just the subatomic kind, as "ubiquitous, interconnected, 'resonance'" (ibid., p. 134), and suggests that nature has a *field-like quality* akin to, but more complex than, Sheldrake's morphogenetic fields (ibid., p. 180).

Dr. Mitchell uses a *dyadic model* for his discussion of the universe, proposing that the interconnected relationship of all things is not dualist, as in Cartesian terms but dyadic: "two inseparable aspects of a single evolving reality" (ibid., p. 159). Mind and matter, religion and science, nature and nurture, particles and waves….good and bad, black and white, liberals and conservatives, secular and non-secular, pro and con, helpers and helped are inseparable parts of the same evolving reality. In effect, *because* of its parts, the larger whole evolves.

He grounds his model in *the zero-point field*: the field of energy that exists at a temperature of absolute zero; that,

> Underlies and is in dynamic exchange with all matter…the basic, infinite, unstructured quantum potential from which existence arose (ibid., p. 160).

Such a description sounds a lot like pure energy, the infinite potential we talked about back in Chapter One. And it – perhaps one could call it Consciousness – only flows in one direction, *towards* an evolving reality.

In NBC, we miss all of this. We forget to be surprised, to be awe-struck by our surroundings. We get caught up in the economic value of things; the education, the religion, the politics that impinge on every thing. It is, after all, pretty extra-ordinary that we're even here, and that our bodies work so perfectly.

B. Mysteries of an Inner Nature

We live "inside" one of the most astounding physical entities on earth. The human body is capable of miraculous and holistic healings, as well as driving out moment-to-moment microbial threats from the environment, the food we eat, the pets and people we love. Most of this we miss because it happens spontaneously and involuntarily. Nevertheless, it's a mystery worth noticing, one that hints at what lies beyond NBC. For example, we miss that:

- Despite containing the "entire blueprint of our destiny", *DNA* is little more "than the most common atoms -- primarily carbon, hydrogen, and oxygen -- glued together by…[a subtle] sequence of vibrations" (Chopra, 1991, p. 135).
- Our brain is 80% water, and uses 20% of the oxygen we breathe and the calories we take in. It is comprised of more than *100 billion neurons*, roughly equivalent to the number of stars in the Milky Way. What's more, the brain never shuts off – *especially* when we sleep (Amen, 2005, pp. 20; 21).
- When the neurons in the brain get excited beyond a certain level, they produce a feeling. Long after the feeling passes, some *residual excitement* remains (Lewis et al., 2000, pp. 44-45), leaving us predisposed to experiencing that same emotion,

or a closely related one, again. One could say it leaves an "imprint" on us.

- Ninety-eight percent (98%) of the atoms in our bodies were not there a year ago. Our skin *regenerates* every month. We "grow" a new liver every six weeks (Chopra, 1989, p. 44). What's more, despite all these "atoms...[passing] freely back and forth through the cells walls" (ibid.), we remain remarkably *un-changed*. Ancient texts tell us this is because we are each comprised of distinctive energy patterns that keep "flashing forth" every moment (Shantananda, 2003, p. 82). These reflect the underlying collective and personal conditioned patterns of the person-self which are replicated over and over again.

Another facet of our bodies we often miss is our ability to hear. Hearing is the most subtle and highly evolved of our senses. Some Eastern traditions believe the universe *began* as sound; as energy pulsating as sound. Deepak Chopra, who was largely responsible for introducing the Western world to Ayurveda, India's ancient system of health and longevity, speaks of *primordial sound*: the "fainter-than-faint sounds" that make up all of nature (1991, p. 131). Through certain special techniques, Chopra suggests we can re-connect to primordial sound and in doing so, deep healing is possible.

Ayurveda breaks down the mind into different levels of *sound vibration*: the outer level is comprised of impressions and informational vibrations; on a slightly deeper level, abstract knowledge vibrates; and at the mind's innermost core, there are the sound vibrations of deep feelings and intuition (Frawley, 1996, p. 224). Emotions, too, carry unique sounds. Negative emotions, for instance, reflect "certain energy...trapped by our... self-centered consciousness" (ibid., p. 228). Mantras, on the other hand, are "specially energized sounds or words" (ibid., p. 225). According to Ayurveda, all conditioning that takes place through words -- as is the case with most social conditioning -- is a mantra of sorts (ibid.); it has the power to capture Mind.

So what other signs of the next state of awareness do we miss? We miss the miracle of the brain's *plasticity*; the fact that the human brain can design "work-arounds" when one part of the brain fails (Doidge, 2007, p. xix). It can, for instance, increase the functioning of one sense, say, peripheral vision, to compensate for a loss of hearing (ibid., p. 296). Moreover, when two different areas of the brain begin to interact (often a higher and lower functioning area), "they influence each other and form a new whole" (ibid., referencing Merzenich and Pascual-Leone, p. 297). In other words, *the dyad evolves*: two inseparable parts of the same evolving reality.

Consider for a moment, another mystery, that of the limbic brain. The limbic brain sets our "emotional tone". It is said to store our most "highly charged emotional memories", control our sleep and appetite patterns, and be "intimately involved with bonding and social connectedness" (Amen, 2007, p. 37). Some studies indicate that the limbic brain plays an integral role in religious and spiritual experiences as well (Newberg, 2002, p. 42).

But what's most intriguing about it is the limbic connection that exists *between* people. We've already said emotions are contagious; recall the depressed friend and how quickly we become the same. This is because when we read other people's emotions, we mirror them and adapt to another's "inner state". This applies to other mammals as well. Another dimension of this, called the "Group Emotional Contagion," pertains to how moods spread through members of a group (See Barsade, 2002). This can have a positive effect, as in the sharing of ideas, or a deleterious one such as in the case of health care reform, office gossip, or bullying at school.

Dr. Thomas Lewis, M.D., coined the phrase "*limbic resonance*" (See Lewis et al., 2000) for how mammals attune, exchange, and adapt to one another's inner emotional states. Much of the research on limbic resonance centers on the mother-child relationship; what psychoanalyst D.W. Winnicott called a "relational organism or *dyad*" (emphasis added; Wikipedia, "Limbic Resonance," 2010). Winnicott found that a child depends on his/her mother for their very *sense of existence*: by "reflecting the child's expressions", the mother conveys to the child that he/she is here and real (Simpkinson, 2003, p. 39; See also, Ainsworth, 1978; Harlow, 1958; and Kraemer, 1985). According to Dr. Lewis, it is the limbic resonance between a mother and child that regulates a baby's physiology: through "mutual synchronization", the mother's responsiveness and emotional and physical contact constantly "fine tunes" the baby's heart rate, temperature, nutrition intake, sleep patterns, hormonal releases, breathing, etc. (Lewis et al., 2000, p. 85; See also pp. 82-86).

But the need for an "outside source of stabilization" doesn't end with childhood. Humans are by nature *social beings*. In their book, *Successful Aging*, Dr.'s Rowe and Kahn found, "Loneliness breeds both illness and early death" (1998, p. 156). When they compared people with strong relationships with those who had fewer and weaker relationships, the later group had a risk of death two to four times as great, irrespective of age *and* all the other factors that come to mind such as "race, socio-economic status, physical health, smoking, use of alcohol, physical activity, obesity, and use of health services" (ibid.). Perhaps the Liberal-Humanist view of "independent, unitary beings" is the wishful thinking of an isolated person-self.

All of this operates largely outside our current state of NBC awareness. In fact, we rarely even take note of it. What's worse, there are many enemies of the limbic brain – stressful jobs, angry people, incessant demands (See Thompson) – which cause us to miss even more, because the brain never gets a chance to rest and replenish.

C. Daily Mysteries

We don't have to look far to see the mysteries that surround us every day. But we do have to look. To:

- Feel the vitality of a hawk sitting eye-level on the side of the road;
- Experience the freshness of New England leafing-out in Spring;
- Revel in the joyful welcome of a loyal dog bounding up to offer a wet kiss after a crummy day at work; or,
- Sense the amazing harmony of birds flying in unison overhead.

Nor do we have to work very hard to:

- Connect on a deeply human level with someone we've just met;
- Make room for an old friend or family member and honor how they've grown and changed; or,
- Ponder the many hundreds of decisions, events, and circumstances that coalesce to make this particular moment as it is.

We can also notice whether we felt what we just read; or did we read it like a grocery list, looking for what's next to feed Mind?

Another important sign of the next state of awareness we routinely miss is our unusual capacity to *observe our self*. This is a capacity no other creature is believed to have. Similarly, we are able to *engage a question* without seeking, or searching, or trying to figure things out. We can ponder the imponderables; such as, what is it that endures? Perhaps it's the process, "dynamic, adaptive, creative" (Wheatley, 1992, p. 98); or the energy emanating from the zero point field. Perhaps it's the "impulse of consciousness": "nonmaterial, whole, dynamic and yet utterly stable, and infinite in its capacity to evolve" (Chopra, 1987, p. 108). Who's to say?

All of this is miraculous. And it's only the beginning. The next state of awareness is changing and will change *everything*. It will change how we see, how we are, and where we're going. We will likely evolve just as these signs suggest: energetically, biocentrically, and limbically; using sound and emotional tones, imprints and qualities, distinctive patterns, plasticity and fields; as the larger, more encompassing dyad itself evolves...inseparable aspects of a single, evolving reality.

Missing the Possibility

In addition to experiencing the mysteries in and around us, signs of the next state of awareness "hide" in the many possibilities that try to grab our attention but we fail to see. As we've said, once we adopt this person-self as our self, the natural progression is towards greater and greater contraction. As we grow in years, we grow stale. Even if we are forever learning new things, it's on a narrower and narrower scale, and often at the expense of other parts of our life.

So we drive to work the same way, listen to the same radio station, and notice the same things along the way, if we notice anything at all. We see the world's events from the same perspective, compare our self with others with the same results, and struggle with the same feelings of discontent and uncertainty. We re-act to differences in the same way, and to suggestions with the same automatic "no" or "that's not possible." We have the same beliefs, the same old tired stories, the same temperament, and live by the same rules. Whatever we are, we become more so. And as we do, we miss the possibilities.

We forget we are able to suspend judgment – an amazingly simple feat. We *can not know*. We can *not* express our opinion and not suppress it either. We can suspend our personalized and collective beliefs and assumptions, and indulge in the ambiguity of the moment. Perhaps you'd like to try it? See what happens if with the next person you meet today, you just smile and listen. You don't offer your thoughts. You don't say what you feel, or what he/she should or shouldn't do. You don't re-direct the conversation back to something that happened to you. You just say, "Wow, that's too bad," or "Whoa, that's incredible" or whatever brief statement seems called for; or nothing at all. Why fill in the space?

We also miss the possibility of *unlocking our emotions* from our

119

responses. Emotions don't have to be automatic. It's possible to watch an event unfold, as if in slow motion, and simply observe how much we *want* to re-act. We can also take one of life's many mini-dramas and respond to it with an, "Oh". It doesn't have to be a life threatening event, but a juicy one, one that might normally drum up a week's worth of stories. To instead just say, "Oh," and let it pass.

We're also able to "see" beyond the problem, beyond that which immediately absorbs Mind. In NBC, we focus on the problem and how to fix it; it clouds out everything else. In contrast, when we see beyond the problem, it's a *different kind of seeing*: it's both broader and deeper, and extends beyond the constituent parts. We're not fixated on the answer or finding a center; nor are we reduced to splitting the difference. Whenever we look for and try to fix "what's wrong", we're falling back on old conditioning, on what we've been trained to do...just as we've been conditioned to see separation and boundaries between objects.

Another possibility we miss is the miracle of intuition. Some people confuse intuition with deductive reasoning: they figure something out based on a given set of facts – some subtle, some not so subtle – and deduce what has yet to be stated aloud. Intuition is an altogether *different kind of knowing*: it's a *visceral* knowing, one that offers us a whole new understanding; where the dyad evolves.

When we're mired in thought, struggling to solve a problem, it's the thinking and the struggle that impede creativity. We're so constrained by what we know that we miss any new or novel energy that's trying to surface to help us out. Worse, when an epiphany *does* happen, we forget to marvel at this "sudden synthesis of existing ideas" (Mitchell, 2008, p. 84). Neuroscientists call these "insights": when the explicit memory – the part of our memory that records serial events as they occur – becomes aware of what heretofore has been implicit. It's an incredible possibility, just waiting to happen.

Intuition is even more fascinating, such as when a dog knows his/her human partner is about to arrive home, two people have the same idea at the exact same moment, we sense an accident is about to happen or experience something inside the body. According to ancient texts, this faculty is unlike ordinary knowing that comes from memory and the senses (Worthington, 2002, p. 78). It's an *understanding from a deeper place*. Perhaps it comes from what psychiatrist and author Dr. Mark Epstein calls "this third place...which is neither inner nor outer" (quoting D.W. Winnicott, 2007, p. 188); a place where transitions occur, a "space of intermediate experience" (ibid., p. 189). Dr. Epstein explains further that in Buddhism, "there is something positive...joyful...creative that underlies all experience" (ibid.). It's called "emptiness" and like space, it's totally full.

When we miss the possibilities, we miss the chance to be fully alive: to be right here with what is, whatever that may be. We miss the opportunity to give up control; to consider for a moment, that maybe we don't *need* to rush headlong into a new project or replace the rug that's been pulled out from under us. We miss that there may in fact be...a "third place".

=============== Missing the Stillness

In NBC, we miss the Stillness. We're too busy thinking. The Voice is simply too loud. In Stillness, we can find the next state of awareness.

Stillness is a quality we each have. It's a quiet sense. If we choose to stand still in one place for a moment and take a long, deep breath, we can feel Stillness. It envelops all things. Out of this Stillness, things seem to emerge and pass: thoughts, memories, events; the smell of coffee, the laughter of friends; a residual feeling, an insight. All of life's events emerge and pass against a backdrop of Stillness.

Eckhart Tolle calls this "the Now". He calls it "the Now" because our **attention shifts from the "content of what happens to the space in which it happens"** (The Flowering of Human Consciousness CD, 2004). The Now is "the undercurrent of Stillness in which everything happens" (ibid.). He says, "You can *feel* it". You can call this backdrop whatever you wish: Dr. Mitchell might call it "ubiquitous, interconnected, resonance" (2008, p. 134); in Buddhism, it might be called emptiness: "a sense of spaciousness that both holds and suffuses the stuff of the world" (Epstein, 2007, p. 189); Dr. Chopra might call it "the *arrangement*, the *organizing power...the intelligence*" (1987, p. 108). You can call it energy, Consciousness, awareness, whatever.

Eckhart Tolle suggests we are ready to enter the Now, to move beyond our current Mind-dominated level of awareness. It is already happening. It doesn't matter whether you believe this. Although it's not altogether different from what Jesus said or the Buddha pointed to so long ago. You can call it heaven or the full emptiness. As Brian McLaren said in his book, *A New Kind of Christianity*: Jesus was pointing to a new era, one that "transcends 'life in the present age'...[which] is soon going to end..." (2010, p. 130). At the time, humanity wasn't ready. Eckhart Tolle tells us the shift is happening now and gaining momentum.

Since the beginning of time, one sure way to enter the Now was through suffering: austere conditions; sickness, disease, grief, and heart-ache; a life-altering event, a life-time of arduous study, meditation and self-deprivation. We suffer so much and to such a huge degree, Mind finally gives up. But this no longer has to be the case. Eckhart Tolle suggests that the current state of human awareness – what we call NBC – is over and we are transitioning to the next state. It's not a central oneness, or some *thing* we have to achieve, or an entity we must believe in and follow prescribed rules. It's an **underlying, surrounding, and enveloping field of infinite potential**. We can feel it because we *are* it.

When we live on the surface as a person-self, everything else -- every other potential -- falls by the wayside. We never realize the effort we put into surviving in a NBC-world is a form of resistance: having to be *somebody*, trying to get our needs met, fighting with our self and others, prescriptive and directive help – it's all a form of resistance. Resistance is just another word for conflict. We're so busy building and believing, reinforcing and refreshing the fiction, we miss the experience. We miss the essence. We miss the mystery that whatever "the Now" is, it can't be understood by Mind. It's beyond Mind.

Helpers Lead the Way

How we help is pointing to the way out -- it's pointing to the next state of awareness. It's a quieter, softer state of awareness: one that "sees" beyond doing and needs and problems, acts outside a personal point of view, and comes with a knowing that is not thought. This shift is more significant than any of the shifts we can recall from the past. It's beyond paradigms and tools, new ideas and inventions. It's more akin to the discovery of the wheel, bipedalism, or the end of the nomadic way of life. The shift beyond NBC will change everything, including how we help.

People are tired of NBC; although we may not realize it's our level of awareness we've tired of. In particular, those who help have suffered enough. Helpers live at the crux of the constant state of conflict. We endure an extra dose of frustration; the frustration that comes from trying to "do help" on a personal, professional, and institutional level. And we're closest to the pain, to the events that remind us that the world couldn't *possibly* be here to make us happy; that such a notion doesn't even make sense. As individuals, many of us have had to face our own frailties, an experience that often comes with the job. Intuitively, we know that what we're doing isn't working. We understand that how we help is a reflection of where we have evolved to as human beings; that *our own life* mirrors the current state of NBC awareness. And that gives us pause.

But this is not a religious book. Nor is it about some great spiritual awakening. It's about the natural progression to the next state of awareness, a state that is hiding in plain sight and is slowly replacing NBC. We've taken NBC as far as it can go. What's left is either narrower or increasingly superficial, with very little originality. Among its many costs has been a deep-set polarization: it has left us painfully divided, with few means of understanding. It is, perhaps, in re-action to the transition that NBC seems to be making a final stand: conditions can sometimes feel as though they're actually getting worse. But that's how all patterns die: they hold on even tighter at the end and then gradually fade away. Meanwhile, the progression continues: just as the universe evolves, so too does human awareness.

Those who help are likely to be among the first en masse to move beyond NBC to the next state of awareness. The fact that how we help is broken – that what should be the very best part of us actually stirs more conflict – is a key indicator that we've outgrown our current state of awareness. It's also the reason those who help will be among the first to move beyond NBC. For our purposes, we will call what follows NBC, **Presence**, because no words suffice. *Presence is Stillness.* It resides in all the things, in each of us and especially in the signs we miss. And it will take the helper in each of us to fully usher in this next state of awareness during our lifetime.

And yet you may ask, aren't the signs we miss just another form of knowledge? Isn't it just ordinary knowledge, the kind that belongs to the reasoning mind? And the answer is yes, in part. Many of the mysteries and possibilities of the next state of awareness sit right on the cusp of a deeper kind of knowing. What distinguishes it from ordinary knowledge is that it is not *self*-serving; we can't self prove with it. It's simply awe-inspiring, a reflection of Stillness.

Presence is what follows NBC. It is not some thing you find. It finds you. It is not knowable by Mind or experienced by the person-self. It manifests as a rooted sense of aliveness. Presence enables us to offer the kind of help that heals -- first, to ourselves.

8 From the Heart and Then Some

A woman stands in front of a class of professionals trying to give a training lecture. She is bouncing off the walls. Her energy is so frenetic, she's difficult to watch.

She's attempting to convince a skeptical crowd of the underlying connection between two seemingly unrelated topics. She speaks of harmony and mindfulness and oneness as she paces wildly back and forth across the room. Somewhat embarrassingly, she offers a five-minute "Body Scan" to "evoke a feeling of inner calm" which she races through so quickly, it's hard to mentally keep up. She then turns to the group and says, unequivocally, "So, you can see the inner ease and tranquility that creates." The whole effort *could* have been possible had she been able to touch something deeper in herself. But the person-self was working way too hard, trying to "be" a certain way. She was *helping by doing*; one person-self to another, wholly out of sync.

When we come from Presence, there's no person-self involved. There's no story telling us who we think we are or who we need to be, no conditioned patterns dictating our re-actions, no core needs driving us on. There's no *somebody* that gets offended, that's hurt or hostile, and ready to fight and fight back. There's no self to prop up, no thing to protect and defend...nothing to prove.

Those who help will likely lead the way from NBC to the Presence state of awareness. They will be among the first to find that "third place" -- to uncover Presence. The point of this chapter is to invite you to experiment with what Presence feels like, without prescribing how or what it *should* feel like for you. The goal is to offer the opportunity to feel Presence, if you so choose. And yet, you may ask, what is this Presence?

Presence

Presence doesn't involve doing, so it basically undermines everything we think we know about living and helping and change. It doesn't involve "being" either, if by being we mean "being spiritual" or being a particular way. Best said, Presence is a state of awareness.

Presence means more than being *present*. It's not about being deliberate or precise, contemplative or introspective. Nor is it an aura or sense of goodness we seek to exude. Presence bubbles up inside. It expresses itself energetically, without being hyper, unsteady, or out of control. It is pure potential, available to each of us to express in a way that's totally our own. Yet Presence has nothing to do with building, or propping up, or adding to the person-self.

You *are* Presence. It's both **the backdrop and the essence of all things**. It generates, comprises, and contains all things; it is each of us and all-encompassing at the same time. It's constant and expansive, flowing and harmonious; the "sense of spaciousness that both holds and suffuses... the world" (Epstein, 2007, p. 189). Moreover, Presence involves no effort. It is *effortless*.

Everything that causes suffering in our individual lives, our relationships, and our institutions is a sign that NBC is receding. The Us or NOT culture, the Daily Discord, the intractable conflict -- all of these are signals that NBC is drawing to a close. For now, however, the reason we find Presence or Presence finds us, remains a very personal one. More often than not, it's an accumulation of Mind-made noise and discontent with daily life that allows Presence to surface; the constant frustration of fighting for something and not being able "to get them to _____". But how do we step out of the old and make room for Presence? For the moment, the reason for doing so is yours. In time, the sheer momentum of Presence will seal its certainty, just as NBC was once unavoidable.

But herein lies an important distinction. As a state of awareness, Presence will never be adopted as unconsciously as we were once indoctrinated into NBC. That's because the **person-self is a stage in development**. And it is likely to remain as such *even after* Presence takes hold because it serves some useful functions. It is not, however, the goal. It's a step. If this makes you feel uncomfortable, you might try asking yourself: Who is it that experiences the anger in conflict? Who feels hurt or jealous, who gets frustrated with daily life? Who produces the mental noise, The Voice, the story, the failed help, and colliding realities? The fact is *no one* does:

> The mysterious aspect of our awareness is that there is no locus in the brain for this sense of I. Science has found no evidence of an independent observer...nor a way for it to interact with physical reality, were it to exist (Mitchell, 2008, p. 174).

"I" is an illusion. It's a fiction. There's no "me" at the controls. It's thought. The person-self may serve some practical purposes, but it's not who we are. It's a frame of reference we live in and rarely, if ever, crawl out of. It's a contracted place, but one subject to evolution like everything else.

When we stop relating to the world through our needs, we can start letting go of the "I". To put it another way, **as we transition away from NBC and into Presence, we move beyond the person-self.** We relinquish the need to control, the need to present our self in a certain light, the need to behave according to an image. We experience more fully, engage in all the mysteries and possibilities; we can feel the energy, touch the Stillness. And when we help, we tap into a different place: we come from the heart *and then some*. In the Presence state of awareness, the person-self is a stage we all must go through. Then, through Presence -- keeping the practical aspects of the self in tact -- we move beyond to all that is possible.

===== Transformational Paths That "Help"

Obviously, the language isn't quite ready to talk about something that isn't predicated on doing: to adopt, to find, even to move beyond, all imply deliberate action of some sort. But because Presence does not involve doing, we can't create Presence or achieve it. Instead, Presence arises. So how do we "get there" if there no place to go to? Typically, at this juncture, we take a turn: we work really hard on the path to transformation.

A. The 7 (or 10 or 15) Steps to Perfection

There are scores of books on the paths to transformation. Surprisingly, many of them reduce the task to a few lessons, principles, habits, or laws. These books are useful in the NBC-world: they're directive and prescriptive; they require that we judge our self and often, contrast our self with others; and they create an entirely new set of needs for us to pursue. What's more, they sound so promising: Mind loves something that sounds simple, completely absorbs our attention, and feeds the fantasy that it really can create some semblance of control. But what's particularly striking about these prescriptive measures is their inherent similarity.

Take, for instance, Stephen Covey's national bestseller, *The Seven Habits of Highly Effective People* (1989). In this book, the path to transformation can be summarized as follows:
- Always take initiative;
- Have a vision to guide you;
- Adhere to the right principles, the right values, and the right priorities;
- Go for the win-win and always be ready to "agree to disagree agreeably" (ibid., p. 219);
- Listen first, empathetically;
- Be adaptable – remember differences are an opportunity; and,
- Have a balance of the physical, mental, social and spiritual in your life.

Who could argue with these "habits"? Let's look at the same goal from a different vantage point.

Maria Bartiroma's book encourages us to follow *The Ten Laws of Enduring Success* (2010). Her laws include:
- Know yourself, meaning, listen to your heart;
- Have a vision to guide you. Ask yourself, "What is your life preparing you for?" (ibid., p. 64);
- Take initiative;
- Have courage: be bold, smart, and fair;
- Maintain your integrity: always do the right thing;
- Be adaptable;
- Have humility;
- Practice endurance;
- Know your purpose; and,
- Be resilient.

In an interview about the book, Ms. Bartiroma explains that by "purpose", she's not just talking about making money: "It doesn't necessarily have to be about stuff...Success is a feeling" that comes from contentment (NPR's *Weekend Edition Saturday*, Scott Simon interviewing, April 24, 2010).

Let's try one more with a slightly different slant. Richard Stengal wrote a book entitled, *Mandela's Way: 15 Lessons on Life, Love and Courage* (2009). As a life worth emulating, Stengal summarizes Mr. Mandela's life lessons as follows:

- Courage is not the absence of fear;
- "Control is the measure of a leader – indeed, of all human beings" (ibid., p. 39);
- Lead from the front, with or without being noticed;
- Virtue takes a team effort;
- Always "look the part" in clothing, stature, and a smile;
- Have a core principle (such as, equal rights for everyone). The rest is tactical;
- Look for the good in others: people are "virtuous unless proven otherwise" (ibid., p. 117);
- Know your enemy, understand him and discover his weaknesses;
- Keep your rivals close;
- It's okay to say no, just know when to say it;
- It's a long process: quick decisions lead to error and gratification often needs to be postponed;
- Love is what makes the difference;
- Quitting is also a way of leading;
- There's "no one interpretation…both may be correct"(ibid., p. 211); and,
- Have a place where you can find peace.

While they differ in tone, all of these conventional paths are grounded in NBC: they are predicated on doing, based on knowing, and driven by needs. They've got all the catch phrases of living on the surface: contentment, control, and proof; rivals and enemies; appearance and stuff; win-win and doing the right thing; courage and virtue, etc. They presume we are masters of our universe, and anything "bad" that happens is just a learning experience in the making. They create a world of should's, must's, and ought to's that we need to live up to.

Conventional paths to transformation are built on the NBC tripod: there's a problem to be fixed, something "out there" will fix it, and we expect the world to deliver because it's here to make us happy. In other words, we're still *self*-serving. And as with all *self*-serving activity, it inevitably leads to conflict and frustration. That's why another especially striking thing about these books is that so many of us have them on our bookshelves… and the lessons remain unlearned.

B. The New Age Let-Down

Like the 7, 10, and 15 steps to perfection, the so-called "New Age" was another promising path to transformation. It, too, proved surprisingly prescriptive.

For example, many of us came to believe that "the problem" was a matter of perspective. We assumed that just *knowing* there was a problem would somehow profoundly change our life. Or worse, we came to believe that it wasn't *what* happened to us that mattered, but how we related to it. We believed in the power of Mind: that with a change in perspective and enough repetition, poof -- we'd be transformed. So we pinned affirmations on the fridge and all of the mirrors: "I have everything I need", "Follow your heart", "I am in charge of my life's path", "Everything happens for a reason." And sometimes they worked; but after awhile, they just became part of the mirror.

For many, the New Age brought with it the spooky notion of a universe conspiring to guide us down a Divine path, if only we would listen. Some people took this to an extreme and underwent a physical and psychological metamorphosis: they *became* "spiritual". They worked very hard at projecting the dogma: calm, unaffected, wise, and all-knowing. They established rigid protocols for others to follow, and required strict adherence to certain practices and daily regiments. They were spiritual masters and as such, they *knew*: they knew how the rest of us should be, what we needed to do, and who we needed to become. They were "helping".

Having found their "Higher Self", these so-called teachers proclaimed: "We're part of a greater whole", "We are all connected", and "Life's events are not arbitrary". Eerily, they told us, "Life's mysteries will reveal themselves to you in time." Suddenly we found our self scouring every challenge in search of its special, highly personalized, and life-altering message. Since nothing was random, we scrambled to find the meaning of each and every event. Healing became a personal obligation which was, unfortunately, often misinterpreted as, "If you're still sick, you have only yourself to blame". In the end, disheartened by the experience, many of us found we *could* heal…and yet still have a disease.

Meditation, too, held great hope for transformation. Meditation is not easy. There are numerous techniques and it can be very difficult; in fact, depending on how it's taught, there are prescribed ways of meditating. Many people labor to this day focusing attention on a single point, witnessing thoughts as they rise and pass, repeating mantras, and attempting various other methods. Some who meditate try to eliminate desire; others, mistakenly, try to stop their thoughts. Some come to see their bodies as a hindrance, others start policing Mind. At a minimum, the experience is effortful.

Some New Agers even managed to make a personal drama out of their meditation practice: they forced themselves to suffer in the hopes of reaching nirvana. They fought to reign in the thinking Mind and suppress the negative thoughts which caused dis-ease; practiced non-attachment in an effort to align with a "higher power"; and strove to be above the fray, in the world not of it…a realized being. Some of us learned to witness our thoughts so well, we found we'd adopted multiple selves who were now in charge: fighting, forcing, competing, prescribing, and judging. We wholly lost touch with the practical aspects of the self.

Despite these stumbles, the New Age experience was an essential part of where we are today. It taught us many techniques for slowing down, and focusing attention. It also showed us *we can be other than how we are*. It introduced the West to many wonderful teachers and thousands of insightful books that draw on ancient texts and traditions, readying us to move beyond NBC. Meditation too, especially what some call "true meditation", can help pave the way. Even affirmations can be useful. In effect, we can choose to believe whatever we want, including that "The path is the goal", "The challenges we face are the lessons we need most", or "Find peace within" -- as long as we recognize that even "good" beliefs can be prescriptive. And when pursued aggressively, they can be abusive to our self and others. As Apollo astronaut and author Dr. Edgar Mitchell cautions:

> Following the feeling nature alone is a mixed blessing…[These] sensations respond not only to conscious thought, but to subconscious activity, internal health, and non-local resonance… [We need to be] aware of the differences in these inner signals (2008, p. 221).

In other words, life's events *may* reveal some profound insight. On the other hand, the message can be totally Mind-made and mean nothing at all.

When we *become* spiritual, or try to *be* spiritual or religious or more evolved than others, we think we're special (Tolle, The Flowering of Human Consciousness CD, 2004). We're attached to an image that makes us feel superior; we're meeting an I-need. We're propping up the self and feeding our own Reality; which is to say, we're still stuck in NBC. In any variety of ways – whether we're trying to be a good Christian, find contentment, deepen our faith, or surrender to the Divine – we're striving to meet some need. We're setting up an expectation and looking for the world to deliver.

What's more, we're fighting our self. In no time at all, the other, more neglected parts of the person-self will surface: we'll re-act angrily to some situation or grow short-tempered with someone. This applies to the "seekers" and "masters" alike. Then we'll be disappointed in our shortcomings…because we're never satisfied.

C. The Hybrid Approach

One additional path to transformation deserves mention. As reflected in his book, *The Seven Spiritual Laws of Success* (1994), Dr. Deepak Chopra suggests a blended approach, melding conventional laws with New Age-type principles. It's a slower method and doesn't appeal to everyone. Dr. Chopra suggests the way to transformation requires that we:

- Recognize that true success is the Divine unfolding;
- Give silently and with intent, and be able to receive as well;
- Make choices consciously;
- Take actions that are motivated by love;
- Focus our attention and use intention to transform;
- Relinquish attachment; and,
- Ask and answer the question, "How can I serve humanity with my unique set of talents?"

One thing these transformational paths all share in common is they usually don't work. As with any form of self improvement or self help, whenever we try to re-make our self, we usually fail. We fail because we're trying to adopt someone else's prescriptive model of how we should be, and we think that will make us happy. The fact is we can't force our self *to be anything*…it's just a slightly more disguised way of trying "to get us to _____."

Not Being a Better Person

There's something else these transformational paths have in common: they all try to make us *a better person*. They too, are built on the assumption that we *are* a person-self and expected to remain as such for a lifetime. They help consolidate the fiction. These paths are predicated on thoughts and thinking, and generate conflict and frustration. They reinforce the Person-Self Cycle. As Eckhart Tolle tells us, **it's not about "improving the person but moving beyond the person"** (The Secret of Self Realization Intensive, 2008). And nothing short of a change in awareness will suffice.

The same is true on a social scale. What makes our current condition so frustrating is we keep applying more Mind to a situation that's calling for something far deeper. Every group comes to a problem with its own distinct perspective and helpful prescription for solving it *their* way. What resolves the problem for one group causes deep consternation for another. We end up with more of the same: our policies grow more abstruse, our issues become obfuscated, and deliberate action becomes all the more unlikely...as rifts within communities and races, among peers and friends become commonplace. It's the same "more Mindset".

Meanwhile the progression from NBC to the Presence state of awareness continues. We can see it every time we look up from our hands; every time we take in the backdrop against which all of this happens; every time we breathe deeply and listen to the Stillness. And the flow can't be stopped because it's the natural unfolding of Consciousness. The only question is how much resistance we'll put up – and consequently, the pace at which the shift will occur.

The point is this: for whatever reason, in NBC, we got stuck at the stage of the person-self. In Presence, we gradually evolve beyond it. Presence is not some thing we can achieve, or conform to, or force to fit. It doesn't involve fighting with our self, or balancing our good and shadow selves, or trying to transform the person-self in a prescribed *or any* manner. Presence is not about doing. In Presence, *the dyad evolves;* the larger whole evolves; *we* evolve, effortlessly. We move from living in our heads to assuming our place as, and in, the evolving reality.

But why begin with me? The answer is simple. Many have come before us and embraced Presence. This is just the first time it's ever been possible on a mass scale. We start with ourselves because we're ready. Even in the time-honored tradition of Buddhism, the epitome of compassion, there are ten stages of becoming a Buddha and "the first seven are working *for your own benefit"*; after that the work is for the benefit of both yourself and others (emphasis added; NPR's *Morning Edition*, Anthony Kuhn interviewing Zen Monk Endo Mitsunaga, May 11, 2010). So we begin with ourselves.

Presence is "in" each of us. It requires only some space and an awareness of "our own" Stillness to arise. **Presence is first a physical sensation. Over time, it becomes a state of awareness.** It's physical first because we are embodied creatures. If helpers are going to lead the way from NBC to Presence, becoming aware of our physical nature is critical to feeling Presence as it arises more deeply. So we start by feeling in the body.

=========== The Knee-Jerk Re-action

It's tempting to want to skip this part. Feeling "in the body" sounds weird. It sounds other-worldly and strange. The fact is many of us checked out of the body years ago and have learned to reside almost exclusively in the head. We regard the body as a tool we must attend to; Mind wrapped in some restrictive casing. But the body is far from a limitation. Without it, we have no means of *experience*. We couldn't touch someone else's skin or feel a hug; we couldn't smell vanilla or a nearby skunk; we couldn't see a poppy bloom, taste ice cream, or hear the wind. The body is *how we feel*, including how we first feel Presence.

But this isn't some "feel good" exercise we do for its own sake. While it may be calming to some, there are at least three distinct reasons for feeling in the body:

- First, it gets us back in touch with our physical nature without making demands of it, which is relatively foreign in the NBC-world. It heightens our sense of what's possible;
- Second, feeling in the body decreases the pull of Mind, making room for Presence. At the same time, it brings us current, into this particular moment, instead of off somewhere thinking; and,
- Third, it gives us a taste of silence which enables a more indepth experience of Presence as it arises. Feeling in the body lays the groundwork for Presence as a state of awareness.

To be "in the body" means bringing our attention to the physical body and learning to distinguish between the inner and the outer body. The outer body is comprised of our skin and outer sensations. Some outer body experiences go slightly deeper, for instance a heart-felt touch, certain smells and sounds. Also, some outer body experiences impinge on the inner body such as how sugary foods taste great initially, but later cause inner upset or agitation.

As physical sensation, Presence arises in the *inner body*. It engages the entire body and at the same time extends beyond it. When we bring our attention to the inner body, it feels alive and energized, flowing and vital. *This is Presence* – it's the Presence that resides "in" us, which is no different than the Presence that surrounds us.

So, perhaps, you might be willing to experiment?

Sitting in your chair, feel what it's like to be in your body. Can you feel the bottom of your feet? Can you feel your calves? Does anything hurt right now? Is there any muscle tightness? Can you feel your bones against the chair? Where do you feel your weight? Does the top or bottom "half" of your body, or left or right side, feel heavier? Is there any part of your body you *can't* feel? Your mid-back? Your forearms? When you bring your attention to those areas, do they suddenly ache or feel any sensation? What happens if you allow a particularly tight part of your body…to relax?

===================   Inside the Casing

What follows is a series of "exercises" for feeling progressively more in the body. The first is preparatory in nature, allowing us to sit and reconnect with our body. The second focuses our attention, and introduces the inner body. And the third draws us directly into the inner body and out of Mind, making space for Presence to "fill in". By working with one or more of these exercises on a regular basis, we deepen the experience.

It's important to note, these exercises have been chosen because they have worked for others. Yet if neuroscience has taught us anything, it's that we can't understand or anticipate someone else's inner experience. So there's no right or wrong way to feel; no performance measures or rule book to follow. Feeling in the body can't be done perfectly or poorly. It's not prescriptive…**it comes from within**.

Opportunity One.

In his book, *A Year to Live*, Stephen Levine offers what he calls the Soft Belly Meditation (Levine, 1997, pp. 32-33). His premise is that we tend to hold certain parts of the body more tightly than others, and some, like the belly, seldom feel relaxed. In this meditation, he advises us to bring our attention to the belly, breathing in and out of it as a way to soften it. He tells us every time we get lost in Mind – in fear, expectations, feelings, etc. -- we can release the belly, take a deep breath, and soften.

A similar exercise involves releasing specific areas of the body where we hold our tension. Many of us, for instance, hold tension in our neck and lower back, and we do so even when we sleep. This exercise is done in bed before falling asleep:

> Lying in bed, notice where you are holding tension in your body. Just notice it; don't judge or reflect on it. Bring your attention to it. Then slowly proceed through a physical review, releasing each area of your body that feels tight, starting with your feet and moving towards your head, spending a fair amount of time focusing on each area.
>
> If you're having trouble feeling in your body, you can try the following: release the bottom of your feet, your calves, and your thighs...and pause; release your belly and lower back...and pause; release your shoulder blades down your back...and pause; release the skin on your face, the skin around your ears, and your eyes... and pause; release your jaw...release your tongue away from the roof of your mouth...and allow the pillow to hold all the weight of your head. Now just be there, quietly.

If you wake up during the night, you might see if any tension has crept back into your body; especially in the jaw and shoulder blade areas which are where many people in the Us or NOT culture seem to hold their stress.

If you enjoy this, there is a more advanced version pioneered by Dr. Jon Kabat-Zinn in conjunction with the Stress Reduction Clinic at the University of Massachusetts Medical Center, called the Body Scan. The Body Scan takes around 45 minutes and involves breathing several times in and out of each area of the body, slowly and with attention, releasing thoughts and tension (Kabat-Zinn, 1990, pp. 75-93). It's available through the Clinic in a pre-recorded format so you can fully explore it, without having to memorize or think about anything.

Opportunity Two.

This next exercise delves more deeply into the inner body. Each of us harbors certain sounds. Sometimes, if we sit quietly, we can hear these inner energetic vibrations. To try it:

> Sit alone, with a set of earplugs in your ears and without the radio or anything playing, or any perceptible noise in the background. Simply sit back in the silence. Feel your physical presence: your body on the chair, the edges of your skin, the contours of your body, the air pulsing against you.

> When you're ready, take your attention inside your body and listen for a sound. At first, there might be a slight ringing sensation. Beneath that, in the recesses, there is often a low tonal hum, a primordial sound. Sometimes it forms a word-like sound. Other times, it's just a hum. Simply sit with the sound if you hear it.

> If you don't hear a particular sound, listen to your own heart beat. Simply sit with it. Notice how full silence can be.

Listening to "your sound" can be very soothing. It also provides an opportunity to see how Mind re-acts: how it wants to run away and think about something; how the story starts up or The Voice begins commentating; how lists appear, discussions are recited, and problems are recounted. It can be fun to watch Mind try to reassert itself and at times, succeed. Some people keep a sheet of paper handy to write down thoughts that might need to be addressed later so they can let go of them now.

In addition to personal sounds, there are also healing sounds. According to Dr. David Frawley, certain words or sounds are "energized" and by repeating them, we're able to change our dominant or repetitive "vibratory patterns" (1996, pp. 225-226). Some people call these mantras, some call them prayers, and some call them healing sounds. HUM, for example, helps dissolve negativity; RAM is calming and restful; SHAM is good for relieving stress (ibid., pp. 232-235). You may even find some of these healing sounds mirror your own inner vibrations put into words.

Working with sound vibrations focuses our attention inside the body. It introduces us to the inner body and to silence. The outer body is how we experience the world, through our senses. The inner body is spacious and still, yet full of energy. It flows and pulsates, like intermeshing waves, and speaks through sound and movement rather than words and judgment.

Opportunity Three.

Conscious breathing draws us directly into the inner body. When we breathe in deeply, we can follow the air as it moves into the inner body. The lungs fill and if we pay attention, we may even feel the breath touch the interior linings of our lungs. Taking a deep, conscious breath periodically throughout the day is one way to refocus our attention on the inner body without any formal practice or effort. It draws us out of Mind and brings us fully present.

To intensify the experience of the inner body, you may like to try this simplified version of an advanced Yogic breathing exercise:

Sitting up straight in a chair with your feet firmly on the floor, breathe deeply, in and out, several times. Feel your outer chest expand and contract with each breath. "Watch" the air move in and out of the inner body.

On your next *exhalation*, see if you feel a *lift* in your *inner body* as you exhale the breath. While this may sound counterintuitive to Mind, allow yourself the experience. On the next exhalation, sense if something in the lower abdomen and up through the inner chest cavity actually rises. After several times, the experience starts to feel quite natural and no longer requires your attention.

Now, breathe with awareness in and out, allow your shoulder blades to move down your back and feel the expanse of your inner body. Can you feel something "flowing into" you, starting with your feet all the way up through your chest, as if it's filling you up inside? Again, just sit with it. How does that "something" feel to you?

In this exercise, with repetition, the lift of the inner body on the out-breath feels natural because we're not really *doing* anything or making something new happen. This is what happens when we breathe. We just never noticed it before.

When we breathe consciously, we have fewer thoughts. In this way, conscious breathing makes room for Presence: Mind recedes, the commentary quiets, and the constant barrage of mental noise settles down. In time, we may begin to feel Presence "fill in" this space. Presence feels alive, dynamic and vibrant. We feel very still, yet full of life. This *is*

Presence. It's the Presence that's inside of us and makes up the body. As we said, we *are* Presence.

=============== The Unfolding of Presence

For many of us, the first thing we notice as a result of these exercises is The Voice in the head. The Voice is the outer world internalized. It's irritating and directive as it tries to siphon off our attention. But now, instead of listening to The Voice and getting swept away by it, we breathe deeply and let it pass. We don't need to *do* anything; we ignore its instructions. Miraculously, nothing happens. No earth shattering catastrophes befall us. That's because The Voice is not who we are. It's just conditioned thought.

But being in the body is just the beginning. It flips the switch. It sets the dominos in motion for a fuller experience of Presence that evolves at its own pace. For those of us who help, being in the body affords us the chance to be *quiet*. We can watch Mind play its games and try to lure us back into the fiction. We can focus our attention and become present. Being in the body draws us out of our heads and creates space. It gives us the *physical* sensation of Presence. It would be a shame to stop there.

The more we experiment with Presence, the more we start to notice certain changes occurring with very little effort on our part. We may notice, for example, that some old habitual patterns don't seem to fit anymore. They're not as attractive or entertaining or addictive as they once were. We might find ourselves letting them go; perhaps initially, just a day or two at a time. Similarly, our physical patterns may change, or the people or groups we care to spend time with change. Again, there's no effort, no pressure; there's no right or wrong way we should be. We intuit what's okay for us right now. And accept that things will change.

In time, our re-actions become less automatic. We find it easier to listen without putting in our two cents. We may notice that we *want* to pause during the day, take a conscious breath and stop Mind flow. We may even devise little reminders to feel Presence, such as "the slow blink": when the thinking Mind takes over, we breath and blink very, very slowly, clearing the mind as we open our eyes and tune back into the backdrop, the space in which everything happens.

As the experience of Presence becomes more frequent, we may discover just how much space we take up as the person-self that needs and knows. We may notice how loud we are or how much talking we do; how we grow quiet to get attention or prepare to recite our victim stories; how often we re-direct the conversation to "me" or have to tell others our problems; how we need to feel important, to have the answers, to know what to do and how to do it. We may ask: How dominant was I at that party last night? Or at that meeting, the dinner table, the church group, or while helping my son with his homework? How much "space" did "*I*" consume? How often did I have to say what *I* thought? We do so not in a critical way, but a pragmatic one: we take note of it and take action if we so choose.

As we grow in Presence, we become less attached to our stories. Our judgments and opinions feel less important, our past and future don't need retelling, and our many pressing needs don't seem so critical. Occasionally, Mind takes a backseat, as it matures into simply the mind; another sense perception, another tool to draw on when the situation calls for it.

Gradually, as we spend less and less time in NBC, the draw of the person-self lessens. It starts very slowly. We may notice, for example, that taking anything personally causes a tightening in the body. When we take things personally, we are neither present nor in a state of Presence. We're ready to protect and defend our self. As we breathe and focus our attention, we find that "personal" doesn't matter as it once did. The convictions we bring to events – what makes them good or bad, right or wrong, with or against us – diminish as well. We don't need to fight to prove who we think we are.

Presence shouldn't be mistaken for some vacuous condition of mind or inactive feeling of oneness with all beings. Presence is a state of awareness: we are fully grounded and even *more* alert, capable, and creative than ever before. To look at us, we don't appear any different. And yet, where our actions come from and how we see ourselves, others, and the world, shifts significantly. In time, Presence becomes the preferred state -- because there's no driving needs, no need to know, no doing for its own sake.

Finding Presence

As we've said, Presence begins as a physical sensation and becomes a state of awareness. The more in-bodied we feel, the less time we spend lost in thought. With fewer thoughts, Mind starts to clear. Slowly we begin to **tune into the backdrop** in which all things happen, what Eckhart Tolle calls the Now, the Stillness. We're able to shift our attention from the "content" that happens -- our story, what went wrong, who we're battling with, why we're so disappointed, etc. -- "to the space in which it happens" (The Flowering of Human Consciousness CD, 2004).

At first this feels very odd. While interacting with the world, we "look for" the backdrop. As things happen around us, people come and go, meetings transpire, activities take place, we're taking a walk -- we notice that everything occurs against **a backdrop of Stillness**. Initially, this requires some effortless practice but soon, it comes quite easily. This is because when we tune into the Stillness that surrounds the "stuff of the world", we tune into the Stillness in ourselves. We experience "our own" Stillness, "our own" sense of Presence. Stillness and Presence are one.

"Our own" sense of Presence is more than sensation. It's deeper than an emotion and greater than a mental phenomenon. Over time, it becomes a natural grounding that accompanies us, because it is us. Conscious breathing is a key step in feeling "our own" sense of Presence. Conscious breathing hones our attention in on this very moment – it brings us here and now. We simply breathe deeply and bring our awareness "forward": our eyes see what's here, our ears hear what's around us, and our whole body is alert and alive. It's as if Mind finally catches up with the present moment and when it does, we realize it's no longer needed.

Gradually, sitting in a chair, standing, moving, with our eyes open or closed, we can go inside and feel "our own" sense of Presence. It starts in the body but very quickly extends beyond it. It pulsates outward; we feel grounded, but it's more than a physical experience. It's a feeling of "being"; that *we are*...here, alive and vital. It comes from a place deeper and wider than the heart. Perhaps we're connecting with pure energy itself, to the field of infinite potential.

Again, **when we tune into the backdrop of Stillness, we tune into "our own" Presence**. We can stand back and notice. We can touch Presence and reflect it outward. We can see it and experience it in others. In that moment, *we step outside our self and Presence evolves*. After all, isn't that what spirituality is?

> Once [you have] the awareness of being aware, you attain a totally different state...You simply stop projecting your sense of self on [a] particular object of consciousness...That is spirituality (Singer, 2007, p. 37).

The more we experience the backdrop, the more it expands and extends and envelopes -- and the more we meld with it and awareness grows. There's a greater sense of clarity, a calm excitement, an expanse, a feeling of awe. We are fully here, but aware that the energy that makes up the body and the mind is the same energy that surrounds us. It's the same space, the same Stillness, the same Presence...the same underlying, surrounding, and enveloping field of infinite potential, emanating from the same zero point field. This is not something we comprehend, it's something we are. It's a deeper kind of knowing, it comes from within.

========= ## Why It Evolves Slowly

Slowly, we transition to the Presence state of awareness. The backdrop, "our own" sense of Presence becomes our state of awareness. We move beyond the surface view, beyond the words; beyond the "me", the person-self. We don't see what happens in terms of fault or blame, cultural or individual, chance or destiny, a challenge or a punishment. It's what is, and it's okay. We can sit with a situation. We don't need to impose a self on it; Mind doesn't need to make it right. We accept that we have a limited understanding of this moment. We can *be* without needing and *know* without thinking.

But we've been trapped in the person-self for a long time. As a result, Presence evolves slowly. The helpers – those who are more than ready for the shift to the next state -- will find it easier to move into the inner body, to breathe and tune into the backdrop...to embody Presence as a state of awareness.

Once again, *Presence won't make us a better person*. It doesn't permit us to be a worse one either. And yet, especially during this interim phase, we will falter time and time again. We will catch ourselves self proving, thinking compulsively, and manipulating to get our way. But the digression will be temporary, because Consciousness only flows in one direction and that's towards an evolving reality. In other words, once we've tasted Presence, we can never go back to NBC for very long. The fit is too perfect; Presence will find you ever time.

It's now time to bring Presence into our daily activities...and rediscover what it means to *help*.

9 How We Help in Presence

In the Introduction, we said we chose to examine how we help for a several reasons: it's something we all do, everyday; it takes place in a variety of settings; and we're proud of it, we value how we help. How we help is a reflection of how we live. We chose help for another reason as well: it's special. How we *help holds the seeds of Presence*: when help is offered without a person-self, it is Presence in action. It's part of what makes us fully human. We could say we do it *now*: it's the moment before we think about what we're doing; when our actions come from a place not filtered through Mind; when they come from that "third place", from the backdrop, from "our own" sense of Presence.

The Presence state of awareness is a revelation. It's a profound shift that transforms everything it touches. It's not a path, or a model, or a prescribed way of getting somewhere. Nor is it a new paradigm: it's not new because Presence has always been with us; it's just been covered up by NBC. And it's not a paradigm: it's the underlying, surrounding, and enveloping field of infinite potential from which everything flows – including paradigms.

Presence is a simultaneous shift in how we see, how we are, and where we're going. It's the next state of Consciousness, an awareness we "bring" to everything. Whatever is touched by Presence changes fundamentally but the transformation is not *self*-serving. It comes from a different place. It's likely to involve a lot of action but very little effort. Increasingly we simply notice…"This isn't working." We acknowledge it, explore it, and act accordingly.

Presence is a discovery, one that happens at its own pace. As a result, during this interim phase as Presence slowly replaces NBC, each of us will be in a different state of Presence. This will, at times, be challenging. For many, Presence will be a space we turn to with increasing frequency; to feel the energy and connect with where creativity, intuition, and imagination arise. Essentially, from hereon in, the transition from NBC to Presence will affect every aspect of our lives…including how we help.

The trick at this point is *not* to be prescriptive -- not to use this chapter to describe what help in Presence *will* or *should* look like. This book wasn't written to give us the answers. It was written to offer each of us a chance to consider how we help and why, and to question the underpinnings of our collective definition of what it means to help. As Presence enters our daily lives, how we help will change dramatically but the specific forms it takes will depend on those who know it best: those who offer advice and counsel everyday to friends and family, the professionals who were once expected to know the answers, the people formerly thought of as on "the receiving end" of help, and everyone else affected by it.

What follows is a general discussion of what help *may* look like in the Presence state of awareness. It is offered in support of all those who will ultimately shape what it means to help in Presence.

Help in Presence

So far we've said that Presence is part of each of us; that it is first a sensation and becomes a state of awareness. We begin by feeling in the body, breathing consciously to make space for Presence, and gradually tuning into the backdrop against which all things happen and which comprises all things. In the next state of awareness, every level of help evolves: everyday, professional, and social help. Presence will change:

- <u>Why we help and where it comes from</u>: In Presence awareness, help comes from a place beyond Mind. We are open to the possibilities and tap into something deeper than knowledge and experience;

- <u>How help happens</u>: In Presence, help is not prescriptive or pre-packaged. No-one is told what to do or how to do it. We're not trying "to get them to _____". Nor does it involve a lot of mental activity, analysis, or deliberation. The process of help unfolds; and,

- The outcomes of help: In the next state of awareness, help fosters individual growth, social change, *and* Presence. In effect, because of its parts, the larger whole evolves.

In other words, in Presence awareness, both the **process and the product of help serve to increase Presence.** We can thus anticipate Presence to manifest in how we help in at least three significant respects.

#1. Help Comes From Within

In the Presence state of awareness, help comes from within. Problems are no longer seen as such: there's no inner need, no glaring deficiency; there's no basis to create a division between us and them, nothing to fix. No-one is broken. And there's no Knower.

Instead there's a *situation* that's happening now and it's broadly defined. For the individual, a situation may cross life areas: family, relationships, work, lifestyle, personal habits, and culture. For professionals, a situation may cut across fields, professions, hobbies, and interests. For organizations, it may span departments, agencies, levels of government; former historical, national, and cultural boundaries. In lieu of fault or blame, a situation is accepted as the by-product of deeply conditioned collective habits: of NBC and Mind, of believing that we are a person-self and building a civilization around that fiction, of the constant state of conflict and frustration we live in.

When help comes from within, the entire process is **elicitive.** To understand the spirit of this term, John Paul Lederach, author of *Preparing for Peace*, contrasts two training events, one prescriptive and the other elicitive. In prescriptive training, the trainer is the presumed expert and participants are there to learn. Prescriptive training is based on the transfer of knowledge:

> The trainer defines the need, names the model, provides the content based on special knowledge, oversees the process, and provides direction and correction. The goal of learning for participants is to understand and master the model (1995, p. 52).

Prescriptive training follows a standard format, beginning with a description of the model and how to use it, followed by "ample opportunities" to test-out the model and apply it in prepared exercises (ibid., pp. 50-51). With its emphasis on skill-building and technique, prescriptive training is generally a "first step" towards applying the model in real cases (ibid., p. 51).

In elicitive training, *the participants* are the "primary resource for the training", while the trainer acts as a "catalyst and a facilitator" (ibid., p. 56). As opposed to the transfer of knowledge, training is an opportunity for participants to identify and resolve *their own* needs. The trainer facilitates a process which builds on the "rich understandings" participants have about their environment, in a setting that is "highly participatory" (ibid.). The entire process is geared towards discovery, creation, and innovation; where results are tested on real-life circumstances and the participants evaluate what works and what doesn't based on "standards and values" of meaning to them (ibid., pp. 60-61). In sum, an elicitive approach:

> Simulates reflection…[It] encourages people to trust their ability yet *transcend themselves* and participate actively in identifying the challenges they face and the means to meet them (emphasis added; ibid., p. 26).

Putting this in a helping context, when we help in an elicitive way:
- The people involved define the situation and shape the actions to be taken, if any;
- The person helping enables, allows, elicits, and supports. The two are co-conversant, in a conversation, not a session, a class or an appointment; and,
- The process is non-directive. There are no absolutes, no One Right Way, no single Truth.

When help comes from within, practitioners hold their knowledge and experience lightly (Winslade and Monk, 2008, p. 114): nothing is imposed, or adhered to, or strictly enforced. There are no expectations, no one way to be. As helpers, we're not searching for something new, or trying to synthesize old and new, East and West, cultural and individual, etc. Instead, the experience of help creates opportunities to engage in all the mysteries and possibilities; to see and change and "be" on a deeper level…in other words, to increase Presence.

#2. The Person-Self Lessens

The second way Presence manifests in how we help is the pull of the person-self lessens. This happens gradually but persistently, and applies to both the helper and those who are helped: as Presence takes hold, the person-self loses its former dominance. As a result, we're better able to:

- Dis-identify with the image, our story, and our set of conditioned behaviors. We no longer need to be a *particular* person-self, attached to our unique skills and abilities. We don't identify with being a helper, or need it to confirm who we think we are. We're able to distance ourselves from our core needs, notice when we're self proving or *self*-serving, and separate our needs from our experience. In effect, we stop fighting so hard; with our self, with others, and with what is.

- **"De-*person*" a situation, conflict, or conversation**. We can explore the role of the person-self without feeling so threatened or defensive. We recognize blame, judgment, and competitiveness when we see it, and know the person-self as its source. We make full use of that mysterious capacity we have to observe our self, to stand back and notice: our personalized reality, how we resist, and where we're attached. In any given situation, it's easier to let go of the "I" and connect to a deeper place. Moreover, we're more comfortable with differences because we understand our differences don't define us, or anyone else.

- Transition from a Mind-made person-self to *a functional self*, keeping what's useful and releasing the rest. We're apt to keep our name for example, and a basic sense of worth and humility. We don't have to work to maintain the fiction; and perhaps, we re-invest that energy in learning to move about more softly. Ultimately, we are left with a self "no longer obsessed with its own solidity" (Epstein, 2007, p. 43), no longer looking to the outside world for its satisfaction.

As we transition to a functional self, we're able to take the recent findings of neuroscience and put them to everyday use. We can appreciate that the brain fights with itself to make decisions; that we "Photo-shop" things in and out of our experience; and that we *feel* what we know and must intentionally construct the point of view of others. These ideas begin to in-form how we deal with our own person-self whenever it tries to reassert itself, and the person-self of others.

As the draw of the person-self lessens, we continue to grow in Presence but that doesn't make us special. A functional self doesn't need to be special; it's just practical. It's also easier to be in the body and breathe, and to look up without thinking. And when we help absent a person-self, it's more than compassionate and non-judgmental: how we help is honoring and unconditional. It embodies giving *and* receiving. Most importantly, **help is offered. We don't serve**. It's not "our" help and it's not an offer*ing*; it's Presence in action.

#3. A New Definition of Help

The third manifestation of Presence in how we help is that a new definition unfolds of what it means to help. Perhaps it will take shape along these lines:

> **Help: 1. To find Presence inside, and offer that Stillness and space to others; 2. To allow those who are helped and the helpers alike, a chance to step outside our self long enough to see the possibilities and hopefully, be engaged enough by the experience to pursue Presence in our own way.**

Living this reality invites us to tap into a different place, beyond traditional knowledge. "Ordinary knowledge belongs to the reasoning mind": it is "thought-based", derived from memory, experience, and the senses (Worthington, 2002, pp. 47; 37). No matter how well developed, "this knowledge is confined to the field of the known" (ibid., p. 47) and as such, is limiting: once we know our self or a situation a certain way, it seals off all the other possibilities.

To "step outside our self long enough to see the possibilities" asks that we move beyond the ordinary and "bring" Presence to what, and how, and why we do things. It suggests that we rekindle an appreciation for the unknown, accept that some things are out of our control, and recognize that we always have a limited understanding of the situation. Moreover, it challenges us to step outside the norm: instead of relying on brainstorming and thinking and solving, we shift to seeing, sensing, imagining, inspiring, and intuiting.

The new definition of help may trigger other changes as well. There's a good chance it will embody some notion of *safety first*, meaning that all help first ensures people are safe -- but beyond that, everything is pure potential. It's also likely to call into question many established conventions, labels, and long-accepted practices. Regardless, the new definition **is grounded in a belief in the capacities of others and a process of "co-engagement"**; one that invites conversation, stimulates reflection, and accords us space to take what we discover and make it our own.

As help transforms, both the process and the product reflect and increase Presence. But it's not for helpers to "spread Presence". We provide the context. The specifics that others walk away with are wholly their own. And we change right along with them. In effect, the dyad evolves: as part and parcel of how we help, Presence increases.

The following sections provide a sketch of what everyday, professional, and social help may look like in the Presence state of awareness. These are not prescriptions. Nor are they naive yearnings or utopist musings; just some renderings. Since each sector builds on the prior, everyday help plays an especially important role in shaping how we help in Presence.

I. Everyday Help in Presence

We've already said that as Presence grows, *we* begin to change: our time-worn patterns feel less comfortable, our re-actions are not as automatic, and the people and groups we once enjoyed seem to diversify. We're mindful of how much space we take up, especially in social situations, and feel less attached to our stories, our past and our future. We find we look forward to pausing during the day, taking a deep conscious breath to stop the flow of Mind, and tuning into the backdrop. We can release our emotional scripts and take fewer things personally. We're not as afraid either: we're neither haunted by an underlying sense of uncertainty nor a pressing need for certainty. There's less mental noise as The Voices quiet down.

On the flip side, as we grow in Presence we feel more alive, more energetic and present. We pay attention, feel attentive, and are generally more alert. We're no longer surprised when others disagree with us: they're not liars and that doesn't make us wrong; the world doesn't feel as hard and fast as it once did. Nor do we need to be perfect or strive to be safe, solid, and secure. In fact, it all seems rather silly... In Presence, we don't need to be *somebody*: we can be however we choose because the person-self no longer dominates our life. And we afford others that same opportunity.

All of this has huge implications for everyday help -- for the assistance, advice, and support we offer others everyday of our lives. As we've said, the specific forms such help takes will depend on each of us, as we evolve in Presence. Here are some possible general trends:

- In Presence awareness, we can anticipate less conflict. That's because the person-self needs conflict to survive and the functional self is just that, functional. We don't need to fight or fight back, or to resist the flow. Yet we're not immobilized either. We simply don't need conflict to define who we are.

Nor do we struggle against life's conditions, the things that seem to happen *to* us; from spilling the coffee, to being late, to not getting what we want. Once we stop resisting, Presence grows…exponentially.

- In Presence, we're more at ease with silence and space. Our manner of speaking may slow. We don't reduce life to aphorisms, invest heavily in self help or self improvement, or grasp at things to have something to hold on to. We don't look for meaning through suffering. Nor do we expect others to fit into the molds we've constructed for them. Instead, we anticipate that people change energetically all the time. And when we relate to the world around us, we're beyond putting our self in another person's shoes: we understand that doing so serves the person-self; that we're still trying to give 'them' *our* answer. We offer others the same silence and space we give ourselves.

- Most importantly, in Presence we engage in relationships differently, without wanting or needing anything from the other person. The "I" that once so desperately needed to be right, diminishes in stature and value. As a result, we're not as compelled to give advice, present our opinions, or need to defend our principles. In fact, it begins to feel awkward to *even consider* substituting our views for someone else's. Nor do we need to change the other person. It's not that the world suddenly becomes a happy place where everyone loves one another. Rather, we **shift in our experience of differences**: differences are okay; maybe even useful.

"Yes but, how do we *help*?" Mind demands to know! What do we do when we're faced with a situation? When someone tells us their problems and asks for our advice? Or we have a momentary lapse of Presence and find our self telling someone what to do?

In each case, we do the same thing: we take a conscious breath and become present, we ground ourselves in the inner body, and we tune into the backdrop. We find "our own" sense of Presence and proceed. However we elect to *offer* help, we do so **in service of the conversation: our actions enable the conversation to continue**. We might:

- Be an inspired listener. When we listen, we do so in Presence. We tune into the Stillness and focus on the person speaking:

> The most difficult part of listening is learning *to leave the other person alone*...listening is not about problem-solving. It is about the gift of our attention. [It] does not demand anything, it allows everything to be just as it is (emphasis added; Smith, 2003, p. 268).

When we listen, we don't speak or think about speaking. We don't over-promise or assume: we don't tell others that everything will be okay, or it'll all be fine in the end because we don't know. In fact, we don't even know what that means to another person. We connect without an opinion: we listen, quietly, inside and out.

- Reflect *First* (Thomas, 2007, pp. 94-98). Reflect *first* is not active listening. Active listening is a skill; it's something we *do* to or for another person: we deliberately paraphrase, as closely as possible, what someone has just said and repeat it back as evidence that we heard it properly. When we Reflect *first*, we use our own words: we reflect our *understanding* of what was said. We reflect what we heard *and* what we felt. It comes from within, from a place beyond Mind.

  Moreover, we anticipate that we may be wrong. When we Reflect *first*, we're not trying to prove what we heard. We're serving the conversation, inviting the other person to say *more*. That's why we Reflect *first*, before we've had a chance to speak. We focus all our attention on the other person. And to emphasize the point, each time we reflect, we end with a question: *not* "Am I right?" but more simply, "Is that it?" There's no "I" involved.

- Support the *truths* of others -- all of them. We offer others space to discover those truths for themselves, and we accept them as *their* truths. We do so whether we agree or not. We accept that some things can only be discussed and not resolved, that few things are ever final, and that most facts are never known for certain.

  Of equal import, we offer our own truths *only* when they are **true *and* useful** (emphasis added; Smith, 2003, p. 269). They must be necessary, fact-based, and clear (Kasl, 2005, pp. 104-106):

--- By necessary we mean we examine our motives. We ask, is this coming from "a sense of caring" (ibid., p. 105) or out of some veiled need or other emotion?

--- Fact-based means we stick with the facts: we say, "You hurt your Father deeply", and not, "You broke your Father's heart. It nearly killed him. He'll never be the same man." We drop the drama and release the story; and,

--- Clear means we feel it inside and express it simply.

We accept that "honesty without sensitivity can be a weapon" (Smith, 2003, p. 269), so when in doubt, we say nothing. Saying nothing doesn't risk shutting down the conversation.

In Presence, help comes from within. It's not filtered through a person-self and isn't based on needs. So when we offer everyday help, we don't *need* to have a come-back (re-act) or present our beliefs as fact (defend); we don't need to challenge what other people say (compete) or tell them what to do (prescribe). We offer others an opportunity to fully acknowledge their situation, as it is. We support them as they feel *their* way through *their* situation and reach *their* point of relative comfort. We might ask:

- What's at the heart of this for you?
- What do you need to make it through today or this week?
- What happens if you do nothing?
- How do you want to proceed?
- How do you take all that's been said here, and make it your own?

In other words, we co-engage in the relationship. We give one another a chance to step outside our self long enough to see the possibilities, to become aware of the resources at our disposal, and to shape whatever comes next. The dyad evolves: the dyad of viewpoints, the many dyads within us, and the dyad of two or more people in relationship. We are both changed by the experience. Presence increases.

II. Professional Help in Presence

In Presence awareness, what it means to help professionally changes dramatically. For the individual practitioner however, the bases remain the same as in everyday help: we take a conscious breath and become present; we feel the inner body and ground there, where Presence arises; and we tune into the backdrop, the expanding, extending, enveloping field of energy. We find "our own" sense of Presence and proceed.

Again, without making any prescriptions, professional help will likely shift just as the signs pointing to the Presence state of awareness suggest: energetically, biocentrically, limbically, and beyond; where being with a situation, connecting innately with others, and allowing Presence to enable and support shifts form the foundation of professional help. What follows are some possibilities.

=========== The Demise of "I Know"

As the person-self lessens, we become comfortable *not knowing*. For the scholar and layperson alike, whenever we help, we hold our knowledge lightly: we don't need to speak or prove it. We appreciate that much is unknown.

For those who help professionally however, this has even broader implications: professionals no longer *need to know*. We don't need to be the knower. As we grow in Presence, we're able to dis-identify with the image of the one who knows "what to do and how to do it for someone else." Initially, this means that every encounter is a chance _not_ to teach or train, or prescribe what to do. At first, it's an effortless practice. In time, it's liberation.

In Presence awareness, the professional adopts a "Beginner's Mind" (See Suzuki, 1997). A Beginner's Mind is not cluttered with preconceptions, professional opinions, and accumulated experience. We're able to observe our self and catch the contracted patterns, the seasoned and habituated practices that arise from the person-self. We can breathe deeply, relax our shoulder blades down our back, and sit back in the chair. We come from a place of Stillness. We don't need to have the answers. We're here as Presence: to support, not to fix.

With a Beginner's Mind, **the principal "work" of the helping professional may be being *with* a situation**. When others bring their situation to us, we're not trying to solve it or label it, or reduce it to a diagnosis, because there isn't one, there are many. Situations span multiple areas of people's lives. Moreover, **only those who are *in* the situation understand it fully and know what's best for them** because it's their reality. As we've learned from neuroscience, we can't possibly know the experience of another. Instead, our "work" is to be *with* a situation.

Being with a situation means we give others the opportunity to tell their full story, in their own way, and meet it face-to-face. We offer them a safe place where they are honored, and give them our full attention. We are open to the full range of possibilities, including those that come from unlikely places and are far outside our control.

When we are with a situation, we Reflect *first* and often. We reflect what we see, hear, and feel. We reflect any patterns or recurring themes *they* notice in their self. We allow those involved in the situation to connect the dots: to become aware of the needs, the unenforceable rules, and the self proving woven throughout the various parts of their lives; to determine what's important, what needs expressing, and what remains hidden; to decide what it all means, and what has meaning for them.

We also reflect any shifts or changes in how they perceive the person-self, the situation, one another, or another party (See Bush and Folger: Recognition Shifts, 2005). We reflect any gray areas or openings that may inspire or spur the imagination (See Chasin et al., 1996; See also Public Conversations Project, Training Series 1, 2009). As professionals, we're not pushing any agenda: we're reflecting what we think we see and stand ready to be corrected. We follow; we don't lead (See Bush and Folger, 2005).

Being with a situation means we serve as guides: we allow, enable, accord, yield, and support. We say very little. When we do speak, we do so "not as pronouncements" from some "expert authority" but as "those of a co-conversant with different experiences and viewpoints" (Chasin et al., 1996, p. 329). We offer only what is true *and* useful. When we are with a situation, we have faith in the ability of others. We believe that those involved are fully capable of "identifying the challenges they face and the means to meet them" (Lederach, 1995, p. 26). We offer them the opportunity to gain an initial understanding of their situation *as they see it*...and build from there.

An Innate Connection

In NBC, there's a problem and a solution, a helper and those helped, a doing and a prescribed way, a seeking and a known, those who change and those overseeing the change. In Presence awareness, all of this shifts because we are inseparable parts of a more encompassing, evolving reality. In Presence, we explore a situation together, equally engaged in a conversation. More than present, we're interconnected *as if by intermeshing fields*. What this means for practitioners is that in the Presence, **the value of professional help may rest with our ability to connect in limbic resonance with those involved in the situation.**

When we connect on a limbic level, we listen *viscerally*. We feel what it's like to suffer *as others suffer*. We "hear" their reality: the dark corners where fear resides; the deeply held beliefs that are "in-bodied" but not known; the painful memories, the physical and emotional stockpiles of anger, hurt, and hope. We harmonize with, and co-stabilize one another. Rather than the "calm dispensation of tidy data packets" (ibid., p. 171) from the knower, we attune, exchange, and adapt to one another's emotional inner states (See Lewis et al., 2000).

Moreover, one person doesn't go there alone. The professional and those involved in the situation travel the limbic path together. We share in one another. Speaking of therapy in particular, Dr. Lewis says:

A therapist loosens his grip on his own world and drifts...into whatever relationship the patient has in mind...[because] when he stays outside the other's world, he cannot affect it [limbically] (ibid., p. 178).

Together we throw out the rule book and the formulas. We practice reading emotions, connecting empathetically, and interacting on a feeling level. When emotions are present, we lean into them (See Bush and Folger, 2005). We're not invasive or voyeuristic, but we don't shy away from emotions either. As professionals, we attend to the experience, reflect the emotions, and notice their contagion effect: how energy flows into a room, how emotions rise and fall, and rise again. We feel without interpretation, without Mind.

Yet Presence invites us to go beyond emotions and grow in Presence. Thus, in the safety of the limbic connection, we **"de-*person*" the situation**: we experience the situation as a projection of "me" and what it might mean to move beyond that place...even slightly. This is not pushed or prescribed, or envisioned as a series of steps the professional administers. It proceeds if and when others desire, and at a pace they choose. For the professional, it means tuning into the backdrop and finding "our own" sense of Presence. Then together, we:

- Listen in on The Voice, unlocking emotions from re-actions to look at them -- not critically or analytically, but to elicit a deeper knowing;

- Unpack the story from the facts, and imagine what the situation looks like absent the drama and self-proving;
- Uncover the patterned ways we think and behave, the core needs that drive those habits and the recurring circuitry that keeps repeating them, irrespective of outcome;
- Challenge the "I", exploring its needs and expectations, its fears and deeply held convictions -- what we once called "the truth"; and,
- Unmask the ways in which culture, individual and collective conditioning colors our world and our thoughts, forcing us to see separation and grow isolated.

This is a very intimate experience. In effect, through the situation at hand, we meet the person-self and get to know it. We learn what props it up, where its attachments lie, and how it generates conflict. We rely on our capacity to self observe; to engage questions without seeking or searching, or trying to figure things out; and to open to the mysteries and the possibilities. Throughout, we have moments of simply "being"; where the person-self no longer dominates our awareness and Mind is not in charge...where we step outside our self and simply *are*.

As part of such an experience, we affect one another limbically and beyond. A dependency develops (Lewis et al., 2000, pp. 171-172). Not a cycle of dependency as in NBC, but an intermeshing relatedness. Without it, nothing changes; with it, *we both do* (ibid., pp. 178-184). Through mutual exchange and change, those involved can transition from *how they see the situation* to a deeper understanding of *what is*. They can fully *acknowledge* the situation as it is, if they so choose.

=========== An Iterative Conversation

In the Presence state of awareness, professional help is elicitive. The people involved in the situation define it and express their own multiple truths. They decide what can and can't change, and how; and what's best for them. Rather than a pre-scripted strategy or standard solutions, the **process of help unfolds**, it comes from within. The professional and those involved are co-engaged in an iterative conversation: they feed off one another in a process that evolves. The process is one of discovery and exploration, creation and innovation. And the decisions rest with those involved.

Help in Presence means we never substitute our views for someone else's: we don't interrupt, offer our opinion, or seek to impose our "solution" on someone else's "problem". Nor do we expect others to follow. We are totally at ease with how people relate to one another and how they relate to us. We have no single frame of reference, no One Right Way. Since there's nothing we *do* per se, there's nothing we do that might trigger resistance. Nor is it our job to ensure the process is self-determined. Instead, we attend to our own non-directive behavior: we yield to those involved and follow their lead.

As a guide, we support conditions conducive to shifts. We communicate compassion without saying a word. We may spend long periods in Stillness where only Presence is expressed. We see those involved as the primary resource, and have faith in their abilities. We are open to the full range of possibilities and hence, **together, we tap into a different place**. We may:

- Experiment with primordial sounds, feeling in the body, meditation, breathing, and other ways to find comfort in silence;
- Devise experiential and/or participatory "exercises" to attend to mental noise, release emotions, or uncover unexamined patterns;
- Employ different ways to notice the nature of Mind, the shifting nature of energy, or the changeable nature of thoughts;
- Practice observing the person-self in action, sitting with others who have strong emotions, or being with differences; and/or,
- Discover how to imagine, intuit and create possibilities, uncover unexpected resources, and unleash unrecognized potential.

As a professional, our role may be as simple as offering others a chance to notice the daily mysteries that surround us. Regardless, we forever grow in "our own" Presence without ever feeling special.

In an iterative conversation, it's likely we will use questions in a unique and provocative way. Again, not in an invasive or intrusive manner, professionals who help in Presence may pose questions that inspire reflection, foster inquiry, kindle insights, decrease certainty, explore assumptions, create alternatives, and expand choices (Public Conversations Project, Training Series 2, 2009). Such "wise questions" take a long time to develop. They may encourage "multiple and even competing perspectives" or promote "fresh ways" of being with a situation (Chasin et al., 1996, p. 329). Wise questions are asked carefully and with curiosity (ibid., p. 325); they are always asked in service of the conversation. Most importantly, they're often asked *without seeking an answer*; to instead, just sit with… in silence.

Irrespective of how help unfolds, professional help will adhere to some broad parameters, such as being non-directive, non-invasive, and non-intervention-based; where the latter is a blend of safety first, do no harm, and not creating resistance in another. It won't involve a lot of mental work, analysis, or deliberation (See Figure 8). As professionals who help, our job is to offer others space and Stillness to take whatever they discover and make it their own. Then *they shift in their own way*. Those involved decide what works for them. They grow as they deem fit. They pursue their best action for this moment, *their* balanced response to the situation. For them, the situation is "solved" for now.

All the while, we take time to care for ourselves. This is especially true when we're part of de-*person*ing a situation. As a professional, de-*person*ing requires that we are grounded in Presence: that we can touch that sense and reflect it outward. Equally, that we can see Presence, and experience and reflect it in others. *When we reflect one another's Presence, we accelerate its growth.* We both grow in Presence. Those involved may begin to experience how energy emerges and passes; how they can breathe and go inward, and use silence as a refuge; how their life situation is just that, surface level, and there's something beyond whatever that current situation happens to be. Again, it's not for professionals to spread or create or shape Presence in others. Helping means supporting the conditions for Presence to evolve. And Presence will evolve…because that's what Presence does.

Figure 8.1

Professional Help In Presence	
Core Qualities Of Professionals	What Professionals Bring
Don't *Need* to Know Establish a Limbic Connection Be the Space and Stillness for a Deeper Knowing to Evolve	• Our "Own" Presence • A Beginner's Mind • Ability to be *With* a Situation • Inspired Listening • Faith in Those Involved • Capacity for Limbic Co-Dependence • A Willingness to Change • An Openness to Possibilities • Questions that Inspire Non-intervention, Non-Invasiveness and "Non-Directiveness" • Capacity to Support Conditions Conducive to Shifts • Movement towards a Functional Self Help that Unfolds
What's Elicitive	**What's Offered to Others**
• *Their* Description of the Situation • Their Multiple Truths • Their Hidden Discourses • Their Sense of What Can and Can't be Changed • Their Emotions • Any Shifts or Changes • Any Gray Areas and Openings • Their Insights and Epiphanies • Their Decisions • Their Best Actions	A Safe Place Where They are Honored and a Chance to: • Tell Their Story, Their Way • Separate Facts from Story • Feel Heard • Examine Patterned Behavior • See Self/Others in Different Light • De-*person* the Situation • Tap into a Different Place • Find Comfort in Silence • Feel Part of an Intermeshing Field • Explore the Possibilities • Find Their Own Way • Grow in Presence

III. Social Help in Presence

In the Presence state of awareness, social help changes too; it's just slower to transform. Steeped in an Us or NOT culture, dominated by Daily Discord, controlled by groups which are often embroiled in intra- and inter- group conflict, and committed to preserving the institution as we know it, it is here that the starkest dyadic contrasts exist; where,

"When we create a person-self, we create a fiction. When we build a civilization around it, we institutionalize that fiction…" meets,

"To allow the helper and the helped alike, to step outside our self long enough to see the possibilities and hopefully, be engaged enough by the experience to pursue Presence in our own way."

These are, nonetheless, inseparable parts of the same evolving reality. Eventually, as everyday and professional help continue to grow in Presence, the next state of awareness will flow into the social help arena – into the organizations, non-profits, agencies, foundations, corporations, and institutions which provide it.

But why is this so? What makes this possible? The answer is this: since those who help will be among the first to usher in the next state of awareness, millions of people will be accorded a direct experience of Presence. They will seek advice or go to a professional for help and find something altogether different – something fresh, energetic, and alive. They will experience the new definition of help, grow in Presence and, in turn, affect others. Gradually, it will become commonplace to look at a situation and simply notice: "This isn't working". Not to judge or criticize or point the finger of blame, but to acknowledge it, explore and discover, and then act in a creative and conscious way. Before long, rapidly increasing numbers of people *will want* to experience Presence. They will realize that compared to NBC, Presence is spontaneous and original, dynamic and yet grounded; that it's a revelation, a profound shift that transforms everything it touches. And gradually, Presence will become *the* state of awareness.

As such a groundswell of Presence transfuses the organizations of social help, change will once again come from within -- from beyond traditional knowledge and accumulated experience, and the process will be elicitive. Those effecting the changes will include people both inside and outside the organization, who have grown in Presence, as well as those affected by the process and product of help. Ultimately, the larger whole will evolve. While the discussion that follows assumes organizations and professions continue to exist, we may find that Presence quickly takes us beyond such conventions.

=========== Different Organizations

In the Presence state of awareness, we stop looking to organizations to tell us what to do and how to do it; for prescriptive mandates of what's good or right, what's needed or "should be" on a social scale. Nor are organizations responsible for spelling out what it means to help in Presence; this is left to everyday and professional help to expound. Instead, Presence-inspired organizations play a supporting role: they **serve to support the new definition of help as it unfolds.**

These refashioned organizations will be more fluid, organic, and temporary than the immutable fixtures we've come to know in NBC. In Presence, *life creates organizations* – they are there to support *us*, instead of taking on a life force of their own. This changes everything we think we know about social help organizations. For starters, organizational charts of static boxes arranged hierarchically for a single purpose agency will give way to more illustrative, versatile, and dynamic ones. One or more organizations may elect to represent themselves in a multi-dimensional model comprised of many interconnecting fields that intersect other professions, levels of government, institutions, and the public; where energy flows in and thru, "in-forming" every level and facet of the operation. Moreover, these models will change regularly, as organizations adapt to keep pace with how help in Presence unfolds.

In their supporting role, organizations will shift away from continuously fighting for their own survival, and re-invest their energy in more reflective and transformational pursuits. They're likely to begin with a "self" review, inquiring into the innermost nature of the organization:

- How have we contributed to the Us or NOT culture? The Daily Discord? How do we benefit from these conditions?
- How do we promote the institution's need to survive? Where and how has the "help" we've provided *hurt*?
- Who are we fighting with and why? How do we add to the constant state of conflict, where we're left splitting the difference?
- How do we institutionalize the fiction of the person-self? The fear of "Other"? And most importantly,
- How do we transition to an entity that is *not* rooted in the assumption of *more*?

Once these matters have been "experienced" – sat with, discussed, and allowed to mature and assimilate, as opposed to analyzed, brainstormed and fixed – organizations may turn to other matters, such as how they affect people. They may ask:

- How do we create an environment that is both non-directive and "non-direct*ed*"? Where in both process and product, we draw from "all sides-in" as well as bottom-up and top-down?
- How do we stick to the facts without getting caught up in our own stories and needs: in lofty mission statements and inveterate goals, or trying to protect the institution's historical dictates and doctrines?
- How do we embody non-doing and effortless-ness in the organization? Where have we grown too complicated? Where do people take a backseat to policies and procedures?
- How do we reduce distracting mental noise, eliminate invasive rules, create an atmosphere of calm, and foster the feeling of space and the quality of silence?

As Presence grows within and around organizations, this inquiry will deepen significantly. Organizations may begin exploring:

- How do we create an organization that doesn't *need* to know? That allows those who understand a situation best to decide what works?
- How might we engage in relationships differently? How do we move from giving advice, stating opinions, and defending principles, to allowing, enabling and supporting?
- What does it mean to support and not lead? How do we transition from protecting the organization against outsiders to *protecting the outside* as part of our everyday activity?
- What does "unfold" mean in an organization? Where can we let go of the need to control?
- How can we be inspired listeners? How do we offer only those truths that are both, true and useful? And finally,
- How do we "de-*person*" the workplace, taking the "I" and the "us and them" out of what we do?

As a continuous work in progress, organizations will also shift in their experience of differences. As opposed to being threatened and having to hold on even tighter to old, established ways, they will come to see differences as useful, even essential to their evolution. Differences become especially important in an organizational culture that values **regeneration**

and renewal, energetic qualities likely to be at a premium in the Presence state of awareness. Thus to remain viable and agile, organizations may adopt multiple means to routinely invite reflection, counteract certainty, explore assumptions, and expand opportunities, producing "uncertain, even chaotic circumstances" (Wheatley, 1992, p. 109). They may wonder: What does it mean for us to change in a conscious way? What do we regularly miss or gloss over, and how might it matter? How can we put the foundations in place to allow us to readily disband, merge, or morph into something new as Presence evolves?

Most importantly, organizations will be quick to realize that the answers to these questions are not found by doing; or by doing something new, synthesizing the old and the new, or through new policies, paradigms, programs, initiatives, or procedures. They flow from one underlying question:

> How do we "bring" Presence to work? To our workplace, our relationships, and what we do? In effect, how do we allow Presence to inform every aspect of this organization?

From there, all the other answers unfold.

================ Different Professions

In Presence, the professions too, will re-cast themselves in accordance with the new definition of help; to support an experience of help where practitioners are *with* a situation, the connection is more innate, and Presence enables and supports shifts. Rather than problems or challenges, they'll approach this transition as a series of "situations" that span departments and divisions, districts and agencies, levels of government, and beyond. They'll draw on an essential knowing, the universal truths and Nature, as well as a multiplicity of viewpoints, from history and different cultures.

There's a good chance they'll start with the standard divisions that exist between disciplines. Instead of the separation we've been conditioned to see, they may ask: How can we harness the energy that exists across professions? How might we relate to one another as if connected by *intermeshing fields*, where because of the parts, the larger whole evolves? This inquiry will go a long way towards regenerating the professions and dissolving the traditional barriers that exist between say, professionals and para-professionals, administrative and direct service providers, public and private, academic and therapeutic, as well as a host of others.

The professions will also encounter the practical considerations of what it means to help in Presence, now that help no longer attends to needs or problems, or seeks to prop up the person-self. Such a pursuit may well turn entire mission statements on their head. Again, tuning into the backdrop and calling upon "their own" sense of Presence, both independently and collectively, the professions may consider:

- How can we "de-center" this field, removing the central role of the knower and creating instead "a sharing of the power and responsibility" (Hedeen, 2005, p. 188)?
- How can we connect limbically with our students, clients, patients, etc.? How do we honor those we work with?
- What does it mean for us to offer and not serve? To allow help to unfold? To give as well as receive?
- How can we support conditions conducive to shifts? How can we convey our faith in others' capabilities, and enable those seeking help to become their own primary resource? And,
- How can we foster reflection, value originality, honor non-conceptual understandings, and uncover hidden cultural discourses?

In effect, the professions face the same underlying question as organizations: How do we allow Presence to inform every aspect of how we help? They will have to "un-pack" many of the established conventions, labels, and long-accepted practices that comprise the helping professions; the notion of "services", service "delivery", whether "clients" are "identified", etc. They will decide what "safety first" means in application; how to test results using "real-life circumstances"; and how to evaluate based on the "standards and values" of those involved (Lederach, 1995, p. 60). As a result, some professions will cease to exist. Others will change fundamentally.

Just briefly, we spoke earlier of mediation. In the Presence state of awareness, mediation changes too. As we've stated, it takes two person-selves to show up to make a conflict, and one to step outside its self for the conflict to be resolved. As such, mediation is a natural setting for Presence to arise. In Presence, mediation is likely be a place where those involved: (a) can replay their situation and "get clear" about how *they* see it; (b) gain a deeper understanding of the role the person-self plays in the situation, the stories they've created around it, and the needs it fulfills; and (c) are offered many, and perhaps unusual, opportunities conducive to shifts, where they can fully acknowledge what is and then decide what works for them.

If the profession of mediation continues, the role of the mediator will be non-directive, and the process, non-intervenient and non-invasive. The mediator will become **the space for whatever happens**. There will be no goal, nothing to steer towards. We won't seek to change the nature of the conversation, although it may; or the people involved, although they may. What will change is where the conversation comes from: by being the space for whatever happens, the mediator reflects "his/her own" Presence outward, and sees and reflects that same Presence in others. As a result, both grow in Presence.

As Presence evolves, mediation may well change from a profession to a way of living. Then *every* situation becomes a chance to increase Presence; each of us becomes the space for whatever happens. At any moment, we might realize a deeper truth, find a peaceful place inside, or experience an instant when we step outside the self and pursue Presence in our own way. Like its fellow professions, in undergoing this re-birth, mediation will re-discover **what it is that gives help meaning** and channel that into action. We will ask more than we know, yield more than we seek, and open to possibilities never before imagined in NBC.

═══════ Different Means and Methods

In the Presence state of awareness, unconventional means and methods are apt to be the norm. This applies to organizations, the professions, professional and everyday helpers alike. To begin with, we can expect a greater use of dialogue. Dialogue promotes discussion and conversation. It allows us **to hold two seemingly opposing views or ideas at one time and *see what happens***. It often results in creative and conscious action.

Dialogue differs from debate "which involves taking positions and challenging others", and also from group therapy processes "which focus more on an individual's internal personal dynamics" (Dressel and Rogge, 2008, p. 211). Dialogue is a "specialized" form of discussion, "designed to remove the focus from winning, or even compromising, to mutual exploration and understanding" (Lowry and Littlejohn, 2006, p. 413). In a dialogue:

> Participants…are able and willing to express what is most important to them while also hearing and understanding the experiences and values of others (ibid.).

Dialogue works in service of the conversation: it enables the conversation to continue. It's a special "way of relating" to one another predicated on mutual respect, curiosity and interest, and attention to what and how we say things (Chasin et al., 1996, p. 325). Through dialogue, we can:

- Appreciate "the complexity of others" as opposed to reducing them to their positions or opinions;
- Raise sensitive issues, giving voice to what we want but are afraid to say;
- Elicit personal as opposed to "group-approved" positions and issues;
- Broach ideas and topics that might otherwise be "dismissed or omitted" (ibid., pp. 334-335);
- Involve a wide range of people, including members of the community and others traditionally left out; and,
- Gain an awareness of and sensitivity for the ideas, rituals, customs, practices, and values of others.

In addition to dialogue, other, even more unusual methods are likely to be used. They will be geared towards enabling individuals and small groups to move beyond Mind-made boundaries: to transition from brainstorming, thinking, and struggling to find the answer…to creative seeing, sensing, intuiting, inventing, and imagining. These methods will come from within. They will be highly participatory and experiential and at least initially, outside our comfort zone. They will reveal old habits, de-program re-actions, and deconstruct assumptions; dismantle realities and challenge embedded discourses; encourage us to see beyond the problem, beyond the words, and tap into a different place.

We may find ourselves heeding intuitive hunches, welcoming the element of surprise, exploring quantum leaps, and working through silence. The techniques may border on the strange: connecting with the zero point field, tuning into energy vibrations, playing with non-local correlation, letting go of thoughts, and dis-engaging the knowing Mind. They may involve breathing, sounds, smells, and colors; experimenting with qualities, feeling in the body, and "seeing" without labeling; working with the energy chakras, releasing thought, focusing attention, and balancing left and right brain activity. Experiences such as these will generate very different and conscious alternatives, choices, and decisions that come from within. They will also increase Presence. So in both process and product, Presence grows.

IV. The Outcomes of Help

Given what's been said about help in Presence awareness, it's reasonable to wonder whether most people are ready for this kind of help. This applies as much to administrators, professionals and everyday helpers as to those involved in a given situation. It is however, a question better suited to NBC where we help by imposing prescriptive solutions on others and expecting them to live up to our expectations. Very often, the people on the "receiving end" of NBC-help are not ready for what's prescribed. They "waste their chances," game the system, or run through a catalog of services as professionals try to force-fit one "solution" after another onto "the problem". It's frustrating for everyone.

When help comes from Presence, the professional is not in charge of solving the problem. Nor is he/she expected to have the answer. The process is one of discovery and exploration, creation and innovation, mutual change and exchange, whereby those involved *figure out for themselves* what they need and what actions they can take. This happens in a very special setting: one that is safe and honoring, limbically connected, and iterative. Through such a setting, *they* decide what they're ready for. Whereas in NBC we try "to get them to _____," in the next state of awareness, help means we grow in Presence, at its own pace and in our own way.

A more difficult question to answer is this: What are the social implications of help in Presence? What does it mean, for instance, for the groups we belong to; the ones who stand ready to fight and try to impose their collective prescriptions on others?

In the Presence state of awareness, the impact help has on the rest of society depends on the course of everyday help. This is because everyday help affects the most people and will spread the fastest; it's so much a part of our lives. As the new definition of everyday help evolves, we'll find our tolerance for the Daily Dose of Discord decreases. We'll be far less willing to listen to the banter or put up with the showmanship. Increasingly, two sides of the issues will represent only the beginning of the discussion, and binary choices will be a thing of the past.

Soon we'll be able to "de-*person*" a situation on our own before it ignites into a conflict; and only on rare occasions will we have to protect and defend our self. At some point, we'll notice a conversation *in progress* and simply say, "This isn't working…Surely there must be someway to move beyond demonizing one another and obsessing over this with our family and friends." Sometimes we'll walk away. Sometimes we'll talk it out. Other times, we'll tap into a different place and try something altogether different. In any event, the dyad evolves because we didn't waste time fighting.

As Presence becomes *the* state of awareness, we will slowly dis-identify with the collective person-self as well. We will recognize the baggage that comes from needing to belong: how it divides us, forces us to speak as one voice when clearly there are many, and vilifies people we don't even know. As Presence grows, these traits will start to feel unnecessary, unreasonable...even foreign. Moreover, we'll know from experience that **connecting feels better than belonging**. While there will still be groups, they will be smaller, more fluid, and temporary in nature, attending to a given function and then dispersing. And dialogue will play an essential role, enabling group members to talk about our fear of "Other" and explore any lingering grand narratives we may harbor.

Regardless of how this actually plays out, the key to any social change is that it comes from within, from those affected by the change. At least initially, this will stir some tension between our old prescriptive ways and a more elicitive approach. We can get a taste for what this kind of tension might look like from a discussion concerning the very volatile and disturbing issue of stoning women in Islamic countries.

In the conversation, Mr. Tariq Ramadan, an Islamic professor from Oxford University, is being interviewed by an NPR-program host, Melissa Block. Mr. Ramadan has called for a moratorium on stoning to allow Muslim scholars a chance to go "back to the texts" and re-consider the issue. Ms. Block suggests that a moratorium, by definition, implies the practice may be resumed and asks, "Why not just say that it's wrong?" Mr. Ramadan responds:

> You have to understand...how this has to be contextualized. If you deal with Muslims, you have to come with Islamic arguments... You [can] condemn it, but you're not going to change [it]...I want the people to understand, come from within, a civilization...it has to be consistent from within (NPR's *All Things Considered*, Melissa Block interviewing, April 29, 2010).

As we live in Presence, conversations like this will take place everyday, in every conceivable sector. Gradually, the results will start to dismantle the Us or NOT culture. Presence will enable us to examine the building blocks of our society and question their utility, many of which will become vestiges of an old NBC. In the meantime, we won't attack. We won't be at our worst. We won't even try to fix the situation.

In the Presence state of awareness, we'll go back to the basics: we'll take a conscious breath and become present; we'll feel the inner body and ground there, where Presence arises; and we'll tune into the backdrop, the expanding, extending, enveloping field of energy. We'll find "our own" sense of Presence and proceed...and Presence will grow.

===================== But What If

Presence is first a sensation. It becomes a state of awareness. It is up to each of us to feel and then grow in Presence. But what if we slip up? What if we get lost in old habits and needs, in group loyalties, professional in-fighting and institutional mandates? What if something terrible happens: we loose someone we love or find out we have cancer? How do we hold on to Presence *then*?

The answer is we don't. Presence doesn't involve doing. We can't create Presence or become it or achieve it. It's not a means to an end: the fact that in Presence, we become more creative or inventive is not why we grow in Presence. It's just a side-bar, an added benefit. We don't grow in Presence to get something out of it.

More importantly, Presence isn't an "it". This is something we have to remind ourselves time and time again. Presence is not *some thing* we aspire to. It's not a way we're supposed to be or a persona we need to maintain. When we hear our self saying such things, we're trying to force Presence into a NBC-frame of reference: we're making it yet another transformational path, a *self*-serving track to get us somewhere. We forget that we don't *put* Presence into practice...it's the awareness that informs, underlies, envelops and inspires our practice of help.

Presence is the next state of awareness; it's an end in itself. It arises. It is effortless. It only requires some space and an awareness of "our own" Stillness to arise. But as Eckhart Tolle says, "Daily life is our practice." The point is this: **we can't hold on to Presence**. In times of great fear, Presence holds us. When we trip up, we simply find a quiet place and sit. We allow the situation to inspire Presence. We become the space for whatever happens. We might quietly walk ourselves through the following:

- Sit with the situation. Just be with it.

- Listen to The Voice in your head – the tone, the words, the re-actions it calls forth in you. Know that you are not that voice; it's just a thought, an opinion.

- Ask yourself, what is it about this situation that really bothers me? Can I reduce it to one word?

- Describe the situation again. Ask, is there a good metaphor for how I feel right now?

- Just sit with this description. Experience what comes from it. Don't judge, just be with whatever comes up.

- Ask yourself, what is this all about? Give the answers some space in which to arise.

- Now, take the "I" out of it. Ask, what does this situation look like if there's no person-self involved? Tap into a different place. Take whatever comes and make it your own.

In the Presence state of awareness, help builds on the "rich understandings" of those involved. It connects and fosters shifts on a limbic level and beyond. It engenders inner-directed change such that everyone involved grows in Presence. It's precisely the kind of help we've been looking for: it's beyond knowing, beyond knowledge and training, beyond advice and prescriptions; it's beyond right and wrong...beyond NBC and the person-self. It's beyond one more thing as well.

10 An Abiding Presence

We really don't know how help will unfold in the Presence state of awareness. The truth is we really don't know much at all for certain. We think we're doing the right thing, but we don't know for sure. We think we're living our life right, but there's no guarantee. We could say the whole Us or NOT culture – the entire way we live – is a re-action to fear... to the fear of finding out that we're not who we think we are. So Mind keeps us forever engaged, trying to avoid confronting this ultimate fear. Until one day, as Presence trickles in, for an instant, we *stop thinking*. Our head clears; The Voice stops and the mental noise quiets down. At that moment, we understand for the first time. The turning point is when we stop thinking.

Presence is, in the words of Eckhart Tolle, "Consciousness without thought" (The Doorway into Now Intensive, 2008). Initially, it grows in fits and starts as we're dogged by Mind-made needs and the demands of the person-self. But once it takes root, Presence grows more rapidly. As it does, the next state of awareness invites us to give up our most addictive habit, our most deeply ingrained collective pastime -- that of compulsive thinking. It's not that we stop thinking about our self, or start thinking more about others. In Presence, we actually stop thinking. We move beyond needs. We move beyond the person-self. And we move beyond thinking – that's the "one more thing" Presence is beyond.

At first this sounds preposterous! Bigger brains are better brains, we've been taught that since grade school. Thinking is what makes us intelligent. It's why we are *the* dominant creature on the planet; it's why we're in charge. And besides, we __need__ to think. How else will we figure things out? How will we fix all the things that are wrong on the planet? *How will we know what to do?*

Thinking drowns out Presence. It suppresses Presence and covers it over as we get swept away in a maze of thoughts. Each of us has been conditioned to see the world through a veil of thoughts: to dissect, analyze, generate opinions, label, interpret, compare, project, and judge. Yet *nothing makes thinking necessary.* Thoughts are not directives we must follow. They are not the truth or inherently correct. They're just thoughts. Because you think your wife has never lived up to her part of the bargain, or bosses need to respect their employees, or school prayer is completely acceptable -- doesn't make it right. Because you believe you're a born entrepreneur, you deserve an extension of your unemployment benefits, or God opens a window when he closes a door -- doesn't make it so. Moreover, why bother thinking this stuff at all?

Thinking is the third part of the Person-Self Cycle that keeps NBC and the person-self intact; it breeds conflict and frustration. As we start living in a state of Presence, we let go of the need to think. Thinking becomes… optional.

=========== ## What Presence Is and Isn't

We've been talking about how we help -- how it comes from within and is elicitive, how we de-*person* conversations and situations, connect more deeply with others and tap into a different place. We've also been talking about Consciousness; because what we do and how we do it is a function of our awareness. Awareness and Consciousness are one in the same. NBC generates a certain end-product that is predicated upon needs, grounded in thoughts and thinking, and props up the person-self. Presence awareness is profoundly different.

In NBC, the way we help is broken. That doesn't mean there aren't many, many people who are sincerely dedicated to what they do and aiding others. It means that the way we help – and the way we live --reflects a state of consciousness that presumes we are a person-self that needs and knows. This brings us down and it brings down how we help right along with it. The cure isn't to change the system, or knock it down and start over, or install a new paradigm. Such efforts – and they are both plentiful and effortful – only prolong and aggravate present conditions because they're not accompanied by a change in the consciousness which created the situation in the first place. Nothing short of a change in awareness will suffice.

Meanwhile, the next state of awareness is unfolding, waiting to be uncovered both individually and collectively. As we transition from NBC to Presence, conditions will change just as how we help changes. We will move from being stuck in our heads, *not* to our hearts, but deeper, to Presence. Figure 9.1 reviews what Presence is and is beyond, and the many assumptions we ascribe to that Presence invites us to reconsider.

Figure 9.1

What Presence Is and Is Beyond	
What Presence Is	What Presence Is Beyond
The Next State of Awareness	• Another Paradigm • A Vacuous Feeling of Oneness • Compassion and Non-Judgment • Thinking More of Others • Being Spiritual or Any Certain Way • Ordinary Knowing • Being a Better Person • Following Your Heart • Guaranteed Happiness or Satisfaction

Some Assumptions Presence Invites Us to Reconsider
• Help means doing for or to someone else • What we see is the one reality everyone sees • Needing is part of being human • Conflict is natural, it's part of life • There are two sides to every issue and they both can't be right • We are independent, unitary beings • We are solely responsible for our self and our actions • If a second person confirms an opinion, it must be true • Conflict is caused by competing interests or needs • Two different views of the same situation means one person is lying • Bad things happen to us • What's "out there" is separate and distinct from "me" • The mind is the source of all intelligence • People who seek help can't solve their own problems • There can only be one truth • There's always one right thing to do • Most problems are personal problems • Help means transferring tools and knowledge to those who need it • We can solve other people's problems • Many people need or want to be told what do to • Group members share the same views on important topics • With enough repetition, affirmations come true • A change in perspective changes the problem • A group's representative speaks on behalf of the group • Truth is always best, honesty is always the best policy • Conflict and debate drive out the truth • Talking things out is always best • The key to life is to know your self

But Not Thinking…?

In the Presence state of awareness, the need to think deceases significantly. That's not to say we never think again. Rather, we stop thinking *compulsively*; the mind is clear of thoughts for increasingly longer stretches of time. Not thinking creates space for Presence.

Compulsive thinking is a straightjacket we wear when we're lost in NBC. It keeps us locked in a closed loop we repeat over and over again. When we think, one thought feeds the next. At any moment, we identify with a given thought and it sets the wheel in motion: "He's got his nerve, buying all sorts of new stuff when he said he couldn't afford to go on vacation...He's just thinking of himself...He's always been selfish...It might have been better if I hadn't needled him about it...I guess I was a nag, but my feelings were hurt...Well he should have told me the truth... But he wants stuff instead of *me*, what does that say about us?...Maybe he's not the man for me after all...Oh no, what do I do now?...How should I approach this the next time we talk?...Maybe I could..."

This kind of wave-like thinking is even more intoxicating when two or more people are involved: almost irrespective of topic, we engage in a thought-feeding frenzy that seems to overtake us. If you don't believe this, sit in a café and listen...in NBC, thoughts are almost irresistible. As we've said before, compulsive thinking strengthens the person-self; that's why we do it. It makes the person-self feel real, gives it an identity, and keeps it distracted. Thinking also sustains the myth that Mind is in charge; that it's on top of things and has matters under control. Excessive thinking is its own form of suffering: while issues can be rationalized and put aside, they never really go away...they can pop up at any point, over almost any trigger. Every thought brings with it a new set of needs and more thoughts, and the wheel starts again.

As we grow in Presence, the need to think subsides. This is because we have less to think about. The moment the pull of the person-self lessens, so too does the drama. We're left with just the facts and no need to *person-alize* the situation. The harassing nature of Mind no longer has the material it needs to construct an uninterrupted flow of thoughts and emotions; there's nothing to demand, nothing to be offended by, and nothing to judge or fight about. In the situation above for example, it *doesn't matter* that the man chose to buy things over going on vacation. He made a choice. Period. It feels unnecessary and monotonous to keep mulling over the same set of facts. Stillness becomes preferable to the endless chatter, as we begin to question the utility of thinking; what purpose it serves, why we do it at all, and what it might feel like to stop.

================   Not Thinking Happens

When we say Presence is beyond thought, we're not saying we're against knowledge. The problem is that all too often we define our self in terms of what we know. And we define others, groups, organizations, professions, societies, etc. the same way. We allow our knowledge to define us, instead of simply being an aspect of our lives.

Knowledge serves many useful purposes, *it's just not primary.* Consider, for example, the information being generated about the brain and brain plasticity. These discoveries have led to many new therapies that teach clients and patients how to "rewire" the brain's circuitry, such that upsetting memories and fears, unsettling emotions and longstanding narratives can be overcome (See Siegel, 2010. See also Fosha, 2000; Frederick, 2009). In the Presence state of awareness, these therapies may become part of a more elicitive approach to help. They may assist in allowing us to "be with" a situation; to breathe through it and experience it as energy that emerges and passes. They may also aid in "de-*person*ing" a situation, or freeing our capacity to connect limbically. If so, they will move outside the person-self and the helped/helper context and potentially, enable us to move beyond thought.

Of course, we can't force ourselves to stop thinking. Even in, or perhaps, especially in meditation, the "goal" is not to suppress thoughts. Many meditation techniques emphasize *watching* one's thoughts but not trying to stop them; we notice their redundant, addictive, and changeable nature, and feel how there's nothing tangible to hold on to in a thought. Rather than try to force ourselves to stop, **thinking subsides...just as Presence arises.** We breathe consciously and allow it to happen. It's effortless. It involves no doing.

Moreover, *we've already had the experience.* We've been "not thinking" for periods of time since we began feeling the inner body. Feeling in the body draws us out of Mind. The more in-bodied we feel, the less time we spend lost in thought. Recall that the brain can only run one emotional model at a time -- so when we're in the body, we're not thinking. When we're fully present, we're not thinking. When we tune into the backdrop or find "our own" sense of Presence, we're not thinking. Living in Presence consumes all our attention.

As soon as we stop thinking, *we see through our eyes and not Mind.* We don't look at the people across the street and think, "What the hell are they doing?" We don't look at the garden and think, "I have got to get to that weeding." We look at the people, we see the garden. We see absent the baggage, without the veil of thoughts. We don't have a discussion with our partner anticipating his next sentence. We don't approach a friend mentally reciting the many ways she's hurt us. We don't see an ex-inmate walking out of a parole office who's probably a crack-head and looks pretty scary so we better protect our self. The discourses fall away, the running narrative fades. Instead we see a fellow human being, which enables us to try something completely different...like saying hello.

Often we see for the first time. It can be very startling. We literally wake up from a lifetime inside our head, dictated by perceptions. Suddenly we notice the strange habits we have to keep our self immersed in thought: we read street signs aloud in the car, sing the same song in our head for days, or talk to our self (or others) incessantly. We count our steps, unconsciously check for messages or reach for the remote, or mull over a single event that happened once, many years ago. We work hard to fill Mind with something – *anything* -- to keep us occupied and avoid the silence. When we finally look up and *see without thinking*, we wonder where we've been all along. How did we miss what's plainly right here?

There are some preliminary "exercises" to ease into not thinking. Sitting in silence is always useful. When we sit in silence, we get comfortable *not* being entertained which is a precursor to not thinking. That is perhaps why some people meditate daily. You can also try closing your eyes as though you were closing down your mind. Sometimes it helps to feel as if the corners of your eyes are extending out horizontally, far outside the body, as a curtain comes down on the mind, and sitting in that space for some time.

Another preparatory technique involves the feeling of rising above the mind. Sitting quietly in a dark room, you can close your eyes and breathe deeply. When you're ready, keeping your eyes closed, look upward. Imagine you have risen above the thinking mind and are suspended in a space at the crown of your head, in a place of emptiness. Release your jaw and your tongue if it's pressing against the roof of your mouth. It may help to feel a clearing, beginning above your eyebrows and rising to the top of your head. Stay in that space as long as you like. If thoughts emerge, just allow them to be and look up again, to that space "above thought".

Not surprisingly, the quickest way to stop thinking doesn't involve doing at all. It involves accepting.

======== Accepting What Is

Accepting what is means accepting conditions as they are right now, without fighting against them. It's synonymous with not resisting, what some people call "surrendering". According to many teachers including Eckhart Tolle, **the simplest way to stop compulsive thinking is to accept what is** (The Doorway into Now Intensive, 2008). That's because most of our thoughts have to do with resisting our life situation or trying to change it. Whenever we complain, worry, judge, impose, manipulate, defend, compare, argue, strategize, re-act, etc., we're resisting what is. We're trying to make this moment into something other than *as it is*. As odd as it sounds, most of the time we spend thinking is spent wrestling with what already is.

Throughout this book we've talked about resistance in various forms: needs are a form of resistance, as are re-actions, fighting, and fighting back; when we conflict with our self, with others, and in groups, we're resisting; clients resist our "help" when its done in NBC; and living as a person-self, striving to maintain the fiction, trying to be a certain way or impose our way on others – all of these are ways we fight what is. Struggling against "what is" is a habit we're taught from a very young age. As babies, when we don't get what we want, we cry and miraculously, things seem to change. Unfortunately, we retain this wish long into adulthood. Now, when traffic slows to a crawl and we're late for a meeting, we pound the dashboard, lean on the horn, and rail at the universe…as if that might make a difference.

Of course, not accepting what is comes with a built-in dilemma: *it already is.* If we're feeling sad or missed the appointment or wrecked the car, that's the situation. People may say, "Hey, it's not the end of the world" but that's their opinion; it may well be the end of the world to someone. The fact is -- it already is. There's nothing we can do about that. Only Mind believes otherwise. So the person-self wails and moans, and resists until we tire our self out, which changes nothing. And more often than not, by struggling, we make matters worse.

When we wrestle with what is, we assume it's a mistake. We assume traffic *should* be moving along smoothly; our daughter should have called; the man at dinner shouldn't have been so rude, bickered with his wife all evening, or be so self-righteous. But he was, and he did, and he is. When we assume "what is" is a mistake, we focus our full attention on it and make it into a problem (Tolle, The Doorway into Now Intensive, 2008).

We feed it energy. We *identify* with it which creates more needs and sets the wheel of thoughts and thinking in motion again.

In contrast, when we accept what is, there's very little to think about because there's nothing to fret over, nothing to change or fight against. It simply *is*. Accepting "what is" is why when we help in Presence, as discussed in chapter 9, we **acknowledge the situation**. By acknowledging it, we accept it as it is. We don't engage Mind or ignite the person-self. We don't accept some drama we've whipped up about it. We reduce the situation down to the facts and accept what is. We acknowledge, explore and discover. We become the space for whatever happens: acceptance creates both the space and the Stillness to proceed consciously and allow Presence to inform our actions.

As we grow in Presence, accepting what is comes quite naturally and the need to think subsides. At first, there are tiny gaps of quiet. In those spaces, the world comes into much sharper focus and feels intensely alive. Slowly, the little spaces elongate. The mind feels clear and unburdened. The brain-burning sensation that accompanies compulsive thinking is replaced with a sense of ease. Presence flows more freely.

=============== Spaces of No Thought

Again, we're not trying to stop ourselves from thinking or suppress our thoughts. We move *beyond* thinking. We experience spaces of no thought which gradually grow longer. As Presence becomes *the* state of awareness, we'll find the majority of our thoughts are unnecessary, perhaps as high as eighty percent. Moreover, in Presence, when we *do* think – when we *elect* to use the mind as another sense perception – we're much more creative and inventive (Tolle, The Secret of Self Realization Intensive, 2008).

Once we stop thinking compulsively, we begin to notice some immediate and profound changes in ourselves. For example, we stop fixating on how the world *ought to be*. That is to say, we no longer need the world to be a certain way in order for us to be okay. Irrespective of the conditions of our life situation – our relative success, physical health, quality of housing, partner or lack thereof, employment status, family relationships, etc. – we are, in our essence, okay. We'll still have happy and sad moments, feel grumpy or joyful at times, but *the events in our life don't determine how we are*. We're "free from dependence on outer circumstance" (Shantananda, 2003, p. 35).

Nor do we need any *thing* in particular to be okay. When we don't need, we're not beholding to any one or any thing. We don't need to think about what we want, or work to get it, or struggle against something that impedes us from having it. We don't have to wait for some event to happen or not happen to finally feel alive. We're like a spider cast out into the wind, with perhaps a few more navigational devices, but wherever we land, we're okay.

Another change we notice is we stop looking to our thoughts to tell us who we are. We *see* that the only part of us that relies on thoughts is the person-self. So when the person-self loses the high-powered, impressive job, it's devastated. It doesn't know who it is without that job. It thinks: "Who am I without my staff? What about my authority? I won't have an office to go to, important meetings to attend, projects to complete, clients to serve? What's left?" As thinking subsides, *we don't allow our thoughts to define us*. We have a deeper knowing.

Similarly, we don't look to others to validate us. We're not defined by the events of our past or our future prospects, or by what other people think. We stop validating others as well. We stop asking, "Are you okay?" because by doing so we think we're "helping": we're imposing our image of who we think the other person is or should be. We appreciate that thinking about how others should and shouldn't be is a waste of time; it serves no purpose at all.

Finally, as the spaces of no thought lengthen, we notice we feel better. We *have the energy of the universe at our back* rather than in our face. Of course, you're free to try it both ways. The next time something disagreeable happens, get upset: rant and rave, think about it obsessively, lose sleep over it, pace the floors, talk about it incessantly, complain to others, write an editorial. Now try a different approach: sit with it, acknowledge it, and allow it to be. When you've fully accepted the facts of what is, act accordingly. Which felt better?

When we think less, our mind isn't blank, it's just uncluttered. It can rest and renew. It becomes like any other tool. We use it to attend to the functional self and our logistical issues. It serves as a conduit for creative, original, and intuitive insights when called upon. As we move beyond thought, we can readily tap into a different place and be filled with Presence. We find we don't *want* to be burdened by thoughts, by the false intrigue or the petty drama. It feels better in Presence.

The less time we spend absorbed in thought, the faster the person-self fades. The world is no longer a projection of "me". We can step outside the pool of patterned re-activity: there are fewer buttons to push and fewer needs we identify with. The props start to fall away. We remain actively engaged in the world; in fact, we have more vitality than ever before. And we fully enjoy whatever we do...we just don't need to *own* it. We're open to the possibilities as opposed to re-acting from a contracted place.

But this leads to a quandary. As Presence replaces NBC, we have fewer needs; fewer needs mean the draw of the person-self lessens; a substantially reduced person-self means we have less things to think about; all of which increase Presence. But *which comes first?* The answer is it doesn't matter. It's not something we control anyways. They are all mutually reinforcing. Presence begins as a feeling in the inner body and becomes *the* state of awareness. As we start living in Presence, we move beyond NBC, beyond the person-self, and beyond thinking. It all happens simultaneously and according to a design we don't need to understand...or think about.

Isn't Illness a Special Case?

Illness feels like it should be a special case. Illness is so scary, so life-altering. It provokes all the person-self's greatest fears. We feel so helpless in the face of an illness; we want to scream and thrash at the world for what's happening to us. The weekends spent waiting for test results, the apprehension that awaits every phone call, the cloud that hangs over us during treatment, that fear that's right there, long into remission. Illness shoves death right in our face and we can't look away like we usually do. It doesn't matter if it's a sudden heart attack, a prolonged illness, or those penetrating words, "I'm sorry. The cancer's back".

When we have a disease or an illness, it doesn't seem fair to expect that we'll accept what is and experience increasingly longer spaces of no thought. Instead we should fight the disease, attack it as the enemy and wage war. Or learn from it; make it into an ally, a friend, or a teacher. Or perhaps, we should see it as a test: a chance to live with dignity and show others "the way". In his book on life with Parkinson's disease, Michael J. Fox refers to his disease as a gift -- a "gift that keeps on *taking*" (emphasis added; 2010, p. 87).

In Presence awareness, we accept what is whether it's pleasant or not. Even short of a disease, life can get pretty ugly: days go badly, projects fail, family members can be unkind, marriages fall apart, people and pets and dreams die, and love affairs meet daily life. What's more, we often **confront our most serious life situations *after* Presence arises**. It is then when we face our most pernicious patterns, the one or two contractions that were imprinted on us at such an early age, we didn't have a choice. Typically, they appear with a vengeance. We find ourselves totally wrapped up in the story with the drama in full swing, gripped by facets of our self we felt for sure we'd moved beyond. We are living in our heads and stuck in "me" -- either far off into a future of fear and worry, or way back in a past of anger and resentment. When the person-self rises up like this, it can feel as though it will last forever and we'll never climb out.

But we do, because Presence is there regardless. At those times, when we face sickness, or heart-ache, or a pernicious pattern, it's important to maintain contact with the *physical feeling* of Presence, both inside and around us. We tune into "our own" sense of Presence and be; quietly. We touch it and reflect it outward. When we're ready, we reduce whatever we're experiencing to the facts we are facing at *this very moment*: our friend is dying, there's not much time left and we want to be there, if she wants us there. The more we accept what is, the less absorbed we are in thoughts and thinking. Once the burden of obsessive thoughts and fears lifts -- even slightly -- Presence flows through us more freely.

Of course, we're not saying that we're happy being sick or hurt or grieving, or that we try to be cheerful and keep a stiff upper lip. Rather, we accept whatever we're facing as it is and accept ourselves as we are right now. We acknowledge it, explore it, and proceed, taking whatever conscious action works for us or no action at all. If that action means we fight the cancer, then that's what works for us. If it means we plant a tree every time we go to chemo, then that's what we do. If it means we lighten our load, then so be it. The key is that we first accept it, as it is *and as it changes*. As thoughts subside, we can see that who and how we are does not depend on life's outer circumstances. We are not our illness.

===== What This Means for How We Help

As we live in Presence awareness, with fewer thoughts and far less thinking to get in the way, we experience a stream of realizations. These cannot be forced. Rather, they arise at their own pace. Several seem more universal in nature and especially relevant to how we help in Presence.

To begin, we realize **the world is not here to make us happy**...and it never was (Tolle, The Doorway in Now Intensive, 2008). This shatters a huge delusion we've lived with our entire lives. As it turns out, conflict and frustration are part of the plan. We think things happens *to* us, we believe we don't deserve it, and we try to fight against it, but **conflict and frustration are here for a reason**: to jar us out of our habitual patterns and wake us up so we can *see without thinking*. Every life situation holds the potential to increase Presence; to allow us to be with whatever the situation is, to accept it as it is, and to take conscious action when we're ready. To loosely paraphrase Deepak Chopra: if there is a hidden meaning behind life's events, it's to further our evolution (1994, p. 60), to increase Presence. That's what it's all about.

Once we realize this, we don't expect life to go smoothly. We see conflict and frustration as an indicator that it's time to stop and take a deep conscious breath. We tune into the backdrop and "our own" sense of Presence, and breathe. For those of us who help, this means we become better listeners. We're able to be with a situation without interpretation or opinion, and free of our own mental chatter. We really hear what another person is saying and connect viscerally with what they're feeling. We Reflect *first* and hear the many truths.

We also realize that **the universe supports us in ways that extend beyond our personal happiness**. That doesn't mean it's conspiring to guide us down some Divine path. Rather, opportunities open up. Synchronicities happen. In Presence awareness, coincidences are an everyday event, often occurring in strange and humorous ways. In Presence awareness, we finally stop pretending: we *fire* Mind. We relieve it of its impossible task of creating some semblance of control. We stop believing that Mind can set matters right; that our thoughts can make things happen or the power of knowledge will save the day. We understand the only person Mind affects is our self (Singer, 2007, p. 10). Whatever happens in the world… is beyond Mind.

As Mind retreats, we realize we have a huge reservoir of energy at our disposal:

> If you watch carefully…you have a phenomenal amount of energy inside you. It doesn't come from food and it doesn't come from sleep. This energy is always available to you. At any moment you can draw upon it (ibid., p. 43).

This energy has always been with us, it's just been covered over by Mind. It's the source of our mood swings, that feeling of being "in the zone", the days we're on top of the world and the lethargy and fatigue we feel when it's obstructed (ibid., pp. 42-43). Thinking, opinions, preferences, beliefs, judgments, needs, conflict – all these inhibit the free-flow of energy. But once they subside, we can draw on this reservoir of pure energy. As a result, when we help, mysteries and possibilities happen spontaneously. We can use this energy to support conditions conducive to shifts, create wise questions, and tune into the Stillness. As we've said, we tap into a different place.

Another realization is even more unsettling. We realize that **while everything around us changes, something *in us* remains constant**. To be sure, parts of us change rapidly: our thoughts, our desires, emotions and moods, our bodies. But *something* remains constant; something that *itself* is not subject to change. How do we know this? Eckhart Tolle uses the example, if everything in the world was blue, we couldn't recognize blue. But we do recognize change: something in us is able to watch what changes. It's the same part that observes our self. So, we can say we're not our thoughts because we're able to watch our thoughts. We can say we're not the person-self because we can watch the person-self. Something in us remains constant and watches what changes.

As we start living in a state of Presence, we come to see that the "something in us" that doesn't change is the same as the backdrop in which all things happen. This is not to be known or understood by the thinking Mind. **The part of us that watches is the same as the backdrop in which all things happen; in fact, it's *the same backdrop*.** We <u>are</u> the backdrop: the same space, the same Stillness, the same Presence…the same underlying, surrounding, and enveloping field of energy that comprises and embraces all things that change. As Eckhart Tolle says, "We are not what happens, we are the space in which it happens" (The Flowering of Human Consciousness CD, 2004).

This is the realization Mind fears most of all; it's *Mind's* ultimate fear. For the first time, we understand. We are not The Voice, or the person-self and its stories. We are not Mind or our thoughts. When we strip away all the superficial stuff that we think we are, what's left is Presence…**it's the Presence that *we are*** (The Flowering of Human Consciousness CD, 2004). What's more, it's the Presence that we *all* are. The Presence that surrounds us is no different from the Presence that we are, which is no different from the Presence that everyone is. One text describes it this way:

> If the [teachings] only explained the true nature of an individual and the true nature of…creation" that would be very helpful but they go on to "establish a truly radical unity" not only "behind different objects" but "between subjects and objects" (Kaji, 2001, p. 98).

So it's not exactly correct to say we "bring" Presence to anything, because we *are it*. Nor can we really talk about "our own" sense of Presence. We all share the same Presence. We share, not so much a unity or oneness, but an essential same-ness; as Dr. Mitchell said, "inseparable aspects of a single evolving reality" (2008, p. 159). **It's the Presence that we *all* are.**

For helpers, this realization brings with it a shift in our nature: we are graced with **an inner sense of quiet.** An inner sense of quiet is a deep feeling of ease, a comfort with whatever is, an abiding Presence. With an inner sense of quiet, there is very little to say. In professional help, we may sit in Presence through an entire conversation with another person and utter only a few words. In everyday help, we may listen to a friend recount his situation and say almost nothing. We breathe before we speak. We focus on what's true and useful. And we tune into the backdrop *that we all are.*

It is this inner sense of quiet we bring to how we help. It *replaces thinking.* Figure 9.2 portrays how help changes from NBC to the Presence state of awareness.

Figure 9.2

Help in NBC and Presence Awareness	
Help In NBC	Help In Presence Awareness
Prescriptive Assume I Know One Truth Directive	An Inner Sense of Quiet Spaces of No Thinking We Accept What Is The Part that Watches is the Backdrop
Competitive One Reality Either/Or Thinking Need to Win	An Innate Connection Visceral Resonance Temporary Co-Dependence De-*person* the Situation
Defensive One Right Way Attached to Specifics Judgment/Blame	A Fading Person-Self Dis-Identify with Image Functional Self Only The Other is the Same Backdrop

==================== Living Presence

How we help is a reflection of where we have evolved to as human beings. As cataclysmic or near catastrophic events grow more common, as do the number of problems that lack any sort of viable solution, conditions are signaling the end of NBC and that the next state of Presence awareness is unfolding.

In the Presence state of awareness, help comes from within. It doesn't come from a person-self, nor is it done to one. It's not driven by needs, nor is it based on thoughts and thinking. Help comes from the very essence of what we are. It comes from Presence. It's all that matters. Many gifted and creative people before us, including Einstein, have had glimpses of Presence. It's now time for all of us to progress from NBC to Presence. Our future depends on it. It rests on the shoulders of all those who are willing to move beyond help.

Epilogue

Since helpers are likely to lead the way and usher in the next state of awareness, there may be some lingering questions which deserve our attention.

Are you saying that no-one is helped by the way we help now in NBC?

No, certainly not. However, most of what we define as help in NBC is (1) aimed at making someone a better person-self, so it's surface-level change and often doesn't last; (2) imposed or forced on others which cause them to re-act by resisting. They also grow to doubt their own capabilities; and (3) someone else's prescription of what "the Other" needs, so the fit is never precise and sometimes, not even close.

Why not just work to improve help and make it better?

This book looks at the human condition through the prism of how we help. In NBC when something is "wrong", we try to fix or improve it. Our solutions are shaped by our needs, by the person-self and thinking. This is why, for instance, we swing back-and-forth between the "solutions" of two political parties and are never satisfied with either.

When we try to fix help in NBC, we each bring the person-self that needs and knows to the table. That is, in turn, reflected in our solutions. This book suggests we move beyond these mentally conditioned constructs, and help in Presence; where we can de-*person* conflicts and situations, engage in an iterative and elicitive conversation, and tap into a different and more resourceful place.

I don't think I live in an Us or NOT culture. People aren't loud or abrasive. Groups don't conflict, issues aren't "laced with violence". It's just a small community. Where's the Us or NOT culture?

Depending on where and how we live, we can avoid certain aspects of the Us or NOT culture, but not all of them. To experience the Us or NOT culture, turn on the radio, work in a competitive environment, drive down a highway, or try reaching a large corporation by phone with a question. Look into any important issue and listen to the angry discord: social security COLAs, automatic citizenship for illegal immigrants, tuition assistance, spending on the arts, offshore drilling. Try citing anything and watch the violence erupt – a mental health facility, a power plant, a waste treatment place, a group home. Turn on a Congressional hearing and feel the Us or NOT culture in surround sound. Watch everyday people turn into raging maniacs over gay marriage, capital punishment, school aid, property taxes, etc. And notice how, with increasing frequency, alarming events are affecting small-town communities.

In contrast, culture in Presence is totally different. It "sees" beyond doing and needs and problems; acts outside a personal point of view; and comes with a knowing that is not thought. Presence is changing and changes *everything*.

"De-*person*ing" sounds important. What does it actually mean?

"De-*person*ing" means to come face-to-face with the person-self and know, on a deeply profound level, it is not who we are. It means unlocking our emotions from our re-actions, separating our stories from the facts, and exploring the beliefs and personal and collective habits that seem to drive us. It also means noticing the Voice in our heads and watching our thoughts. We notice what motivates and challenges the "I", and when and why it feels threatened, strengthened, criticized, or superior. We examine what we're attached to and where we resist. We also come to know we are more than this "I". We grow aware of our awareness. We become aware of the awareness that *we are*...which is so much deeper and vaster than the Voice, our stories, needs, and Mind.

So the steps are: we feel Presence, we grow in Presence, we bring

Presence, and finally, we live in a state of Presence awareness. Is that right?

Presence evolves. It's easy to try to reduce Presence to a series of steps and that's just what Mind wants to do. But Presence evolves. It's uncovered by each of us at its own pace and expressed in our own unique way. The place to start is with feeling the inner body. Everything else will unfold from there.

Does Presence signal the end of training? Of supervision and authority? And of thinking?

That will depend on all of those who decide how to effectuate the new definition of help in the next state of awareness. It's likely there will still be some notion of training but it won't involve "empowerment", because nothing will be "given" to trainees per se. For example, to the extent in Presence that mediation or counseling become non-directive and enable us to get outside our self, it's possible these areas may have mass utility across fields. Some type of non-directive "training" in these areas that increases Presence may be offered.

Insofar as thinking is concerned, thinking will become another tool. Once we stop thinking obsessively, the thinking we do will be far more creative. But whatever thinking we do, it will probably center on how to communicate meaning, connect limbically, dis-identify with an image, etc, as opposed to figuring things out and "solving" ours or other people's problems.

Will we still have needs in Presence?

Yes, but they won't be driving needs and we won't re-act if they're not met. In Presence, we can anticipate our needs will be more aligned with the larger whole. We'll have the energy that surrounds and comprises all things at our back and not in our face. In addition, personal and collective needs will lose importance, while the need for connection and meaning will increase.

What does it mean to accept "what is"?

There are at least two aspects of accepting what is: we accept our inner states as they are and our outer circumstances as they are. Chances are, for many of us, some pieces of the person-self and its issues will remain even as the person-self lessens in Presence. As a result, we'll be confronted with inner states that need to be honored and outer circumstances that need to be acknowledged. By honoring and acknowledging these conditions, we accept what we are experiencing and "see" it as a projection of "me". We stop resisting and remove ourselves from a place of re-activity. From there, we can take conscious action when we're ready. That's what accepting "what is" means.

Aren't you really just talking about introducing more balance into our lives?

In Presence there is more balance but it's not something we seek. When we try to impose conditions on our lives, on our self or others, we are seeking something. We're identified with it and it becomes a need we must fulfill. In other words, we're *self*-serving and the situation will ultimately end in conflict and frustration.

Presence evolves. It is effortless. With it comes greater balance but it is not something we seek, or strive for, or create. In Presence, we're no longer trying to force the person-self to be "x" – better, happier, thinner, smarter, more balanced. Presence is a discovery of who and what we are.

Why doesn't a simple change in perspective work? For example, aging can be seen as having fewer and fewer choices. Alternatively, we can understand that it's not the choices that matter; it's the journey that's important?

A change in perspective is still Mind, and often requires force to believe or remember it. When our adult child takes away our car keys and with it, our independence, it's hard to find solace in knowing it's all part of the journey.

On the other hand, every life situation can increase Presence once we accept what is. The experience of aging may allow us to be gentle with ourselves and through gentleness, Presence grows. It's not that we're gentle for a reason, or with an end-product in Mind; or because we can't be gentle with others until we learn to be gentle with our self. There's no thinking and processing and unenforceable rules involved. We simply apply gentleness to the situation and grow in Presence through aging.

Isn't Presence really what the rest of us call "God"?

Well, it's possible Presence is what some people call God. Presence is not prescriptive or directive. It's not imposed on others, there's no One Right Way, and it's not about knowing or needing. If people call that

God or Allah, or Consciousness or awareness, it's not the label that's important.

Will help be exclusively elicitive forever?

We may swing too far the other way and have to rebalance the elicitive with the prescriptive. We're so prescriptive now it's hard to imagine that happening any time soon. And some industries will be more affected than others. The mainstream media, for example, will have to work with the public to decide what constitutes news in Presence, how it's delivered, and by whom.

How does Presence differ from being religious or spiritual?

As a state of awareness, Presence is beyond what we in NBC, traditionally call "religious" or "spiritual". It's beyond say, coming from the heart; Presence is deeper than that. It's beyond learning to love your neighbor; Presence is wider than that. And it's beyond being a certain way: wise, centered, learned, contemplative, all-knowing, etc. When Mind clears and we stop wrestling with what is, we naturally gravitate to a more "de-*person*ed" sense of aliveness. We can *live* the Presence that we are; that everyone and everything else is as well.

Isn't elicitive the same as getting others to "buy into" a project, an approach or other effort?

No. "Buying into" is too easily reduced to "buying off". It's a good example of what we mean when we say in NBC, we need "to get them to _____" – in this case, to support the project or initiative we want. Elicitive is more than letting people decide for themselves. It's a change in where help comes from, how it happens, and what results. An elicitive approach changes the whole reason for help: it comes from within, there's no One Right Way, and no-one's broken, no-one knows.

How will we know we've slipped back into NBC?

We'll be engrossed in Mind, looking for thoughts and knowledge to save the day. We'll be driven by needs and directed by The Voice; struggling to be right, to win, to feel safe and okay. We'll hear the remnants of NBC:

- "You need to do it because it's the right thing to do" – as opposed to *"It's what I think (or feel) is the right thing to do"*;

- "He's lost sight of what's important in life" – instead of "what's important *in my life*";
- "If I were you…" – yes, but you're not;
- "They're either lying or incompetent" – chances are there are other explanations as well;
- "It's not our fault so we shouldn't have to pay" – as opposed to "*We've all* benefited and we'll all have to pay, it's a matter of how much".

Our discussions will be contentious and high-pitched. It will feel as though we're splitting hairs. Whatever "solutions" are generated will add layers of complexity to an already labyrinth-like situation and feature repetitive ideas that have never worked in the past.

As we've said repeatedly, nothing short of a change in awareness will suffice.

I know *a lot* of people who need to discover Presence. What do I do about that?

Perhaps a handful of people have uncovered Presence fully. They are rare and the exception. This book encourages us to focus on ourselves: on moving beyond knowing and needs, beyond the person-self and doing help. For now, that's a pretty tall order. Once we discover Presence, it speaks for itself.

So nothing lasts? We just get sick and die?

In NBC, the person-self goes through life trying to last in a world where no-thing does. Only Presence lasts. Presence is the real meaning of eternity (Tolle, The Flowering of Human Consciousness CD, 2004). Once we experience ourselves as the backdrop in which all things happen, we can feel our essence as Presence. That's what lasts. The person-self may die, but our essence contributes to the dyad which continues to evolve. It's the part of us that watches…the part that doesn't change…the part that is eternal.

I don't see it. I just don't see Presence arising. Now what?

What's important is that you read this book and that means you have started to uncover Presence in yourself. You may find you are drawn to Silence more than in the past. Your tastes may change. Your preferences may not be as stark. You may feel less vocal and yet, be more approachable as the various props that once supported the person-self begin to fall away.

In time, you'll see you reflect Presence outward and reflect the Presence in others.

Of course, on the cusp of Presence, people can turn away and grow even more attached to NBC. It's only temporary. Slowly, everyone discovers the fiction: our needs will not be met, our time here is limited, and we cannot think our way out this time. In the meantime, Presence continues to unfold. The hope of this book is that we can uncover Presence in our lives sooner rather than later, and go on to help in Presence.

List of References

Alexander, Nadja. 2008. "The Mediation Metamodel: Understanding Practice," *Conflict Resolution Quarterly*, Volume 26, Number 1 (Fall).

Amen, Daniel G., M.D. 2005. *Making a Good Brain Great*. New York: Three Rivers Press.

_____. 2007. *The Brain in Love*. New York: Three Rivers Press.

Avlon, John. 2010. *Wingnut: How the Lunatic Fringe is Hijacking America*. New York: Beast Books.

Bannick, Fredicke P. 2007. Solution-Focused Mediation: The Future with a Difference," *Conflict Resolution Quarterly*, Volume 25, Number 2 (Winter).

Barsade, Signal G. 2002. The Ripple Effect: Emotional Contagion and Its Influence on Group Behavior," *JSTOR: Administrative Science Quarterly*, Volume 47, Number 4 (December).

Bartiromo, Maria. 2010. *The 10 Laws of Enduring Success*. New York: Crown Business.

Bureau of Labor Statistics, US Department of Labor. May 2008. National Occupational Employment and Wage Estimates, on the Internet at http://www.bls.gov/oes/2008/may/oes_nat.htm

Bureau of Labor Statistics, US Department of Labor, Occupational and Outlook Handbook. 2008-9 Edition. Social Workers on the Internet at http://www.bls.gov/oco/ocos0606.htm

Burton, Robert. A., MD. 2008. *On Being Certain: Believing You Are Right Even When You're Not.* New York: St. Martin's Griffin.

Bush, Robert A. Baruch, and Joseph P. Folger. 2005. *The Promise of Mediation: The Transformative Approach to Conflict.* San Francisco, CA: Jossey-Bass.

Chasin, Richard, Margaret Herzig, Sallyann Roth, Laura Chasin, Carol Becker, and Rober R. Stains. 1996. "From Diatribe to Dialogue on Divisive Public Issues: Approaches Drawn from Family Therapy," *Mediation Quarterly,* Volume 13, Number 4 (Summer).

Chopra, Deepak, M.D. 1987. *Creating Health: How to Wake Up the Body's Intelligence.* Boston, MA: Houghton Mifflin Company.

_____. 1989. *Quantum Healing: Exploring the Frontiers of Mind/Body Medicine.* New York: Bantam Books.

_____. 1991. *Perfect Health: The Complete Mind/Body Guide.* New York: Harmony Books.

_____. 1994. *The Seven Spiritual Laws of Success.* San Rafael, CA: Co-published by Amber-Allen Publishing and New World Library.

Coleman, Peter, Antony G. Hacking, Mark A. Stover, Beth Fisher-Yoshinda, and Andrzej Nowak. 2008. "Reconstructing Ripeness 1: A Study of Constructive Engagement in Protracted Social Conflicts." *Conflict Resolution Quarterly,* Volume 26, Number 1 (Fall).

Covey, Stephen R. 1989. *The Seven Habits of Highly Effective People: Powerful Lessons in Personal Change.* New York: Fireside Books.

Della Noce, Dorothy J. 2009. "Evaluative Mediation: In Search of Practice Competences," *Conflict Resolution Quarterly,* Volume 27, Number 2 (Winter).

Dessel, Andrienne, and Mary E. Rogge. 2008. "Evaluation of Intergroup Dialogue: A review of the Empirical Literature," *Conflict Resolution Quarterly,* Volume 26, Number 2 (Winter).

Doidge, Norman, M.D. 2007. *The Brain the Changes Itself.* New York: Penguin Books.

Easwaran, Ecknath. 1992. *Dialogue with Death: A Journey Through Consciousness.* 2d ed. Berkeley, CA: Nilgiri Press.

Eire, Carlos. 2010. *A Very Brief History of Eternity.* Princeton, New Jersey: Princeton University Press.

Ellison, Sharon Strand. 1998. *Taking the War Out of Words.* Deadwood, Oregon: Wyatt-Mackenzie Publishing, Inc.

Epstein, Mark, M.D. 2007. *Psychotherapy without the Self.* New Haven, CT: Yale University Press.

Folger, Joseph P., and Robert A. Baruch Bush. 1996. "Transformative Mediation and Third-Party Intervention: Ten Hallmarks of a Transformative Approach to Practice", *Mediation Quarterly,* Volume 13, Number 4 (Summer).

Fosha, Diane. 2000. *The Transforming Power of Affect.* New York: Basic Books.

Fox, Michael J. 2010. *A Funny Thing Happened on the Way to the Future.* New York: Hyperion.

Frawley, David. 1996. *Ayurveda and the Mind: The Healing of Consciousness.* Twin Lakes, WI: Lotus Press.

Frederick, Ronald J. 2009. *Living Like You Mean It.* San Francisco, CA: Jossey-Bass.

Friedman, Gary, and Jack Himmelstein. 2008. *Challenging Conflict, Mediation Through Understanding.* American Bar Association.

Hedeen, Timothy. 2005. "Dialogue and Democracy, Community and Capacity: Lessons for Conflict Resolution Education from Montessori, Dewey, and Freire", *Conflict Resolution Quarterly*, Volume 23, Number 2 (Winter).

Hofstader, David. 2007. *I am a Strange Loop.* New York: Basic Books.

Kabat-Zinn, Jon, PhD. 1990. *Full Catastrophe Living.* New York: Dell Trade Books, Dell Publishing.

Kaji, Dhruv S. 2001. *Uncommon Sense about Uncommon Wisdom: Ancient Teachings of Vedanta.* Honesdale, PA: The Himalayan Institute Press.

Kano, Susan. 1989. *Making Peace with Food: Freeing Yourself from the Diet/ Weight Obsession.* New York: Harper & Row.

Kasl, Charlotte, PhD. 2005. *If the Buddha Got Stuck.* New York: Penguin Compass.

Lanza, Robert, M.D., with Bob Berman. 2009. *Biocentrism.* Dallas, Texas: Benbella Books.

Lederach, John Paul. 1995. *Preparing for Peace: Conflict Transformation Across Cultures.* Syracuse, New York: Syracuse University Press.

Lehrer, Jonah. 2009. *How We Decide.* New York and Boston: Houghton Mifflin Harcourt.

Levine, Stephen. 1997. *A Year to Live: How to Live This Year As If It Were Your Last.* New York: Bell Tower.

Lewis, Thomas, M.D. 2009. Lecture Series, Pepperdine University School of Law/Strauss Institute for Dispute Resolution and Vermont Law School, *Neuro-Collaboration*, Woodstock, Vermont.

_____. 2009. *Empathy*. Self-Published Article.

Lewis, Thomas, Fari Amini, M.D., and Richard Lannon, M.D. 2000. *A General Theory of Love*. New York: Vintage Books.

Liu, Aimee. 2007. *Gaining: The Truth about Life after Eating Disorders*. New York and Boston: Wellness Central.

Lowry, Carmen and Stephen Littlejohn. 2006. "Dialogue and the Discourse of Peacebuilding in Maluku, Indonesia", *Conflict Resolution Quarterly*, Volume 23, Number 4 (Summer).

Market Data Enterprises Market Report. 2005. at http://answers.google.com, "Self Help Industry".

McLaren, Brian D. 2010. *A New Kind of Christianity: Ten Questions That Are Transforming the Faith*. New York: HarperOne.

Medscape.com: Beauty Today.

Menand, Louis. 2010. "Head Case: Can Psychiatry Be a Science?" *The New Yorker* (1 March 2010).

Mitchell, Edgar, PhD, with Dwight Williams. 2008. *The Way of the Explorer*. Franklin Lakes, New Jersey: A New Page Books.

Moore, Christopher. 2003. *The Mediation Process*. San Francisco, CA: Jossey-Bass.

Myss, Carolyn, PhD. 1996. *Anatomy of the Spirit: The Seven Stages of Power and Healing*. New York: Harmony Books.

Newberg, Andrew, M.D. 2002. *Why God Won't Go Away: Brain Science and the Biology of Belief*. New York: Ballentine Books.

National Public Radio (NPR), *All Things Considered*, Matt Martinez, Supervising Senior Producer (in order of reference):
-- 31 March 2010, Obama Opens Up East Coast for Offshore Drilling
-- 7 April, 2010, 'Churchgate': The Scandal That Won't Go Away
-- 29 April 2010, Formerly Banned Muslim Scholar Tours U.S.

_____, *Morning Edition*, Madhulika Sikka, Executive Producer (in order of reference):
-- 7 July 2010, Social Media Spread Hatred against BP's Hayward
-- 7 April 2010, Dander Up in Israel over Proposed Fur Ban
-- 25 March 2010, Senate GOP Forces Health Care Bill Back to House
-- 11 May 2010, Monk's Enlightenment Begins with a Marathon Walk

_____, *This American Life*, produced by Chicago Public Radio, Ira Glass, Executive Producer:
-- 27 March 2010, NUMMI

_____, *Weekend Edition Saturday*, produced by Deborah Amos:
-- 24 April 2010, CNBC's Maria Bartiromo Shares Her Laws for Success

Pfaff, Donald W., PhD. 2007. *The Neuroscience of Fair Play: Why We (Usually) Follow the Golden Rule*. New York: Dana Press.

Powell, Jim. 1998. *Postmodernism for Beginners*. Danbury, Connecticut: For Beginners, LLC.

Public Conversations Project. 2009. Training Series 1: *The Power of Dialogue*.

_____,. 2009. Training Series 2: *Inquiry as Intervention*.

Rowe, John W., M.D., and Robert L. Kahn, PhD. 1998. *Successful Aging*. New York: Dell Publishing.

Ruiz, Don Miguel. 2004. *The Voice of Knowledge*. San Rafael, CA: Amber-Allen Publishing.

Shantananda, Swami, and Peggy Bendet. 2003. *The Splendor of Recognition*. South Fallsburg, New York: SYDA Foundation.

Siegel, Daniel, M.D. 2010. *Mindsight, The New Science of Personal Transformation*. New York: Bantam Books.

Silver, Robert B., and Deborah Coe Silver. 2009. "The Sieve Model: An Innovative Process for Identifying Alternatives to Custody Evaluations", *Conflict Resolution Quarterly*, Volume 26, Number 3 (Spring).

Simpkinson, Anne, and Charles Simpkinson. 2003. "Feeding One Another", *The Wisdom of Healing*, edited by Mark Brady. Boston, MA: Wisdom Publications.

Singer, Michael A. 2007. *The Untethered Soul, The Journey Beyond Self.* Oakland, California: Noetic Books, New Harbinger Publications, Inc.

Smith, Robert. 2003. "Listening from the Heart", *The Wisdom of Healing*, edited by Mark Brady. Boston, MA: Wisdom Publications.

Stengal, Richard. 2009. *Mandela's Way: 15 Lessons on Life, Love and Courage*. New York: Crown Publishers.

Suzuki, Shunryu. 1997. *Zen Mind, Beginner's Mind*. 37th Printing. New York and Tokyo: Weatherhill, Inc.

Tannen, Deborah. 1998. *The Argument Culture: Stopping America's War of Words*. New York: Ballentine Books.

Tesler, Pauline H. 2008. *Collaborative Law: Achieving Effective Resolution in Divorce Without Litigation*. 2d ed. American Bar Association.

The Environmental Report, Lester Graham, Senior Editor and Mark Brush, Senior Producer:
    -- 5 April 2010, Decision Coming on Cape Wind

Thomas, Camaron, PhD. 2007. *People Skills for Tough Times: The Keys to Getting Along*. Self Published.

Thompson, Michael G., Ph.D. Undated. "Learning the Dance of Limbic Resonance: The Life of the Spouse of the Head of School" at website of National Association of Independent Schools (NAIS).

Tolle, Eckhart. 1999. *The Power of Now*. Novato, California: New World Library.

_____. 2005. *A New Earth: Awakening to Your Life's Purpose*. New York: A Plume Book.

_____. 2002. *In the Presence of a Great Mystery*, CD, New World Library.

_____. 2004. *The Flowering of Human Consciousness*, CD, Sounds True.

_____. 2008. *The Secret of Self Realization Intensive*, CD, Eckhart Teachings Inc.

_____. 2008. *The Doorway into NOW Intensive*, CD, Eckhart Teachings Inc.

Wheatley, Margaret J. 1992. *Leadership and the New Science*. San Francisco: Berrett-Koehler Publishers, Inc.

Winslade, John, and Gerald Monk. 2008. *Practicing Narrative Mediation: Loosening the Grip of Conflict*, San Franscisco: Jossey-Bass.

Worthington, Roger, PhD. 2002. *Finding the Hidden Self: The Study of the Siva Sutras*. Honedale, P.A.: Himalayan Press.

Zaidel, Susan, PhD. 2008. "How Collaborative is Collaborative Divorce?" *Family Mediation News* (Summer).

Index

38, 43-44, 85, 90; Person-Self Cycle and, 16; purpose it serves, 182; truth and, 43-44, 96; ultimate source of, xxii, 36-38

Conflict Trap, 32, 33-36, 85

Consciousness, xxi, 13, 111, 115, 116, 121, 122-123, 140-142, 143, 171, 172-174

Constant State of Conflict, xx, xxi, 3, 23, 29, 30-33, 37, 47, 53, 62, 76, 85

Constructionist View: culture and, 80; discourse and, 80-81, 87-88; language and, 81, 82-83; power and, 80

Core Needs, 9-10, 14-15, 20, 36, 51-52, 59, 92-93

Cracks in NBC, 28, 76, 78, 106-107, 111-112, 126, 186

Cycle of Dependency, xvii, 57, 60, 95, 156

D

Daily Dose of Discord, 83-86, 87, 90, 93-94, 167

Deeply Conditioned Collective Patterns and Habits, 4, 7, 12, 22, 29, 58, 62, 81, 83, 89, 97, 145

De-Personing, 147, 155-156, 158, 167, 176, 188

Discourse, 80-81, 87-88, 96, 103

Dyadic Model, 114-115

E

Eating Disorders, 26-27

Education as Social Help, 95-96

Einstein, Albert, xxi, 16, 111, 186

Elicitive, 145-146, 150-151, 156-158, 160, 168, 191

Energy: coming back in kind, 20, 85; pure energy, 4-5, 29, 113-114, 115, 116, 126, 183; sound vibration, 116; the infinite, surrounding field, 115, 121-122, 141-142, 143, 157, 168-169, 183-184; universal, 180

Eternity, 97-98, 192

Everyday Help: as provoking conflict, 53; disguises of, 51; One Right Way, 49; meeting needs, 51-52; need to know and, 51-52; prescriptive and directive, 52-54; wanting others to change, 51

Everyday Help in Presence: engaging in relationships and, 150, 152; importance of, 149, 167; inspired listening and, 150-151; multiple truths, 151-152; Reflect *first*, 151; the experience of differences, 150; true and useful, 151

F

Fear of "Other", 81-82, 86, 87, 88, 94, 104, 105, 161, 168

Fiction of the Person-Self, 31, 106, 127

Fighting: as Mind-made, 106; at our worst, 85, 88, 94, 104-106; brain with itself, 23-25; fear of "Other" and, 81-82, 86, 87, 88, 94, 104, 105, 161, 168; in and among groups, 90-92; in Presence, 149-150; over thoughts, 38, 43-44, 90-92; with others, xvi, 32-36, 90-92; with self, xx, 26-27

Functional Self, 147, 149

G

Groups: conflict and, 90-92, 93, 94-95; fighting within and among, 90-92; group proving, 91; in an Us or NOT culture, 88-90, 93, 94; in Presence, 168; needing to belong, 89, 168; Social Help and, 92-93, 94-101; the collective person self and, 88; the desire to hurt and, 91, 94

H

Head: living and stuck in the, 8-9, 11-12, 36, 92

Help: a rare truth about, 76; as a contraction, 53; as adding or stirring more conflict, 51-52, 53, 59-60, 93, 94-95, 101, 104-105, 123; as broken, xvi-xvii, xxi, 47, 51, 53, 54-57, 58-59, 60, 62, 72-75, 76, 94-95, 100-101, 105, 106, 123; as Mind-made, 47, 57, 75; as needing "to get them to _____", 60, 72, 93, 95, 97, 103, 132, 144; as prescriptive and directive, xxi, 52-54, 57-59, 69, 72, 92, 93; as sending a message, 76, 111, 112, 122; definition of, xvii, 49, 53, 62; disguises of, 51; Everyday Help, 49-53, 149-152; help by doing, 49, 58-59, 60, 61, 76, 95, 125; in the next state of Awareness, 144-166; knowing and, 48-49, 51-52, 92-94; meeting needs and, xiv, 49, 51-52, 59, 61, 71-72, 75, 76, 88-89, 92-93; Professional Help, 53-59, 152-159; selfless acts of, 61; Social Help, 77-78, 92-93, 94-101, 104-106, 160-169; when it hurts, 59-60, 104-106; when the person-self helps, 12, 49, 51-52, 53, 57, 60, 76, 94-95

Helpers as Leading the Way, 122-123, 133-134

Helping Professions: xv, xvii, xxii, 61, 64, 70, 163-165

Help in Presence: absent the person-self, 143, 148; acknowledging the situation, 144, 152, 156, 160, 179; as offered, 148; as the space for whatever happens, 165; co-engagement in, 148, 152, 154-156; comes from within, 145-146; de-personing and, 147, 155-156, 158, 167, 176, 188; dis-identify with an image, 147; elicitive, 145-146, 150-151, 156-158, 160, 168, 191; Everyday Help in, 149-152, 168; functional self and, 147, 149; how help changes in, 144-145; new definition of, 148-149, 161, 163; person-self and, 146-148; Professional Help in, 152-159; situations in, 145, 153, 163; Social Help in, 160-169; social impli-

cations of, 167-169; they know best, 146, 149, 153, 158, 167

I

Identified with Being a Helper, 53, 57, 76

Identity, 4, 6, 8, 11, 15, 21, 29

I Know: as a core need, 15; conflict and, 36-38; helping and, 48-49; need to know, xvii, 9-10, 36, 51; the professional "I know", 57-59; the social "I know", 92-94

Illness, 181-182

Image of Who We Think We Are, 5, 7-9, 10, 15, 29, 31-32, 43, 76, 91

I-Needs, 21-22, 24, 30

Infinite, Surrounding Field, 115, 121-122, 141-142, 143, 157, 168-169, 183-184

Inner Body, 135, 136-138, 139, 142, 150, 153, 168, 176, 189

Inner Sense of Quiet, 185

In Service of the Conversation, 150-152, 158, 165-166

Intuition, 120-121, 139, 157, 166-167

L

Liberal Humanist View, 78-80

Limbic Resonance, 117, 154-156

Listening: as an inspired listener, 150; becoming a better listener, 183; for assumptions, 83; for sound vibrations, 137; in service of the conversation, 150-152, 158, 165-166; in traditional training, 41

M

Mantras, 116, 131, 137

Mediation: controlling and, 70-71; example of broken, 72-75; needs and, 64; prescriptive and directive, 69-72; reflecting, 66-67; reframing, 68-69; self determination and, 63, 69, 75; self proving and, 71-72; steering and,

205